MW01322868

A LEGAL HISTORY OF ADOPTION IN ONTARIO, 1921–2015

PATRONS OF THE SOCIETY

Blake, Cassels & Graydon LLP
Chernos Flaherty Svonkin LLP
Gowlings
McCarthy Tétrault LLP
Osler, Hoskin & Harcourt LLP
Paliare Roland Rosenberg Rothstein LLP
Torys LLP
WeirFoulds LLP

The Osgoode Society is supported by a grant from
The Law Foundation of Ontario.

The Society also thanks The Law Society of Upper Canada
for its continuing support.

A LEGAL HISTORY OF ADOPTION IN ONTARIO, 1921–2015

LORI CHAMBERS

Published for The Osgoode Society for Canadian Legal History by
University of Toronto Press
Toronto Buffalo London

© Osgoode Society for Canadian Legal History 2016
www.utppublishing.com
www.osgoodesociety.ca
Printed in Canada

ISBN 978-1-4875-0101-3

♾ Printed on acid-free, 100% post-consumer recycled paper with
vegetable-based inks.

Library and Archives Canada Cataloguing in Publication

Chambers, Anne Lorene, 1965–, author
A legal history of adoption in Ontario, 1921–2015 /
Lori Chambers.

(Osgoode Society for Canadian Legal History)
Includes bibliographical references and index.
ISBN 978-1-4875-0101-3 (cloth)

1. Adoption – Law and legislation – Ontario – History.
2. Adoption – Ontario – History.   I. Osgoode Society for Canadian
Legal History, issuing body   II. Title.   III. Series: Osgoode Society
for Canadian Legal History (Series)

KEO228.C53 2016   346.71301'78   C2016-902990-5
KF545 C53 2016

University of Toronto Press acknowledges the financial assistance to its
publishing program of the Canada Council for the Arts and the Ontario Arts
Council, an agency of the Government of Ontario.

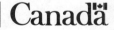

Contents

FOREWORD vii

ACKNOWLEDGMENTS ix

Introduction 3
1 The Origins of Adoption Legislation 13
2 Mothers and the Meaning of Consent in Adoption 26
3 Putative Fathers and Newborn Adoption 42
4 Child Apprehension 52
5 Secrecy and Disclosure in Adoption 63
6 Open Adoption 78
7 Step-Parent Adoption 91
8 Same-Sex Parents, Assisted Reproduction, and Adoption 104
9 Indigenous Children and Adoption 116
10 International Adoption 135
Conclusion 153

NOTES 157

INDEX 225

Foreword

THE OSGOODE SOCIETY
FOR CANADIAN LEGAL HISTORY

Ontario's first Adoption Act was passed in 1921, less than a century ago, and since that time adoption has been an integral part of the history of what we now term family law. Lori Chambers of Lakehead University traces the legal history of adoption from 1921 to the present. She details the origins and passage of the original legislation and its operation through the early decades. Much of this volume is then taken up with the history of more recent decades. Like so many aspects of family law, such as divorce and spouses' relationship to family property, the recent history of adoption has witnessed a series of profound changes and controversies that have resulted from rapidly evolving ideas about "appropriate" family units and parental and children's rights. This volume details the socio-political debates and consequent legal changes in a diverse set of areas – the meaning of consent by birth mothers, same-sex adoption, adoption of Indigenous children, international adoption, adoption and immigration policy, and secrecy in adoption records. In analysing the development of the law, Chambers skilfully weaves together statutes and cases with extra-legal debates. Because so many of these controversies have arisen only in the last few decades, this is very much a modern legal history of adoption law. Because the law cannot be said to be settled in so many of these areas, the volume also provides those engaged with adoption law with invaluable historical background.

The purpose of the Osgoode Society for Canadian Legal History is to encourage research and writing in the history of Canadian law. The Society, which was incorporated in 1979 and is registered as a charity, was founded at the initiative of the Honourable R. Roy McMurtry and officials of the Law Society of Upper Canada. The Society seeks to stimulate the study of legal history in Canada by supporting researchers, collecting oral histories, and publishing volumes that contribute to legal-historical scholarship in Canada. This year's books bring the total published to 103 since 1981, in all fields of legal history – the courts, the judiciary, and the legal profession, as well as on the history of crime and punishment, women and law, law and economy, the legal treatment of ethnic minorities, and famous cases and significant trials in all areas of the law.

Current directors of the Osgoode Society for Canadian Legal History are Susan Binnie, David Chernos, J. Douglas Ewart, Timothy Hill, Ian Hull, Mahmud Jamal, William Kaplan, C. Ian Kyer, Virginia MacLean, Roy McMurtry, Yasir Naqvi, Dana Peebles, Paul Perell, Paul Reinhardt, William Ross, Linda Rothstein, Paul Schabas, Robert Sharpe, Jon Silver, Alex Smith, Lorne Sossin, Mary Stokes, and Michael Tulloch.

The annual report and information about membership may be obtained by writing to the Osgoode Society for Canadian Legal History, Osgoode Hall, 130 Queen Street West, Toronto, Ontario, M5H 2N6. Telephone: 416-947-3321. E-mail: mmacfarl@lsuc.on.ca. Website: www.osgoodesociety.ca.

Robert J. Sharpe
President

Jim Phillips
Editor-in-Chief

Acknowledgments

Encouragement for this research came from many sources and individuals. Financial support was received from the Social Sciences and Humanities Research Council. To the individuals who reviewed grant applications, I give my thanks. Len Husband and Wayne Herrington at the University of Toronto Press have, as always, guided me through the process of publication with patience and enthusiasm for my work. Curtis Fahey gave superb editorial support. Angela Pietrobon supplied excellent indexing services. Anonymous reviewers at the Osgoode Society for Canadian Legal History provided important criticism that helped me to clarify my arguments; in particular, Carol Rogerson, who kindly allowed herself to be identified to me once the review process was complete, suggested detailed revisions. These were very helpful and I thank Carol for her generosity of time and spirit. Philip Girard and Jim Phillips also gave essential feedback on earlier versions of this manuscript. Heather Hillsburg, former student, now post-doctoral fellow, and colleague, has read, re-read, and commented upon multiple versions of various chapters of this work. Numerous colleagues, at Lakehead University and beyond, have been generous with their time and intellectual energy. Special appreciation must be expressed to my department, Women's Studies. Sadly, during the period of research for this book, we lost our colleague Helen Smith. Helen's joie de vivre is greatly missed by us all. To the remaining members of my department, Pam Wakewich, Jen Roth, and Jane Nicholas (now at the University of

Waterloo), thank you for your intellectual support and your day-to-day kindness. Lakehead colleagues outside my home department, including Paul Berger, Susan Forbes, Gary Genosko, Anna Guttman, Lori Livingston, Helle Moeller, Chris Mushquash, Tom Potter, Scott Pound, Connie Russell, Teresa Socha, Nadia Verrelli, and Bruce Weaver, have ensured that work is a place of laughter and kindness. Special thanks must go to Rachel Ariss, Kristin Burnett, Jason Maclean, and Ed Montigny, who have all talked endlessly with me about this project and provided unfailing personal as well as intellectual support. Christine Davidson and Jim Phillips have provided not only constructive criticism and laughter but also, on occasions too frequent to count, a home away from home in Toronto so that I could complete my research and writing. Thank you both for everything. Friend and sounding-board Steph Ross, who discussed this book on many occasions, passed away before its completion. She is deeply missed. To the friends with whom I walk my dogs, run, cycle, play hockey, and otherwise retreat from the world of academia, thank you for the joys that allow me to continue to return to research and writing.

My family has provided essential, but too often uncelebrated, support. My parents, Kay and Dave Chambers, and my uncle, Bill Chambers, have always believed in me, teased me, challenged me, and loved me unconditionally. My sister, Mary Catherine Chambers, has debated the arguments presented in this book on occasions too frequent to count and is an astute critic. Her move to Thunder Bay has allowed me the pleasure of participating closely in the lives of my niece and nephew, Sarah and Jonathon Friesen. For this I am eternally grateful. My partner, Michel Bedard, has been unfailingly supportive of this project. Our shared love of food and wine, our laughter, and our family life sustain me. I dedicate this book to our children, Geoff and Catherine, now adults making their own ways in the world. In all that I do, you are with me and bring me my greatest joy.

A LEGAL HISTORY OF ADOPTION IN ONTARIO, 1921–2015

Introduction

Adoption has fascinated the public for centuries and adoption themes are prominent in ancient fairy tales and modern literature and film alike;[1] this curiosity is not surprising since adoption is both complex and ethically challenging. Historians in Canada have also recently turned their attention to the transfer of children, but such historians have paid scant attention to the law with regard to adoption despite the centrality of law in the regulation of families.[2] This book thus fills an obvious lacuna, providing a detailed history of both legislation and the interpretation of the law of adoption in the Ontario courts from the passage of the first Adoption Act in 1921[3] to the present. Law is a particularly fruitful institution for analysis. Common law in Ontario has framed (and frames) what was (and is) possible with regard to the formation of families outside of biology and reflects particular values that are legitimized through its operation. These rules of Western law are not neutral and value-free and the study of adoption clearly reveals the hierarchies – of race, gender, class, and ability – that permeate legal structures and the society they uphold.

Historically, in Western societies and under Canadian law,[4] adoption was (and often still is) believed to be an altruistic mechanism for "saving" unfortunate children; as Karen Dubinsky argues, "ideologies and images of rescue"[5] are foundational to adoption practice. But from what and whom were (and are) children to be saved? How have unwed mothers, impoverished mothers, Indigenous[6] mothers, and mothers in poor or war-torn nations been discursively constructed in order to justify the removal of their children into the homes of privileged white North American families? What rights have women been accorded in the relinquishment process? What role have fathers played? Under what circumstances have older children been removed from parental care? What alternatives to apprehension have not been explored? Why was adoption shameful and secretive in Western cultures in the past? How have open adoption and knowledge about birth families come to be understood as enhancing the well-being of adopted children? How has adoption been used in the creation of blended, step-parent families? How has adoption law been applied in the context of same-sex relationships and new reproductive technologies? Why and how were, and are, the adoption of Indigenous children and international adoption particularly ethically and legally complex? How can we understand both the promise of adoption for the care of children in need and the potential exploitation of birth parents, families, communities, and nations in the adoption exchange? How has law mediated these conflicts? And how can these questions be asked while remaining respectful not only of adopted children and disadvantaged biological parents but also of adoptive parents who long for children, who have often suffered through infertility and failed reproductive interventions, and who represent the positive potential of loving beyond biology? This book explores these questions.

Such a study of adoption through the lens of law is timely. The rise of a vocal adoption-rights movement, debates about secrecy and open adoption, controversies about Indigenous and international adoption, and the sheer popularity of adoption and reunion stories in the media and popular press all illustrate public interest in the issue. In this context, Canadian historians have begun to explore adoption and three recent histories of adoption in Canada frame the discussions that follow. Veronica Strong-Boag's social history of adoption in English Canada, *Finding Families, Finding Ourselves*, reminds us that the regulation of adoption is part of the nation-building process, and that, by establishing rules for adoption, provinces also established "rules for the forging and control of diverse communities," defining who was in, and out, of families in much the same way that immigration operated on a national level.[7] Karen Dubinsky's *Babies without Borders* challenges previous understandings of the international exchange of children and moves "our understandings of interracial and international adoption beyond the false dichotomy of imperialist kidnap and humanitarian rescue."[8]

Her work forces readers to confront the moral complexity of adoption. Karen Balcom's history of the cross-border exchange of children between Canada and the United States, *The Traffic in Babies*, illustrates that "as babies crossed borders ... adopted children, adoptive parents, and birth mothers disappeared in the space between two (or more) sets of child welfare and immigration policies and laws," highlighting the fact that adoption could, and sometimes still does, occur outside the law.[9] All three authors explore the vulnerability of birth mothers and the intersections of race, class, ethnicity, and nationality in the exchange of children. Insights from these books are foundational to this study. Yet gaps in our knowledge remain, especially with regard to the law. In particular, Dubinsky and Balcom do not explore the full scope of changes in the domestic law of adoption. Strong-Boag provides more detail about adoption legislation in English Canada; however, her work is a general overview of all of the English-speaking provinces, preventing a comprehensive discussion of court cases despite their importance in the evolution of the law.[10] Importantly, also, the work presented here expands on the themes raised in these books by exploring twenty-first-century developments in adoption law.

This book focuses on a single jurisdiction, Ontario. As Canada's largest province, Ontario provides an excellent case study with which to begin exploring the specifics of adoption law. Not only has the volume of litigation in Ontario been enormous, but also Ontario is a province with a diverse population, including remote First Nations communities. Through much of the twentieth century, Ontario was perceived in Canada and beyond as a leader in child welfare; legislation in Ontario was frequently enacted, with limited revisions, in other provinces, and as Strong-Boag notes, Ontario was "often the most visible in its adoption initiatives."[11] A number of exceptionally important decisions have come from Ontario courts and Ontario decisions have had disproportionate impact outside the province.

The changes charted throughout this book had their origins in multiple, overlapping, and contradictory social movements of the early twentieth century. Industrialization, urbanization, and immigration were perceived to threaten the primarily rural and Anglo-Saxon nature of (English) Canadian society. New attitudes towards children in the nineteenth century, ones that framed them as innocent tabula rasa, ensured that reform efforts would be centred on the young. The Great War provided the moment at which concrete proposals for reform coalesced and achieved widespread social legitimacy and support.

Adoption legislation was passed in 1921 as part of a wider child-welfare package and adoption was immediately popular with the public; not only was there considerable positive discussion of the legislation in the press, but also the number of children adopted under the new legislation was immediately much higher than had been anticipated by reformers. The children adopted in Ontario were, until the 1960s, overwhelmingly those born to unwed mothers. Adoption was associated with the shame of illegitimacy and the stigma of infertility and was shrouded in secrecy. Challenges to this regime were limited before the 1960s. For this reason, although my book explores the legal history of adoption from 1921 onwards, by necessity the emphasis is on the last fifty years since much more change occurred in these decades.

The number of domestic babies available for adoption plummeted after the 1960s with the legalization of birth control, the partial decriminalization of abortion, the creation of universal social-welfare programs, and, eventually, the elimination of the legal category of "illegitimacy."[12] In this context, while previously adoptive parents had exclusively sought healthy infants who could be racially matched to their new families, older, mixed-race, and disabled children now became "adoptable"; adoption also became more visible and ideas of shame and secrecy were challenged. Simultaneously, families were changing with the rise of divorce, step-marriage, and, by the 1980s, open same-sex unions. As a result of rising divorce rates and the women's liberation movement with its early emphasis on formal equality, gender-neutral language was established in divorce and child custody law;[13] gender-neutral laws created the possibility that birth fathers – and even unwed fathers – might have new roles in adoption proceedings.

Most importantly, during the second half of the twentieth century, children came to be seen as rights bearers. As Michael Wald, the most influential international advocate of children's legal rights, asserted in 1974, "the idea of children bearing rights is a revolutionary one."[14] Child savers in the nineteenth century argued that children were malleable and that they could be saved from penury and delinquency through positive family influence. These ideas challenged patriarchal control of the household and provided the justification for child apprehension and adoption. However, even the most committed reformers did not contextualize these concerns in the framework of children's rights. This development occurred only in the second half of the twentieth century and is best illustrated in the documents promulgated by the United Nations. The 1989 Convention on the Rights of the Child stated that "in all actions concerning children, whether undertaken by public or private social welfare institutions, courts of law, administrative authorities or legislative bodies, the best interests of the child shall be a primary consideration."[15] Ontario was perceived to be in the vanguard of children's rights in adopting the "best interests" standard early and unequivocally. But how were a child's best interests to be determined? Who would speak for the child when the child could not speak for her or himself?[16] This question is crucial in the adoption context.

Adoption was and remains an issue of great complexity and must be studied not simply as a series of individual transactions in which new adults become the parents of particular children, but as a system or institution that reflects and reinforces existing social hierarchies. As Twila Perry argues in the context of cross-racial adoption in the United States, "just as feminists view marriage as an institution warranting an analysis that goes beyond individual couples, adoption must be approached with a similarly broad perspective. Adoption, like marriage, involves issues of hierarchy and power."[17] Veronica Strong-Boag adds that adoption has been but one piece of a system which has controlled women's reproductive capacities in myriad ways in a "hierarchy of preferred babies and mothers. All too often, white middle class women have been pressed to procreate, poor white women, especially the unwed, pressed to surrender offspring, and racialized minorities pressed to restrict their supposed excess fertility,"[18] sometimes through sterilization against their will.[19] The ability to release a child for adoption, unfettered by the state or by the whims of the genetic father of the child, has been and remains an essential component of women's reproductive freedom, but women have also faced constrained choices and sometimes coercion.

This book uses a wide range of primary and secondary sources, including legislation, parliamentary debates, and popular commentary from contemporary magazines and newspapers, in exploring the history of adoption law. Most importantly, I devote considerable attention to court cases and adoption-agency case files, both of which have been underutilized by previous historians of adoption. In the years immediately following the legislation of 1921, adoption decisions were rarely challenged and reported cases were uncommon. For this period, therefore, my analysis examines Children's Aid Society (CAS) case files produced under the Children of Unmarried Parents Act,[20] companion legislation to the Adoption Act of 1921. Such files provide crucial information with regard to the treatment of mothers who were relinquishing their children for newborn adoption. As Karen Dubinsky succinctly notes, "historical traces left in the case file are, mostly, told to and through the social worker"[21] and give us only glimpses of lived experiences. They tell us much, however, about the power of law and bureaucracy.

For the period as a whole under study, 1921 to 2015, I systematically canvass all reported court cases for the province of Ontario and all Supreme Court of Canada cases involving adoption. Court documents were particularly important in understanding changes since the 1970s. In the context of feminist challenges to the sexual double-standard and restrictions on reproductive autonomy, the rise of gender-neutral family law, and a rights revolution for children, adoptive parents, birth parents (mothers and fathers), and adoptive children have contested multiple aspects of the regulation of adoption in the Ontario courts. Birth mothers challenged restrictions on their right to revoke consent. Birth fathers sought a voice in adoption placement. Parents subject to the apprehension of their children challenged definitions of the best interests of the child. Adopted children and birth mothers confronted the secrecy surrounding adoption. Open adoption was promoted as a solution for the care of children previously considered unadoptable. Biological fathers contested adoptions of their children by step-parents. Lesbian couples used the step-parent analogy to expand their right to form families created via artificial insemination. Indigenous communities challenged the removal of children without community consent. And well-to-do parents sought children through international baby markets.

In recent decades, the guarantee of equality in section 15 of the Charter of Rights has been central to these disputes.[22] Adoption cases reveal the limitations of equality in the post-Charter era: birth mothers, particularly poor and racialized birth mothers, remain vulnerable in the twenty-first century; fathers have successfully challenged women's reproductive autonomy in the adoption context; alternative family formation remains available only to the well-to-do; and many children, particularly those of Indigenous descent, remain outside the adoption regime, languishing instead in the foster-care system. The stories recounted in courts and in this book about individual adoptions are often challenging and complex, engaging empathy for children, birth parents, and adoptive parents simultaneously. In difficult and complex contexts, how has the law determined with whom an individual child should reside? The format for the exploration of these issues in the remainder of the book is outlined below.

The first chapter details the origins of adoption law. Before the passage of adoption legislation, formal adoption was possible only through private members' bills in the provincial legislature. Adoption legislation was intended to make formal adoption more accessible and was explicitly linked to nineteenth-century legislation which legitimized state removal of children from homes deemed neglectful, to community responses to child poverty, and to popular concerns about rising illegitimacy rates. Legislators foresaw adoption being used as a solution to child-welfare challenges with regard to two specific groups of children: the children of unwed mothers and those who were removed from parental care under child-protection statutes. In practice, however, crown wards, taken from their families later in life than illegitimate infants, were viewed by the public as less desirable for adoption and the vast majority of children adopted domestically in Canada until the 1960s were born of unwed mothers.

The next three chapters explore the question of how children became available for domestic adoption. Chapter 2 examines the conditions under which unwed mothers gave consent to relinquishment of newborn babies. Using case files produced under the Children of Unmarried Parents Act, this chapter illustrates the social and institutional coercion that was prevalent in adoption practice. In a few cases in which women challenged these powers in the 1950s and 1960s, courts critiqued the coercive techniques employed by the Children's Aid Society. In cases since 1970, however, the Supreme Court of Canada has restricted women's right to change their minds about relinquishment of infants.

In contrast, the rights of fathers have expanded. This is the subject of chapter 3. Uninvolved, unmarried fathers were initially constructed as irrelevant in the relinquishment of children. But in the 1970s unmarried fathers with existing relationships with older children were determined to have a right to contest the relinquishment of such children for third-party adoption. Unwed fathers' claims were based on the concept of "social fatherhood," referring to actions by the father that reflected extended investment in the well-being of the child. Recent legislation has recognized a wide range of unmarried men as fathers, listed circumstances under which paternity will be presumed, and allowed the use of genetic testing. Even these expanded definitions have been challenged and increasingly genetic fathers without any social connection to their newborns have nonetheless been able to participate in the relinquishment process, limiting women's reproductive autonomy.

Chapter 4 focuses on the involuntary apprehension of children. While the right to remove children from parental care was affirmed in nineteenth-century legislation, in practice apprehensions were uncommon until the 1950s. In the 1960s, new and dramatic medical concern about physical child abuse led to mandatory reporting regimes and a precipitous increase in apprehensions; racialized and Indigenous children were particularly likely to be apprehended or "scooped." By the late 1970s, however, it was understood that far too many children remained in foster care, without adoption placements, and that long-term outcomes for such children were poor. This led to amendments to child-welfare law in 1984[23] which emphasized working with families to prevent neglect and maltreatment and therefore apprehension. Yet such efforts were never adequately funded and, in a context of government retreat from investment in the poor and a number of high-profile child deaths, in 1999 Ontario returned to a child-welfare regime that emphasizes apprehension.[24]

Secrecy and openness in adoption are explored in chapters 5 and 6. As chapter 5 illustrates, into the 1980s, Canadian courts consistently held that secrecy was essential to the security of adoption placement; courts continued to assert that relinquishment was shameful and that knowledge of one's past could harm children and undermine the security of adoptive families. Then, with the rise of a vocal adoption-rights movement, closed adoption records were challenged. The Ontario legislature moved to provide a means by which adopted children and birth parents could obtain non-identifying information about each other and initiate searches for the purposes of meeting. In 2005 the Ontario legislature passed the Adoption Information Disclosure Act,[25] which would have given all adult adoptees and birth parents an absolute right to information about adoption. However, in a controversial court decision, the legislation was determined to violate privacy rights and compromise legislation was passed.[26]

The purpose and value of open adoption, the subject of chapter 6, has been closely linked to debates about secrecy. Open adoption emerged as a result of three interrelated changes in the adoption landscape: stepparent adoption; the open-records movement; and the push for the adoption of racialized, older, and special-needs children in the 1960s. Since 2006, birth parents whose children have been removed from their care through crown ward proceedings have been able to apply for access orders after adoption.[27] But, in all cases of voluntary relinquishment, including newborn relinquishment, birth parents are dependent upon the goodwill of adoptive parents to ensure that the terms of pre-adoptive agreements are respected. Open adoption is often opposed because it raises the potential that children will have more than two recognized parents. Open adoption, however, is not the only context in which children may have multiple parents; step-parent and same-sex second-parent adoption also raise this possibility and, perhaps not surprisingly, both practices have been controversial in part for that reason.

Step-parent adoption is the subject of chapter 7. Under the legislation of 1921, an unmarried mother had the sole right to relinquish a child for adoption and she could therefore allow the adoption of her child by a new husband. Yet, without an exemption, such an adoption would have required the mother to relinquish her own custody. Legislators therefore created a mechanism which maintained maternal custody in cases of step-parent adoption. By the 1970s, in a context of rising divorce and remarriage rates, formerly married mothers were attempting to use this exemption to exclude ex-husbands. Courts came to hold a strict standard that allowed adoption by a step-parent only rarely. Courts also carved out exemptions to permit ongoing contact with birth fathers, providing the first examples of open adoption. Issues with regard to multiple parents have not, however, been resolved. In the absence of legal adoption, what rights and obligations apply to step-parent relationships after marital or quasi-marital breakdown?

The step-parent analogy has been central in obtaining rights for lesbian couples in second-parent adoption in cases involving new reproductive technologies, particularly anonymous sperm donation. These issues are explored in chapter 8. Same-sex couples in Ontario were long denied access to step-parent or second-parent adoption, but in 1995 four lesbian couples convinced a provincial court judge that denial of same-sex adoption constituted discrimination against both same-sex parents and their children.[28] In 2006 lesbian couples challenged the vital-statistics regime and achieved the right to include the names of both same-sex partners on a child's statement of live birth in cases of anonymous sperm donation.[29] Surrogacy has also raised issues closely related to adoption. While open adoption could provide some protection in multiple-parent situations, clarification of parentage legislation, as has been undertaken in British Columbia, would solve many of the dilemmas raised in the context of assisted reproduction and has been advocated by contemporary legal critics.

The adoption of Indigenous children is the subject of chapter 9. The "sixties scoop" – the intentional placement of Indigenous children in white homes off-reserve – raised profound questions for (settler) law. If adoption represented an absolute severance of the relationship between birth parent(s) and child, did First Nations and Inuit children lose status on adoption? The legality (at least in the minds of settler society) of formal adoption, and the fact that the child would retain Indian status, was confirmed by the Supreme Court of Canada in 1976.[30] Despite this decision, or perhaps because of it, Indigenous opposition to adoption out of communities led, in 1984, to an amendment to Ontario adoption regulations requiring that courts considering the best interests of Indigenous children acknowledge "the uniqueness of Indian and native culture, heritage and traditions"[31] and that adoption into white homes be allowed only as a last resort. Notwithstanding this reform, resources remain inadequate and colonialism and structural racism mean that disproportionate numbers of Indigenous children continue to be apprehended and to languish in foster care and group homes.

International adoption is the subject of the final chapter of the book. International adoption emerged in the context of the post-war refugee crisis, the Cold War desire to prove the superiority of the West, and a dramatic decline in the availability of healthy babies (and Indigenous children) for domestic adoption. International adoption scandals prompted the promulgation of the Hague Convention on the Protection of Children and Cooperation in Respect of Inter-Country Adoptions (Hague Conference on Private International Law) in 1993.[32] Very few court cases with regard to international adoption have been heard in Ontario and, when faced with cases in which the conditions of surrender of children in sending countries were questionable, courts have had few options but to formalize adoptions regardless since the children concerned were already landed in Canada.

As this overview illustrates, the issues raised by adoption have been myriad and complex. How we regulate adoption tells us a great deal about how we define appropriate families, about class, racial, and gender hierarchies, and about the value we place on children and their well-being. Problems in adoption law should prompt not only legal reform but also wider discussions about children, their rights, and the diversity of their families.

1

The Origins of Adoption Legislation

Informal adoption has a long history,[1] but legislative adoption in Ontario is a more recent phenomenon, dating to the Adoption Act of 1921.[2] Before this time, legal adoption was possible only through private members' bills in the provincial legislature.[3] Adoption legislation was intended to make formal adoption cheaper and more accessible. Adoption was part of a wider movement for child-welfare reform in a context in which childhood was viewed increasingly as a time of innocence and children as in need of protection. During the nineteenth century, throughout the Anglo-Saxon world, as Shurlee Swain and Margot Hillel note in their study of child-rescue discourse in the United Kingdom, Canada, and Australia, "the child, regarded in law as little more than the property of the father, became ... a citizen or potential citizen with a new status and added respect."[4] With industrialization, urbanization, and rising immigration, child poverty became increasingly visible and reformers responded by creating charitable institutions for poor and neglected children and by developing statutory mechanisms for their removal from parental control. The younger the child, the more innocent and malleable he or she was perceived to be, and, by the early twentieth century, reformers asserted that adoption would be a particularly useful solution for illegitimate children who faced significant social stigma, were disproportionately likely to be impoverished, and could be placed with families at a very early age. This argument gained strength as illegitimacy rates rose during the Great War.[5] Adoption, it was argued, by placing children with parents of means who embodied middle-class values of piety, sobriety, and hard work, would prevent degeneracy, idleness, dependence, and future crime. These beliefs led to the creation of statutory adoption as part of a package of family-centred legislation passed in 1921.[6]

While initially reformers had assumed that some children were unadoptable, by the 1950s, as the rights of the child became an increasingly international subject of discussion,[7] Ontario social workers aggressively campaigned for the adoption of hard-to-place children, including those who were older, suffered from ill health or behavioural problems, or were of mixed race. Institutionalization of hard-to-place children was expensive, and by the 1950s it was also recognized that foster care too often resulted in poor economic, social, and emotional outcomes for children. Not only did the state have a right to remove children from parental care for the sake of wider society, but it was now also asserted that all children had a right to decent treatment and happiness that could be facilitated in families of choice.[8] Adoption, therefore, has been fraught with tensions between the judgment of parents deemed not to meet the moral and economic standards of a middle-class, capitalist society and an altruistic desire to provide opportunity for children born in disadvantaged circumstances.

The most direct antecedent for legal adoption was guardianship provisions which transferred responsibility for children and their property to a caregiver chosen by the biological father. Such provisions had their origins, not in concern for poor children, but in the protection of the property of wealthy heirs. In England's Court of Chancery, well-to-do fathers could assign guardians to protect the property of heirs and to undertake the care and control of such children in the case of paternal death. While the Court of Chancery did not exist in Upper Canada until 1837, guardianship legislation was passed in 1827 specifically to protect the property interests of wealthy families.[9] With the fusion of equity and the common law in 1881,[10] guardianship became more widely available but was largely employed as a means of establishing trusts for wealthy children and testamentary provisions for the care of such children in the case of the death of parents.[11] Guardianship mechanisms provided an example on which to base legislative provisions that might deal with responsibility for poor children deemed in need of state protection. But, first, public attitudes about poor and disadvantaged children had to be transformed.

Attitudes towards poor children historically had not been sympathetic and legislators inherited laws from England which placed the blame for poverty on the poor themselves, even when they were children. Upper Canada excluded England's Poor Laws from reception, believing that poor relief was unnecessary in this land of (supposed) abundance. This left the colony without a system of public relief[12] and authorities filled the void by assuming some responsibility for destitute homeless children by apprenticing them under indentures adapted from English precedents. In 1799 the authority of public officials to indenture children was clarified by legislation. However, the state did not have the authority or the obligation to take a child away from his or her parents, to override the wishes of surviving relatives able and willing to support the child, or to intervene on behalf of children mistreated by their parents. In 1851 comprehensive provincial apprenticeship legislation expanded the categories of children who could be apprenticed by public officials to include orphans, deserted children, children dependent on charity, and those whose parents were incarcerated.[13] Apprenticeships focused on making the child useful to society, but the care provided by the family with whom the child was apprenticed also provided a form of what we might now call foster care and therefore a model for future child placement.

During the nineteenth century, child saving became, as Xiaobei Chen argues with regard to Toronto, "part of a citizenship project"[14] and child savers – loose coalitions of reformers focused on children – created a discursive environment in which removal of children from parental influence was justified for the sake not only of the child but also of the wider society. Concerned, often religiously motivated, groups responded to visible poverty by creating charitable institutions for children. In Toronto the Female Aid Society, later the Protestant Children's Home, was established in 1851, the Girls' Home in 1856, and the Boys' Home in 1859.[15] Many parents used such homes to ensure children's survival in difficult economic circumstances, not because they wanted to abandon their children.[16] Through legislation that facilitated the establishment and operation of such institutions, and through grants to them, the government became indirectly involved in child welfare. A Board of Inspectors of Asylums and Prisons was created in 1860 and later also inspected orphan asylums in receipt of grants.[17] Younger children were sometimes placed in families for informal adoption, but placements were not legally binding. Older children were regularly apprenticed from children's homes, or placed with families as servants, when they could not be returned to their families of origin, but this began to be viewed as inappropriate in a context of universal mandatory education.

Schooling in Upper Canada was inconsistent in the nineteenth century and governments became concerned that children were not adequately prepared for the democratic nation-state and the industrial economy.[18] In 1871 education for four months per year was made a right for children aged seven to twelve and parents who failed to send their children to school could be penalized. Despite mandatory universal education, many children still did not attend school; those not attending were often disadvantaged children who had no choice but to work to contribute to the family economy. Public school boards were authorized to establish industrial schools "for otherwise neglected children." Although the Act to Improve the Common and Grammar Schools of the Province of Ontario did not define the "neglected child," it did provide "that any pupil who shall be adjudged so refractory by the trustees (or a majority of them) and the teacher, that his presence in the school is deemed injurious to the other pupils, may be dismissed from such school, and, where practicable, removed to an Industrial school."[19] However, no industrial schools were established by school boards under the legislation. In 1883 An Act respecting Industrial Schools was amended to allow school boards to delegate the authority to establish industrial schools to philanthropic societies,[20] and industrial schools were thereafter established. But they effectively became reformatories focusing on the delinquency of children, rather than any wrongdoing by their parents.

Juvenile delinquency was linked with child saving in the public mind in profound ways, as is evidenced in the rhetoric and work of the Toronto Humane Society, established in 1887. The agency was cofounded by J.J. Kelso and John Kidson Macdonald, who would later be the superintendent of neglected and dependent children and the superintendent of the Children's Aid Society, respectively. The Humane Society expressed abhorrence of violence against both children and animals, but "neglecting children was [believed to be] a worse sin than being brutal towards them."[21] Evidence illustrated that men were more likely to beat and abuse children (as well as their wives and animals),[22] but mothers were criticized as neglectful. While reformers were aware of the material challenges faced by poor mothers, removing children was "thought of as a remedy to bad housing, immoral home conditions, child labor, and bad companions, and in the end a solution to juvenile delinquency."[23] In 1892 the Children's Aid Society was created to deal exclusively with these concerns regarding child welfare, but it did not have any legal power to enact its programs for reform.

Following extensive lobbying by child savers, this limitation was addressed in 1893 in legislation explicitly intended to empower the CAS to act to protect children from their own parents. An Act for the Prevention of Cruelty to and Better Protection of Children established the province's first comprehensive child-protection system. The legislation was intended to identify neglected and maltreated children, to remove them from their homes, and to provide alternative care. Under the act, anyone "having the care, custody, control or charge of a child" who "wilfully ill-treats, neglects, abandons, or exposes such child, or causes or procures such child to be ill-treated, neglected, abandoned, or exposed, in a manner likely to cause such child unnecessary suffering or serious injury to its health" could be charged with a summary offence. In effect, the act imported the guardianship model from Chancery, taking responsibility for abused and neglected children's well-being by removing them from the legal care of their biological parents and making them what was thereafter to be referred to as crown wards, children under the guardianship of the state.[24]

Not surprisingly, given Kelso and Macdonald's influence, responsibility for implementation of the 1893 act was entrusted to local Children's Aid Societies, staffed by volunteers and a growing cadre of social workers anxious to establish professional legitimacy. Each branch of the CAS operated as a private agency run by its own board at the local level. Although enforcing state policies, workers experienced only minimal government regulation and received limited financial support, rendering each institution dependent upon local charity.[25] The CAS tried to place children in free[26] homes but from the outset had difficulty doing so with older children, sibling groups, and children with health and/or behavioural problems. Middle-class families wanted very young children more like themselves and poor families could not afford extra mouths to feed. In this context, by the 1920s not only were the respectable poor being offered subsidies for foster care, but also CAS workers were increasingly convinced that legal adoption was a necessary addition to the child-protection arsenal.[27]

Concern about infants, in particular illegitimate children, also encouraged the creation of adoption laws. Religious institutions in Ontario focused primarily on older children and the first home in the province providing care specifically for babies appears to have been the Toronto

Infants' Home, which opened in 1875 and received its first government grant in 1876.[28] Such homes had very small staffs and mothers with infants were expected either to live in residence and take care of their own and other newborns or to pay for their babies' upkeep. Infant mortality rates were extraordinarily high.[29] Responding to public concern, in 1887 the Ontario government passed the Act for the Protection of Infant Children, which mandated both annual inspection and regulation of homes caring for more than one infant.[30]

Infant mortality, poverty, and illegitimacy were clearly linked. As early as 1910, Dr Helen MacMurchy prepared reports on infant mortality and child welfare for the Ontario government illustrating that poor families and unwed mothers were particularly likely to suffer the loss of a child.[31] The altruistic rhetoric of child saving was closely linked to the social gospel and Christian-based reform movements that were politically powerful during the Great War and in its immediate aftermath.[32] The rhetoric of child welfare, however, did not absolve poor, particularly unwed, mothers of blame and masked considerable class, ethnic, and racial prejudice. Poor mothering, believed to be particularly common among unwed and immigrant mothers, was perceived to be responsible for disease, immorality, and child mortality,[33] thus adding fuel to the fire for those who advocated removal of children from questionable homes and encouraging proponents of adoption.[34] While asserting that the state must intervene to reduce infant mortality rates and child poverty, for example, the editor of the *Canadian Public Health Journal* simultaneously argued that "intelligent motherhood alone can give to the infant that which neither wealth nor state nor yet science can offer."[35] Illegitimate babies were believed to be at particular risk because their single mothers were disproportionately impoverished and were seen as unfit and unintelligent.

The Ontario laws that condemned the unwed mother and her child to outcast status and poverty originated in England. While married men had exclusive legal rights over their children with regard to custody, guardianship, discipline, and control over education and religion, under the common law the child born to an unmarried mother was a child of nobody. As William Blackstone asserted in his seminal legal treatise, "the incapacity of a bastard consists principally in this, that he cannot be heir to any one, neither can he have heirs, but of his own body. Being *nullius filius*, he is therefore kin of nobody."[36] Upper Canadian legislators made fathers potentially responsible for the support of their illegitimate children in 1837. Under the Seduction Act, anyone who furnished necessaries for an illegitimate child could sue the putative father of the child for the costs of such support. The mother's evidence regarding paternity had to be corroborated by a third party.[37] In cases in which women were successful in affidavits of affiliation, under which unwed mothers tried to prove paternity and claim child support, the liability imposed on the father lasted until the child reached his or her majority; the child did not, however, take the surname of the father or obtain rights of inheritance.[38]

Rising rates of illegitimacy during the Great War prompted fears of sexual immorality, fears that were particularly focused on so-called immoral women and poor mothering, and further fuelled demands for adoption.[39] Increasing concern over the particular disadvantages faced by illegitimate children – legal, social, and economic – was an international phenomenon.[40] In 1915 the U.S. Children's Bureau commissioned a massive three-part series, *Illegitimacy as a Social Welfare Problem*, which was published in 1920. In 1919 and 1920 this agency sponsored international conferences that brought together child-welfare activists to discuss "the legal handicaps facing children born out of wedlock and to formulate broad principles of treatment and legislation."[41] At a 1921 conference in Chicago on the rights of the child, Ernst Freund, a noted professor of jurisprudence, argued that "every effort should be made by the law to relieve the child of the stigma that attaches to illegitimate birth."[42] As Karen Balcom so vividly illustrates, the personal and professional connections between (particularly female) child-welfare professionals in Canada and the United States were extensive, and a significant contingent of Canadian social workers attended this and other conferences.[43] While illegitimacy continued to be condemned, the belief, as prominent Canadian reformer Peter Bryce put it, that "visiting this condemnation on the head of an infant is illogical and unjust"[44] became more widespread in the aftermath of the Great War.

In this context, it is not surprising that the legislature acted to protect children in the years immediately following the war. It is also not surprising that mothers were judged and categorized under such legislation as worthy or unworthy of state support. The first act to assist poor mothers in Ontario, the Mothers' Allowance Act of 1920, provided very meagre support to widows and women whose husbands were incapacitated. All mothers receiving support had to be of "good moral character." Unwed mothers were explicitly excluded.[45] Instead, such children, it was believed, should be removed from their families of origin. J.J. Kelso opined that children, "if taken hold of at the right time,"[46] could be saved from leading lives of worthlessness, poverty, and vice. Such rhetoric justified the invocation of the removal privileges granted to the Children's Aid Society under the child-protection legislation of 1893 and the placement of children in "better" homes through adoption, preferably as early in life as possible. But without an adoption law, what would happen to children removed from parental care or whose mothers were simply too poor to raise them?

Reformers were concerned that commercial adoption, a range of practices involving varying levels of consent by birth mothers,[47] would fill the void, particularly for illegitimate babies immediately after birth. Without a mechanism for adoption, and in a context in which vital statistics were only just being established, it remained possible simply to transfer a child at the time of birth. Social workers, invoking eugenic beliefs, warned prospective parents that profit-driven adoption would lead to dissatisfaction with the children so placed. Charlotte Whitton, a leader in Canadian child welfare, asserted that unmarried mothers were usually of low intelligence and weak morality and that their children must be carefully screened before placement.[48] These problems, child-welfare professionals believed, could be mitigated through careful social-work practice which would differentiate statutory adoption from the for-profit baby market. Much effort would be put by social workers into matching an infant, on the basis of extensive psychological and intelligence testing,[49] with his or her adoptive parents. It should be noted that the major concern expressed regarding adoption placement was not the question of how to ensure that parents were fit and suitable, but of how to reduce the likelihood that adoptive parents would receive a "defective" child.

Legal adoption would also, it was argued, save the state money. Care of children in institutions was prohibitively expensive. It was, as the superintendent of Ontario's prisons and charities put it, "a most extravagant way of dealing with children."[50] Foster care, while widely supported by social workers, also did not solve the problem of the cost of child welfare since subsidies for families had proven to be necessary.[51] As the Social Service Council of Ontario retrospectively admitted in a 1921 memo to the attorney general, W.E. Raney, the purpose of adoption was to place children with "people who have the means and can provide a suitable home,"[52] thus saving the state significant money.

It was in this context – the creation of the state right to remove children from homes deemed inappropriate, rising concern about child welfare and "black market" adoption, sympathy for the unfortunate illegitimate child, blame and shame for unwed and otherwise "neglectful" mothers, and a need to save money – that Canadian provinces passed adoption statutes.[53] In Ontario, adoption was part of a reform package passed in 1921 which consisted of three pieces of legislation: the Legitimation Act, An Act for the Protection of the Children of Unmarried Parents (hereafter the Children of Unmarried Parents Act), and the Adoption Act.[54] While Ontario Premier E.C. Drury's tenuous coalition government could not agree on economic reforms,[55] his family-centred legislation of 1921 garnered wide support. He later described the child-welfare reforms enacted under his administration as "such a program of social legislation as Ontario and indeed all of Canada and North America had never seen, or perhaps thought possible."[56] Charlotte Whitton, a central author of the legislation, also consistently asserted that these child-welfare reforms were among her crowning achievements.[57]

The Legitimation Act allowed for the subsequent legitimation of children, born outside of lawful wedlock, whose biological parents later married.[58] This measure was intended not only to improve the legal and social status of illegitimate children but also to provide an incentive for cohabiting couples to formalize their relationships and for couples caught pregnant to have shotgun weddings; the state rewarded conformity rather than explicitly punishing non-marital cohabitation.[59] Retroactive legitimation represented a dramatic departure from the common law and had previously been rejected "because of the very great uncertainty there will generally be in the proof that the issue was really begotten by the same man."[60] The state would now accept the father's (but not simply the mother's) word regarding paternity. Such a policy may have had particular resonance for the public in the immediate aftermath of war. This legislation allowed couples who married as soon as possible after the war to eliminate the stigma to which their children would otherwise have been subjected and to ensure that such children were not precluded from inheritance.

The Children of Unmarried Parents Act provided a mechanism by which unwed mothers could obtain financial support from the putative fathers of their children, but it did so in a manner that was deliberately punitive and degrading. The act overturned the common law assumption that the mother was the de facto guardian of her illegitimate child. Instead, it provided that "the provincial officer [the government employee appointed to enforce these three acts] may upon his own application be appointed guardian of a child born out of wedlock either alone or jointly with the mother of such child." Moreover, when "the mother ... through lack of means is unable, or through misconduct is unfit to have the care of the child, the child may, with the consent of the provincial officer, be dealt with as a 'neglected child.'" In such cases the child could be summarily removed from the mother's custody. An unwed mother could be deemed unfit purely because of her poverty. The state, not the mother, had the primary right to claim child support from the putative father.[61] The mother could also apply for support from the putative father of the child, but any such applicant had to bear the cost of the proceedings herself. The term "putative" father illustrates the distrust of women that underlay this ostensibly child-centred legislation; as one forthright Ontario judge put it in 1942, the court was inherently "doubtful of her [the mother's] veracity."[62] When convinced by the evidence, the judge could declare "the person named to be the father."[63] The sum to be awarded was to be based, not on need, but on the father's "ability to provide and [his] prospective means." The putative father could not be required to pay beyond his means, but without paternal support, the mother might find her child dealt with as a "neglected child."[64] The state had provided mechanisms for legitimating the child and it was clearly the preference of the state, when legitimation was not possible, that the mother release her child into the care of a more suitable family. The Children of Unmarried Parents Act, not accidentally, created conditions under which relinquishment of illegitimate infants for adoption would be common.

The Adoption Act, the final act in this child-welfare reform package, provided a mechanism for the permanent adoption of children either by strangers or by kin. Ontario based its legislation explicitly on that of Massachusetts, the first U.S. state to amend the common law by providing means for formalizing adoptions, and on the Children's Code of Minnesota.[65] The Adoption Act granted jurisdiction to magistrates and judges in county, juvenile, and family courts to award adoption orders.[66] For a child to be eligible for adoption, the child's former guardians or lawful parents had to sign consent to adoption forms. In cases of illegitimacy, only the consent of the mother was required.[67] Consent could be granted by the judge, even against the express will of the parents, if such parents were deemed unfit to give consent, if the parents were imprisoned, or if the child were deemed neglected or mistreated and had been made a crown ward; what would be required to deem a parent "unfit" was not defined, leaving tremendous room for discretionary interpretation of the statute by social workers in the Children's Aid Society and by the courts. The judge could grant an order for adoption only if "satisfied of the ability of the applicants to fulfill the obligations and perform the duties of a parent towards the child to be adopted." The child had to have "lived for at least two years previously with the applicant and ... during that period the conduct of the applicant and the conditions under which the child has lived have been such to justify the making of the order." The CAS was made responsible for deciding whether proceedings would be instituted against fathers under the Children of Unmarried Parents Act, selecting adoptive parents, and supervising the placement to be approved by the judge.[68] The act also allowed placement of children through the courts under private arrangements; this left a window for private agencies, lawyers, doctors, and homes for unwed mothers to place infants with wealthy families through private adoptions that avoided the scrutiny of the CAS. Although legislators hoped that both illegitimate children and those who had been removed from parental control owing to neglect or abuse would be adopted, in practice the vast majority of children adopted by non-kin until the 1960s were those who had been born illegitimate; such children were desirable because they could be placed immediately after birth and retain the fiction of the heteronormative family.

Under this new legislation, an Ontario adoption order divested "the natural parent, guardian or person in whose custody the child has been of all legal rights in respect of such child." The child became "for the purposes of custody of the person and rights of obedience, to all intents and purposes the child of the adopting parents." The child had "the same right to any claim for nurture, maintenance and education upon his adopting parents as he would have were they his natural parents." The child would be known by the surname of the adopting parents and had, with respect to his or her adoptive parents, rights of inheritance equal to those of children born in lawful wedlock.[69] Since the ties between the child and his/her natural parents were irrevocably severed by adoption, the relinquishing parent had no right to information about the child.[70] The Adoption Act made no provision for the adopted child to obtain information about his/her natural parents. Illegitimacy was shameful and the adoption process was shrouded in secrecy; the natural parent was symbolically erased from the child's life and all original birth records were sealed. In effect, as Katrysha Bracco argues, adoption introduced into Ontario law the "statutory death of the biological parents and the rebirth of the adoptee."[71] Perhaps not surprisingly, given the roots of child-saving organizations and legislation in sectarian charitable institutions, children were required to be placed within their own religious groups, even as their individual identities were completely remade, a fact that led to the development of separate Children's Aid Societies and Catholic Children's Aid Societies in most communities, as well as to separate Jewish agencies, regulating the placement of children.[72]

By 1947, Ontario had forty-six Children's Aid Societies (some ostensibly non-sectarian but effectively Protestant, and others Catholic) in various communities. Maternity homes, children's homes, and adoption centres, both private and religiously organized, also operated, often on a for-profit basis.[73] Demand for babies was so high that adoption became competitive and social workers expressed fear that parents would avoid the requirements of social-service agencies – careful selection of the parents and supervision of the placement – and obtain babies through unregulated means. In 1948 Charlotte Whitton reported that "babies available for adoption are scarce ... [with] rising demand [potential parents] will seek to short-circuit these carefully devised procedures."[74]

In 1954 adoption was incorporated into the wider Child Welfare Act of that year,[75] a move that reflected the increasing popularity of adoption as a means of family formation. In 1957 a reporter in *Chatelaine* asserted that people who wished to adopt faced bureaucratic challenges and long waits, and that "the basic reason is simply that there are not enough children to go around ... last year the Toronto Children's Aid Society had four times as many applicants as children."[76] In part, this shortage of children was created by the desire of parents for babies who resembled themselves so that they could maintain the fiction of the nuclear, biological family. In the 1960s a revolution in sexual morality, the decriminalization of birth control, and the partial decriminalization of abortion[77] reduced the stigma faced by unwed mothers. Moreover, the expansion of welfare benefits under the Canada Assistance Plan of 1966[78] meant that more women could contemplate keeping children born outside wedlock, and rates of relinquishment plummeted. As demand for children increased, older, special-needs, and racially diverse children were also adopted under the provisions of the legislation of 1921; during this same decade the requirement for religious matching was quietly eliminated. Moreover, to meet the demand for children, Indigenous babies and youngsters were apprehended and adopted out of their communities, and, when Indigenous communities protested, international adoption emerged as an alternative source of children.

Adoption is now regulated under the Child and Family Services Act, Part VII, and is an important part of wider child-welfare services.[79] Since the 1980s the proportion of private adoptions has increased steadily; reduced numbers of single mothers relinquish their infants for adoption, but those who do so voluntarily choose not to work with the agencies of the state. For adopters, avoiding government agencies dramatically shortens the process of adoption. For birth parents, it allows the mother to select the new parents for her child, and potentially to maintain contact with the child throughout his or her childhood.[80] Children who are removed from parents against their will, however, are in the public system by default. Such children remain much more likely to be among those in the limbo of foster care. Historically, adoption failed as a solution to wider child-welfare problems. Yet it did provide a means by which infertile couples, same-sex couples, single parents, and others built families of choice which challenged patriarchal and biological definitions of family. It is to the complex history of how the law has regulated these relationships that we now turn.

2
Mothers and the Meaning of Consent in Adoption

The first legal question that arises with regard to the history of adoption is how and why particular children became available for transfer from their birth families into alternative homes. How was a decision made to relinquish a child for newborn adoption and when and why have children been removed from parental care against their parents' will?[1] With regard to newborns, previous authors working on this subject in Canada have paid little attention to the legalities of consent; for example, Veronica Strong-Boag, while noting that "Canadian courts had to interpret what all the legislation relating to consent actually meant in practical terms," devotes only two paragraphs to a brief description of a limited selection of cases.[2] Court cases with regard to newborn relinquishment deserve considerably more study.

This chapter illustrates that the conditions under which women consented to relinquishment were often exploitative. Overwhelmingly, until into the 1970s, children released domestically for newborn adoption in Canada were those born to unmarried women; poor pregnant unmarried women lacked the financial resources to raise children alone and single pregnant middle-class women, to avoid shame and stigma, retreated into homes for unwed mothers where they released their infants in secrecy.[3] The relinquishing mother was often intimidated and harassed, but influence and coercion have been narrowly construed in courts overseeing adoptions. The question of "what constitutes 'free will' and 'understanding' when children are surrendered"[4] was complex and the babies women produced – when such babies were white – were in high demand.[5] Although the Supreme Court of Canada censured the Children's Aid Society with regard to proceedings that pressured young unwed women to release their babies for adoption in a case heard in 1970,[6] since that time the Court has retreated from such protections of mothers. Current provisions that ostensibly guarantee the mother the right not only to make the decision regarding relinquishment without coercion, but also to change her mind within a legislated time frame, have been interpreted restrictively. Exploring the history of the legal interpretation of relinquishment is essential to understanding the hierarchies that underlie domestic adoption.

As already noted, under the Ontario Adoption Act of 1921, for a child to be eligible for adoption, the child's former guardians or lawful parents had to sign consent to adoption forms. In cases of illegitimacy, only the consent of the mother was required. This consent could be granted by the judge, even against the express will of the parents, if such parents were deemed unfit to give consent, if the parents were imprisoned, or if the child were deemed neglected by the CAS and had been made a crown ward.[7] In a revision to the Adoption Act in 1937, the right of the court to dispense with consent was further clarified: "The court may dispense with any consent required by this subsection if satisfied that the person whose consent is to be dispensed with has abandoned or deserted the infant or cannot be found or is incapable of giving such consent or, being a person liable to contribute to the support of the infant, either has persistently neglected or refused to contribute to such support or is a person whose consent ought, in the opinion of the court and in all the circumstances of the case, to be dispensed with."[8] The question of how to determine "whose consent ought, in the opinion of the court and in all the circumstances of the case, to be dispensed with" remained open to considerable discretion.

Further, the rights of mothers with regard to consent would be interpreted in a context in which their babies were in high demand and women were assumed to be inferior parents if unmarried. J.J. Kelso, Ontario child-reform leader, argued that "no unmarried mother can successfully bring up her child and save it from disgrace and obloquy. [But] the child, if adopted young by respectable, childless people, will grow up creditably, and without any painful reminders of its origins." Illegitimate babies were widely considered to be disadvantaged and infertile parents wanted very young children. In 1930 J.J. Kelso noted that, in the nine years since 1921, over 6,000 adoptions had been completed.[9]

While adoption was already popular in the 1920s and 1930s, demand for babies increased further in the immediate post-Second World War and Cold War period. As Wayne Carp argues in the U.S. context, "parenthood during the Cold War became a patriotic necessity. The media romanticized babies, glorified motherhood, and identified fatherhood with masculinity and good citizenship."[10] In Canada as well, the childless were marginalized. It was explicitly babies, not children, who were in demand. Under the influence of popular psychology and the concept of early bonding, in particular the work of John Bowlby in the 1950s, parents sought custody of babies as early as possible. Bowlby asserted that "on psychiatric and social grounds ... the baby should be adopted as early in his life as possible."[11] Many parents also wanted to maintain the fiction of the biological family to the wider world and this was facilitated by adoption of the infant directly from the hospital. Unwed mothers were often impoverished and always subject to stigma and therefore vulnerable. It was in this context that adoption expanded dramatically.

The demand for healthy white babies invited abuse. Evidence from the United States during this period illustrates the existence of a widespread and profitable underground market in white babies. Canadian scandals in Nova Scotia,[12] Alberta, and Montreal also revealed that babies were being sold across the border to American couples.[13] In the United States, it was recognized that the popularity of adoption had created problems for those genuinely concerned about child welfare: "One of the outgrowths of this imbalance between the number of couples who want to adopt and the number of babies available is a practice commonly referred to as the 'black market' – the selling of babies for adoption."[14] Ironically, evidence from the United States also made it clear that some of the worst cases of abuse of power with regard to adoption involved child-welfare agencies themselves.[15] It is possible that some welfare workers in Ontario were also corrupt. Several young mothers hinted at CAS profiteering in the baby racket, asserting that "babies had been sold to the United States without the consent of their mothers."[16]

The vast majority of child-welfare professionals were not involved in such practices and they expressed deep concern about "black market" adoption. Child-welfare workers asserted that all adoptions should be regulated through children's agencies in order to prevent undue exploitation. However, they simultaneously admitted that "agency policy is to have mothers of illegitimate children consent to having those children made Crown wards so that adoption may be facilitated and the process speeded up."[17] As early as 1932, one social worker described the process of obtaining babies from young unwed women in an article for *Chatelaine* magazine: "The particular goods mostly take the shape of babies born of unmarried mothers. They are given up voluntarily – although that isn't the right word – by girls who walk into your office very bravely but without the baby, and tell you of the bitter struggle they have made trying to get along and keep the baby properly. But because of sickness, unemployment, or in most cases the failure of the child's father to help, they have to give up."[18] Social workers did not question the fact that "voluntarily... [wasn't] the right word" or challenge the wider social conditions that made it difficult for single women to raise their birth children. And they had considerable power to influence young women's decisions with regard to relinquishment.

Formally, judges granted final legal approval to adoption proceedings, but the records of the courts provide little detail about the process by which an adoption was organized and secured. Judges relied heavily upon the recommendations of social workers. They did not have the resources, or the inclination, to supervise the details of individual placements. This ensured that the CAS was largely unsupervised and indirectly awarded the agency enormous discretionary power. The case files produced under the Children of Unmarried Parents Act therefore provide one of the few sources of historical information about the means by which decisions regarding adoption placement were reached in the offices of the CAS.[19] Although these records did not begin as adoption files, the mothers who approached the CAS looking for help raising their babies, not relinquishing them, in time became convinced that adoption was their best option. In this context, the case files reveal the conflict of interest that permeated adoption proceedings and the limitations inherent in the idea of consent. While decrying "black market" adoption, social workers failed to recognize that simultaneous control over adoption and affiliation proceedings placed child-welfare workers themselves in a position of undue influence and conflict of interest. This conflict of interest, moreover, was intensified by the financial constraints faced by CAS workers and by ideological presuppositions about the inability of unwed pregnant women to parent adequately. White women were subjected to unrelenting pressure to release their children for adoption.

The Children's Aid Society was chronically short of money and there is little doubt, as one U.S. critic of child-welfare law put it in the 1970s, that "behind the belief that adoption is a good solution is money."[20] Cheap solutions were definitely required. Until 1965 only a limited portion of the costs involved in placing and caring for children was covered by the provincial government; the rest of the money required by the CAS had to be raised through charitable donations and alternative fund-raising.[21] Social workers may have been motivated by the possibility that some wealthy couples might complete the process of adoption with a significant "charitable" donation to a local agency. A Hamilton social worker admitted to one set of prospective, and very wealthy, adoptive parents in 1944 that "a gift from them in such an amount as they choose will be gratefully received."[22] Did such a gift constitute payment for a baby or influence the selection of adoptive parents by CAS workers? More commonly, adoption made it unlikely that a child would be in the care of the state beyond a few weeks immediately after birth, reducing the costs incurred by the agency. Social workers were also aware that the limited costs of placing a child pending adoption could usually be obtained from putative fathers, making adoption even more financially desirable. Although some men fled the jurisdiction to avoid long-term child support, it was rarely worth sacrificing family and community to escape the small, finite debts associated with adoption. And when men failed to pay, the CAS was ruthless about collecting money owed to the agency.[23] Inadvertently, this further empowered ex-boyfriends to exert influence over women to release children for adoption. Finally, it was recognized in the social-work community that, "with the combination of the stigma attached to illegitimacy, and the lack of means of support for the child," many unwed mothers who opted to keep their children later left their infants in institutional care; these older children were then considerably harder to place for adoption.[24]

Unwed mothers were also constructed as delinquent and unstable, unable to be good mothers. One Canadian social worker critical of the adoption mandate pointed out that the description of the unwed mother as sick mandated removal of the child: "If the mother is abnormal it follows of course that she is not a fit person to raise her own child. Obviously, then, it becomes in the best interest of the child to be separated from her."[25] The majority of social workers, however, asserted that adoption was the best outcome not only for children but also for unwed mothers themselves. Adoption, they argued, gave the mother a chance to start over and lead a "good" life – to get married and raise legitimate children for the state. As Veronica Strong-Boag notes, "the promise that they could rejoin the ranks of the respectable if they 'chose' to surrender offspring influenced many unwed mothers well into the 1960s and beyond."[26] Social workers acknowledged that many unwed mothers expressed a desire to keep their babies, but they claimed that this was itself a symptom of sickness. U.S. social workers, whose writings had wide circulation in Canada, claimed that the "healthy, normal unmarried mother has usually faced her situation realistically, has a plan in mind, usually adoption, and will stay with her decision."[27] Popular beliefs echoed such sentiments; as an editorial in *Maclean's* put it as late as 1966, "the best thing for the unmarried mother and for the fatherless child is for her to give up the baby to a home with two parents. Parenthood is a job for married couples."[28]

In the social-work journals, only one Canadian voice offered open critique of this hegemonic discourse. Svanhuit Josie, a child-welfare worker from Ottawa, lamented in 1955 that "it seems to me that casework with the unmarried mother has come to mean the process of convincing her that it is impossible if not absolutely immoral for her to plan to keep her own child. She must be made to face the 'reality' of the situation, which means to give it up for adoption."[29] Josie argued that "social workers do not admit that they encourage the mothers, and they emphasize that they only want the best for the mother and child. But I see encouragement in telling the girl how many good and loving families are willing to take her child and that most of these families are rather wealthy and can give the child everything, even the best education."[30] Her critique prompted a harsh, immediate rebuttal from the supervisor of the Unmarried Parents Department of the Toronto Children's Aid Society, who stated that most mothers keeping their children "were emotionally sick people" and that the social worker therefore "trie[d] to be of assistance in helping her assess the realities of her situation."[31]

Social workers had a responsibility to ensure that mothers were aware of the financial difficulties that they would inevitably confront raising children alone, but lurid descriptions of abject poverty were used to dissuade mothers from keeping their infants. The Canadian Welfare Council advised social workers that "the mother should know that if she keeps her child she may be beset by many difficulties of which she can hardly be aware before experiencing them. She may be censured by relatives and neighbors; she will have, in all probability, acute difficulty in supporting herself and her child."[32] Young women were also routinely warned that the woman who insisted on keeping her child had "less opportunity to meet appropriate men and future husbands."[33] The Welfare Council asserted that issuing such dire warnings did "not disregard the unmarried mother's right of choice, but with more understanding of the complications of the problem, the caseworker is able to approach the situation more objectively and help the unmarried mother arrive at a realistic decision."[34] This "realistic" decision was to relinquish the child; the possibility of challenging the poverty and stigma faced by single mothers was not considered.

In a context in which innumerable challenges awaited single mothers, white women were subjected to unrelenting pressure, some might say harassment, to conform to the adoption mandate.[35] As the Children of Unmarried Parents Act case files illustrate, this did not go unnoticed by unwed mothers themselves. One distraught mother asserted that "all social agencies are anxious that all unmarried mothers give up their children."[36] Another mother, under interrogation in court, echoed such sentiments:

Q: What are your intentions with regard to the child?
A: I am going to keep her and bring her up to the best of my ability.
Q: Has anyone ever explained to you that in the best interest of the child it would be better to give it up?
A: Too many people have told me that.[37]

As this exchange attests, unwed mothers did not always give social workers or the court their complete cooperation. But they were vulnerable.

The high-pressure tactics that Children's Aid Society workers could use to convince women to place children for adoption are well illustrated in a CAS file that resulted in an unreported case that came before the court in Toronto in 1959. Although this case may have been extreme, it reveals the potential for abuse inherent in the allocation of conflicting powers – the right to begin proceedings against putative fathers for child support and the control of adoption – to a single, unregulated, agency. The woman in this case had entered into an agreement with the putative father of her child through negotiations handled by the Children's Aid Society. He had agreed to pay $700 in costs on the assumption that the child would be placed for adoption immediately after birth. At the time of delivery, however, the mother refused to sign release papers and kept her child. She then sought child support from the putative father at her own expense. The CAS countered by seeking specific performance of the informal adoption agreement. The mother's lawyer argued that the father had implicitly admitted paternity by signing the agreement for adoption, that the mother had been unduly pressured to place the child for adoption, and that the agreement could not be binding. Under vigorous cross-examination the mother asserted:

Q: You stated that you had – in answer to your own counsel's questions – been pressed to put your child up for adoption.
A: That's right.
Q: By whom?
A: Mrs. M., the representative of the Children's Aid Society ... Both before and after the birth, and even after the 26 May when Judge B gave me custody of the child, and she still tried to tell me that it was the best thing to give the child up for adoption ... The Children's Aid Society said that this money – I should accept it – otherwise Dr. M. might go away and I wouldn't get anything.

Social workers had emphasized to the mother that she would live in poverty should she raise her child alone and that the "reasonable" approach to the problem was to release the child for adoption. When this tactic failed, they resorted to threats, warning that if she insisted on pursuing her former lover in court she would not only lose but also would be humiliated:

Q: You discussed with her whether or not there was adequate corroboration. You felt that there was no adequate corroboration.
A: I saw Miss R. had yet to provide corroboration. There was no intention at this point at all that Miss R. was desirous of taking this thing to court ...
Q: Well, then is it not true that in the CAS's handling of these cases that they usually handle the cases in which the applicant doesn't have a lawyer and the Children's Aid Society takes them under their wing and looks after them, isn't that right, and the Children's Aid Society doesn't like a private lawyer. I suggest that Mrs. M implied to you that she hoped the child would be adopted ... and that she would be able to get Miss R. to agree to the said adoption.

Miss R. had obtained no legal advice at the time of the agreement and had expressed her desire to keep the child. CAS workers knew, as her lawyer put it, that "if the mother intends to keep the child then the agreement is not adequate." The mother was subjected to a constant barrage of pressure to place her child for adoption, since a "suitable family had been found for the child." She was forced to get a court order confirming custody, at considerable expense. She was threatened that support would not be forthcoming and that it would be difficult, if not impossible, to raise the child herself, and was informed, without legal counsel, that she had inadequate evidence to take her ex-boyfriend to court. Although the presiding judge softened the blow by asserting that "my sympathies are with the mother," he deemed that there had not "been any undue influence on the mother at the time she agreed to accept this amount, and no unfair advantage seems to have been taken of her."[38] He did not define what would, in his estimation, have constituted undue influence or unfair advantage. The CAS lost on the issue of specific performance of the adoption agreement, but the mother would not get any support for the child from its father. This mother was lucky that she had refused to release her child to the adoptive parents; had the child already been with them, reclaiming the infant might have been impossible.

Under such pressure from CAS workers, as well as, frequently, ex-boyfriends and families, it is not surprising that many women relinquished their babies for adoption. As one mother put her dilemma, "I'd like to keep her, if I could, but without money I just can't."[39] An unwed mother might not agree with social workers that "if you love your baby you will give him up" because this is "best for our babies, best for the lovely couple who would be the best people to have our baby, best for our family and best for society."[40] Most, however, realistically acknowledged their limited financial resources and the social stigma they faced. They sought help from the Children's Aid Society because they believed that the financial resources of the fathers of their children should be made available for child support. When the CAS refused to help them to obtain such support, they were desperate. Similarly, middle-class women shipped off to homes for unwed mothers knew that the price of reacceptance into families and society was relinquishment and secrecy.[41]

Women were vulnerable and few had the resources to challenge the CAS in court. Yet the question of how the court responded to the few challenges that did arise is important. Could a mother who initially relinquished her child change her mind? This question, not surprisingly, was the subject of confusion, debate, and judicial wrangling in the years after 1921. Ostensibly, not only did the mother have the right to choose relinquishment in an unfettered manner, but also the child was to be placed in a probationary home pending formal adoption. But, in practice, the conditions under which consent had been granted were rarely questioned. As one judge asserted in Ontario in 1948, despite the fact that an adoption had not been finalized, the child could not be returned to the mother: "Where a parent has signed a solemn consent to adoption under the provisions of the *Adoption Act* and the foster parents have taken the child and assumed their duties with a view to fulfilling the probationary requirements of the act, I do not think that a child is to be restored to the natural parent on the mere assertion of that parent's right."[42]

In the 1950s, however, a trilogy of Supreme Court cases established that, within a limited time frame, mothers had a right to revoke consent and have infants returned to them.[43] In *Martin v. Duffell*, 1950, the mother stated her objections to the adoption promptly, but the adoptive parents, and the adoption agency, refused to return the child. It was found that "at any time prior to the making of the [final] order of adoption the wishes of the mother of an illegitimate child as to its custody must be given effect unless very serious and important reasons require that, having regard to the child's welfare, they must be disregarded."[44] In *Hepton v. Maat*, 1957, the mother and father had initially given up the children because the husband was unemployed, they were very young, and they were recent immigrants from Holland with considerable financial challenges; they quickly regretted the decision and tried to revoke their consent before the adoption was finalized, but the adoptive parents contested. The Court found that "the natural parents of an infant are entitled to its custody unless by reason of some act, condition or circumstance affecting them it is evident that the welfare of the child requires that custody be given to some other person." It should also be noted that Justice Ivan Rand castigated the foster parents for hiding the twins from their biological parents and delaying proceedings: "I should have thought that, to avoid any unnecessary distress to the latter, however temporary it might be, they would at least have allowed the dispute to be determined without delay."[45] In the final case of the trilogy, *Agar v. McNeilly*, heard in 1958, it was found that "the mother of an illegitimate child, who is of good character and is able and willing to support it in satisfactory surroundings, is entitled to the custody of that child notwithstanding that other persons who wish to do so could provide more advantageously for its upbringing and future. This is true even notwithstanding the fact that the mother signed consent to the adoption of the infant if, at the time she seeks custody, the adoption has not yet been completed." The Court also noted that the mother had been quick to revoke her consent and that the adoptive parents, and the adoption agency, had gone to great lengths to conceal the location of the child and to encourage the mother to give up her quest for the baby.[46]

The lone vocal and open critic of the adoption mandate in the Canadian social-work community, Svanheit Josie, lauded these decisions: "There has never been any question of the legal responsibility of the unmarried mother to maintain her child. But the rights of the natural mother have been getting less and less attention. They have been almost forgotten by many who have been all for helping childless couples satisfy their desire for children ... It has been argued in some quarters that the mother should lose all her rights when she signs the preliminary agreement to hand over the child to strangers who plan to adopt it. This in spite of the fact that the law does not permit her to sign away her liability to maintain the child."[47] However, hers was a voice in the wilderness.

The Ontario legislature explicitly attempted to limit the implications of the decisions of the Supreme Court of Canada. In 1951, in response to *Martin v. Duffell*, a legislative amendment reduced the probationary period for adoption from two years to one year, allowing courts to finalize proceedings earlier in order to avoid revocation disputes.[48] In 1958, in response to *Hepton v. Maat* and *Agar v. McNeilly*, the Ontario legislature amended adoption provisions and stipulated that mothers could not give consent before a baby was seven days old. Simultaneously, however, it was enacted that thereafter she had a window of only twenty-one days within which to revoke her consent; after this time the adoption would proceed. Further, another clause in the amendment asserted that judges were to allow revocation only when "the court is satisfied that it is in the best interests of the child,"[49] explicitly limiting the rights of the mother which had been articulated by the Supreme Court and ensuring that, once a baby was physically handed over to an adoptive couple, the mother would face tremendous challenges in reclaiming her child. In 1960 the Social Planning Council of Metropolitan Toronto went so far as to assert that the ability of the unwed mother to change her mind with regard to adoption should be abrogated entirely since she "might delay placement" or "demand the return of her child with disastrous consequences for the adopting parents and child and doubtful advantage for the unmarried mother."[50]

Nevertheless, the Supreme Court continued to expand its recognition of women's rights and in 1970 censured the practices of the Ontario Children's Aid Society. In *Re: Mugford* the Court explicitly acknowledged the problems that young unmarried women faced. On learning that she was pregnant, the mother in this case had moved to live with a married sister in Ottawa. She consulted the CAS and two social workers affirmed that the mother had been "tense and upset" and "in a state of indecision as to what should be done about the child since she would have no way of keeping it." She was nineteen years old and her parents did not know that she was pregnant. She signed the adoption papers but shortly thereafter was so distressed by her actions that she informed her parents of her predicament and sought their help in regaining custody of her child. The child had been in an adoptive home for only a couple of weeks, but the CAS informed the mother that "David has adjusted well to his new environment and we cannot disturb this arrangement." The final order had not yet been granted and the mother had revoked her consent within the legislatively required time period. However, the child was still with the adoptive parents because the CAS had disregarded her revocation. The court of first instance determined that there was "no evidence on the record which suggests that the respondent mother had deserted or abandoned [the] child." Instead, it held that "she was motivated solely by a sincere desire to do what she thought was then in the best interests of her child despite an almost overpowering desire on her part to keep him and be a mother to him."[51] The case was exceptional in that the mother's family had sufficient funds to hire a private lawyer and challenge both the CAS and the adoptive parents who had refused to return the child; families without such resources might simply find themselves without recourse against coercive practices. The Supreme Court's decision to uphold the lower court's ruling was the high-water mark of recognition of the rights of mothers.

In spite of the trilogy and *Re: Mugford*, lower courts after 1970 distinguished the facts in cases before them, negating the protections regarding consent and revocation articulated by the Supreme Court. For example, in a 1973 case the Ontario Court of Appeal found against a mother who had delivered her child to the adoptive parents four days after her birth but who had never signed consent to adoption papers. Although the mother had requested the return of the baby within the first three months of life, the adoptive parents had simply refused to return the child to the mother. Significant delays had ensured that the daughter was four years of age by the time the case came before the Court of Appeal. The custody of the adoptive parents was confirmed. In this case the mother had become pregnant while separated from her husband and wanted to reconcile, but he rejected the child and the court distinguished her circumstances from those of younger women:

> This was not a case, as was the situation in many of the other leading cases on the subject, of an unmarried young woman who found herself with child, having been abandoned by her family without the support of friends and without gainful employment, who delivers up a child to a society or foster or adoptive parents for the welfare of the child. Without in any way casting aspersions on Mrs. Moores, or passing moral judgment on her action, it is important to observe that in this case she was a mature woman with professional training who delivered the child to the Feldsteins hoping that the child would be well taken care of, but not really out of a concern for its welfare.[52]

Despite denying "passing moral judgment," the Court of Appeal did cast aspersions on Mrs Moore by asserting that she was not concerned with the child's welfare. As was later noted by the Supreme Court of Canada, "judicial reaction to the trilogy ... has been uneven and ... [has] moved away from the strict application of the rule approved in the trilogy."[53]

The rule of the trilogy was that the mother had the right to make her decision without coercion, that she could, within a reasonable legislatively determined period of time, change her mind and revoke her consent to relinquishment, and that in such cases the child had to be returned to her. The underlying assumption was that it was in the best interests of the child, absent evidence of misbehaviour or unfitness on the part of the mother, for the child to remain with her. This presumption, however, was eliminated in the 1980s.[54] The standard of the best interests of the child that replaced the emphasis on parental rights was intended to overturn the historical notion of children as property and to ensure that the needs of children were considered in custody decisions. An emphasis on the bonding of the child with the parent with whom he or she has resided and has closest connections makes sense for the older child and was an important child-centred reform. This concept expanded the work of John Bowlby, emphasizing the early bonding of children with their caregivers, and reflected both the growing influence of child psychology in the courts and the work of advocates of children's rights who argued that bonding must be a guiding principle in custody contests.⁵⁵ Moreover, in the divorce context, advocates of children's rights asserted that custody decisions should be gender-neutral and driven by recognition of social parenting.⁵⁶ While recognition of bonding and social parenting are extremely important, newborn adoption was (and is) not like other custody decisions: conditions at the time of birth are unique and require particular attention to the concerns of the birth mother and the context of gestation. Additionally, once they had physical custody of a child, adoptive parents could delay proceedings simply by refusing to recognize revocation and thereby creating the very conditions under which they had bonded with children. As one Ontario court recognized in 1983, "that they can appeal and obtain stays of the Provincial Court decisions is, of course, proper under the present statute. That they could do so repeatedly ... [raises] serious questions about their unfair advantage."⁵⁷ The Supreme Court of Canada, however, did not recognize such differentials in power, and, in a new trilogy of cases in the 1980s, the rights of relinquishing mothers were circumscribed.⁵⁸

In the first case, *Manitoba (Director of Child Welfare) v. Y* (1981),⁵⁹ a nineteen-year-old Manitoba mother had released her child for adoption immediately after the seven-day waiting period, required under legislation, had elapsed. Two days later, she attempted to revoke her consent but was told that the baby had been placed for adoption. Under provincial legislation, the mother had the right to revoke her consent within the child's first year of life or until the baby was placed in a probationary adoptive home, whichever came first.⁶⁰ The court of first instance, therefore, found no strict violation of her rights. On appeal, Justice Alfred Monnin ruled that "in effect, what the Director did by his speedy action was to deprive this young mother of all her rights ... The legislature, having made provision for the withdrawal of a voluntary surrender, expected this right to be of some effect, and capable of being made use of." But the Supreme Court disagreed and and restored the decision of the court of first instance. The legislation did not restrict the right to place the child immediately after the signing of consent, and therefore no rights were deemed to have been violated, and the mother was determined to have effectively abandoned her child by signing the consent documents.⁶¹

The second revocation case was heard in 1983. *Racine v. Woods*, also discussed in the context of Indigenous adoption later in this book, was a landmark case which accepted psychological bonding as an important issue in child-custody determinations.⁶² The Supreme Court of

Canada found that the "law no longer treats children as the property of those who give them birth" and deemed that the best interests of the child would be served by leaving her with the parents with whom she had bonded. Justice Bertha Wilson's assertion that the child is a "human being to whom [the parents] owe serious obligations" was a welcome corrective to historical patriarchal control of children and the decision may have been the only reasonable one given that the child had, by the time of trial, lived with the adoptive parents for over six years. This argument, however, conflated patriarchal rights over children, which historically were absolute and property-based, with those accorded to birth mothers, which are of much more recent, and fragile, origin. Moreover, within the first years of the child's life, the mother had requested her return but the request had been refused by the then foster parents. The child had bonded with the foster/adoptive parents precisely because the courts had taken a very long time in making a decision. It is noteworthy that the Court acknowledged that "consideration of bonding might effectively enshrine possessory rights for the parent who had obtained interim custody."[63] Despite these delays, the Supreme Court refused to consider the possibility, raised at the Court of Appeal, that the adoption be open and that the mother be granted access.

King v. Low, before the Supreme Court in 1985, confirmed these limitations on the rights of the natural mother. The mother in this case was unmarried and feared the anger of her family. She had chosen private adoption in the hope that she might have some contact with the child as he grew up. The child, born in 1982, left the hospital with the adoptive parents five days after his birth and resided with them thereafter without disruption. The mother almost immediately regretted her decision, discussed the situation with her mother, and requested the return of her child within the first three months of the child's life, but the adoptive parents refused. She had to launch complex custody proceedings, despite the fact that she had not yet signed final adoption papers. The case involved a determination of custody under section 28(1) of the Domestic Relations Ordinance of the Northwest Territories. The circumstances of the case were parallel to those in *Re: Mugford*, in which the rights of the mother had been upheld. In this case, however, although the Supreme Court found that the mother had neither abandoned her child nor conducted herself in a manner that meant the Court should refuse to enforce her rights as a guardian, it nonetheless concluded that "the mother's decision to give the child to the adoptive parents

... was motivated by a consideration of her own interests and that she had accordingly been unmindful of her parental duties."[64] Again, a mother was castigated for being "unmindful of her parental duties" in releasing a child. Yet, had the child simply been returned at the time of her request, the bonding that had occurred by 1985 would have been avoided. The circumstances under which she made her choice to relinquish were given minimal consideration and the fact that bonding had effectively "enshrine[d] possessory rights" was ignored.

In the context of the recognition of the pressures imposed on mothers by putative fathers, society, and social workers in the trilogy of cases in the 1950s and in *Re: Mugford*, the retreat from recognizing women's vulnerability is perhaps surprising. By the 1980s, courts appear to have come to believe that women no longer confronted stigma or poverty when raising children alone, and that the choice to relinquish children for adoption was therefore made in an unfettered and equal environment. But mothers continued to face potential penury and denigration, censure and coercion from ex-boyfriends and families, and also pressure, even harassment, from the bureaucracies that were ostensibly charged with helping them. Once children were with adoptive parents, moreover, delays could be invoked that would result in bonding with the adoptive parents. The about-face of the Supreme Court of Canada was influenced by children's rights rhetoric and an emphasis on bonding and social parenting which was appropriate in contexts in which children had established relationships with parents other than the birth mother. Yet, when such bonding had been possible only because of delays in court proceedings, outcomes favouring adoptive parents were unjust for birth mothers in the newborn context. The disempowerment of birth mothers becomes even more apparent when the restrictions placed on women's right to revocation are compared with the expanding rights of birth fathers in the newborn adoption context, the subject of the next chapter.

3
Putative Fathers and Newborn Adoption

Under the Ontario Adoption Act of 1921, a married father was required to consent to the relinquishment of his child for adoption, but in cases of illegitimacy only the mother's consent was necessary. While married men had legal custody of marital children, unwed fathers had no obligations to their children. This resulted in ostracism and poverty for illegitimate children and their mothers. In an attempt to mitigate the social and economic disadvantages faced by children deemed *fillius nullius*, affiliation proceedings were abolished in Ontario on 31 March 1978, and the legal designation "illegitimate" was eliminated in 1980.[1] An explicit intention of the Ontario Family Law Reform Act, which formally separated the issue of child support from marriage, was to "remove disabilities suffered by children born outside of marriage."[2]

In this context of heightened concern about children's welfare, unmarried fathers who demonstrated existing relationships with older children intervened successfully in adoption proceedings in the 1970s. Initially, unwed fathers' claims were based on social fatherhood, particularly evidence that fathers had cohabited with, and supported, their children. More recent parentage legislation has extended recognition to a wide range of unmarried men as legal fathers, listed circumstances under which paternity will be presumed, and provided for the use of genetic testing in the determination of paternity.[3]

While reforms were intended to make it easier for women to make child-support claims against recalcitrant men, expanded recognition of men as fathers also raised new legal questions in the context of newborn adoption. Whose consent would now be required to relinquish a child? Was the mother obligated to notify the father when she became pregnant or to reveal his name to social-service agencies? Although the rights of the father would appear to have been limited by the requirement that they meet criteria for presumptions of parentage, recent Charter challenges have allowed uninvolved men who have not met the definition of "parent" to nonetheless claim an interest in their genetic children. While the rights of mothers in the immediate period after birth have been restricted by the courts, Charter litigation has expanded the rights of fathers to control decisions with regard to newborn relinquishment. In a brief review of the role of fathers in adoption, Veronica Strong-Boag rightly asserts that recent decisions reflect an "unprecedented consideration for the rights of unwed fathers."[4] Feminist legal scholars have argued that such consideration is in conflict with women's right to reproductive autonomy. The history of how and why such rights for fathers have arisen is important but has not been explored by previous authors on adoption in Canada.[5]

Under the Adoption Act and the Children of Unmarried Parents Act of 1921, putative fathers did not have any formal say in the process of relinquishment for adoption; however, evidence from the Children of Unmarried Parents Act files illustrates that affiliation procedures indirectly empowered men to influence former girlfriends (as well as women they had assaulted). Many men simply disappeared before social workers could find them for interviews, thus reinforcing the assertions of social workers that women would face enormous economic challenges in raising children on their own. If a judge felt that a man was at risk of disappearing, he could be "detained as a material witness,"[6] but in practice men who wanted to disappear did so long before cases proceeded to court, and before such procedures could be invoked. One sarcastic putative father taunted his former girlfriend in a letter that he wrote to her after fleeing the jurisdiction of the court: "Since I am now residing in Vancouver, it will be impossible for me to appear on May 3. I would appreciate a more convenient time and place."[7] When interviewed by CAS workers, most men denied paternity and expressed a strong desire that children be relinquished for adoption. Men were not under oath when they were interviewed at the Children's Aid Society and they routinely sought to impugn the reputations of former girlfriends to prevent the CAS from supporting women's claims for child support. As one father admitted, although he had promised marriage, he hadn't really meant what he said: "Was he to be burdened by this for life?"[8] Despite the fact that men had a financial interest in disproving paternity, their veracity was rarely questioned and their denigration of former girlfriends reinforced the pre-existing perception of social workers that unwed women would be poor mothers.

In this context, social workers seem to have introduced the possibility of adoption into negotiations with putative fathers even when mothers were adamant that they did not want to relinquish their children. The informality of negotiations with putative fathers indirectly empowered men to influence the decisions of mothers with regard to the futures of their children. As one father asserted in 1952, "he was not going to do anything more than this $200. If the girl did not take that, he would just live outside of the Province of Ontario and she could not collect anything."[9] Another man threatened his pregnant ex-girlfriend: "If Miss K is prepared to place her child for adoption he would be prepared to enter into an agreement for confinement expenses and maintenance from the date of the child's birth until placement. He stated that if Miss K wished to keep the child that he would be prepared to have the matter brought before the court." Miss K was unemployed, unable to speak English, and, as a recent immigrant, had no local family to help her. It is not surprising that ultimately she accepted her former lover's offer of $120 and gave her child up for adoption.[10] Another father was explicit that he would provide no support "for the care of the child in this case while in the care of her mother" and stated that it was his intention, if an order was made against him, "to leave the province in order that he might not be forced to pay."[11] CAS workers did not use such admissions against men in court; instead, they seem to have assumed that putative fathers would carry through with threats to abscond or to deny paternity, and that it was therefore a waste of time and money to pursue support for mothers. Women themselves recognized the power of putative fathers in negotiations; as one mother lamented, "he is trying to force me to place the baby for adoption so he can evade payment."[12] Social workers were also aware that the limited expenses required to cover the costs of placing a child pending adoption could usually be obtained from putative fathers, making adoption even more financially desirable for the CAS. It is important to note that putative fathers used their influence overwhelmingly to coerce women into relinquishing children for adoption; arguments by uninvolved unwed fathers that they have a right to prevent relinquishment are a very recent phenomenon.

Unlike non-cohabiting unwed fathers, men who had cohabited with the mothers of their children often admitted paternity and agreed to pay child support (although actual payment might not then follow). Although the particular concerns of cohabiting families were not explicitly referred to in the initial version of the Children of Unmarried Parents Act, such families were treated very differently by social workers than were single mothers, in part, perhaps, because their children were not highly adoptable newborns. The interests of unmarried fathers who lived with their children were recognized in an early amendment to adoption legislation in 1929; the Adoption Act thereafter required the consent of a father if the child resided with and was maintained by the father at the time of the application.[13]

The rights of unwed fathers under the Children of Unmarried Parents Act were not formally challenged in any higher court. However, by the 1970s, unwed, but cohabiting or formerly cohabiting, fathers were asserting their rights in other contexts, including adoption. In *Children's Aid Society of Metropolitan Toronto v. Lyttle*, 1973, a father who had cohabited with his child asserted that he should be able to veto the unilateral decision of the mother to release the child for adoption.[14] Technically, the mother was within her rights under the legislative amendment of 1929, since the father was no longer living with her or the child. He had lived with both until the child was two years old, at which time the mother left to live with another man, taking the child with her. Without informing the father, she placed the child with the Children's Aid Society for adoption. When the father learned of this, he contacted the CAS and was told that he had no right to the child. He then sought legal counsel, but by this time the period for contesting the wardship order had elapsed. The adoption order, however, had not been finalized. He argued that the wardship order was void on procedural grounds since he had not been informed; without a wardship order, the adoption could not proceed. The Supreme Court of Canada upheld his claim. Yet, while the father won his right to a day in court, his application for custody was dismissed and the adoption was confirmed.[15]

In 1975 the Ontario Divisional Court considered directly the question of whether or not a mother was obligated to name the father of her child when she relinquished a newborn baby for adoption. The court explicitly distinguished newborn adoption from circumstances such as those in *Lyttle*. It asserted that newborn adoption "discloses an entirely different statement of facts. In the *Lyttle* case, the father not only wanted custody of his son, but also in the registration of the birth, acknowledged his paternity. The proceedings taken by the Children's Aid Society were taken behind his back, although the registration, if examined, would have disclosed his relationship and name." The mother of a newborn, in contrast, would not be forced to disclose the name of the father of her child.[16]

In 1979, however, a contrary decision was recorded. Four Ontario wardship orders were challenged to determine the obligations of the Children's Aid Society in investigating paternity and naming fathers in adoption cases. The Family Court in York County held that a father of a child born out of wedlock was entitled to notice and consent in adoption proceedings. The court asserted that it had to consider the fact that distinctions between married and unmarried parents had been abolished. Perhaps not surprisingly, given the belief that it was better for illegitimate children to be adopted, rights of notice for the father were vigorously opposed by counsel for the CAS. They argued that giving unfettered rights to all genetic fathers would lead to violent men and "sperm donors"[17] being able to interfere in adoption proceedings and would thwart the purpose of legislation by reducing rates of relinquishment. However, the court found that these concerns could be met since the CAS had the right to exclude specific fathers after investigating the circumstances surrounding each birth and potential adoption. All four applications were sent back for consent from putative fathers.[18]

In extensive proceedings in 1987 and 1988, the Family Court in York County and then the Divisional Court again considered the claim that biological fathers were discriminated against by not being notified with regard to the adoption of infants born out-of-wedlock. The baby in this case had been born of a short-term relationship. The mother had not notified the father of her pregnancy, and the court returned the adoption, adjourned the proceedings, and advised the attorney general that the constitutional validity of section 131(1) of the Children of Unmarried Parents Act was in question.[19] Counsel representing the interests of genetic fathers argued that "the mother and the father (married or not) are necessary to conceive the child" and that "the fact of whether or not the parents are married has no effect on the child; and both are presumed to be able and entitled to care for the child." Counsel for the attorney general asserted that "the purpose of the legislation in this regard is to achieve an expeditious adoption" and that "by the fact of birth the mother has at least some minimal involvement with the care of the child, while the fathers, married or not, have no similar involvement." They also submitted that "parental rights of a biological father do not exist 'in a vacuum' equal to those of the mother, but rather are rights which arise, or are 'activated' by some positive conduct being taken by the father." It was argued that, because the Children's Aid Society was obligated to investigate the circumstances surrounding pregnancy, the only father who would be excluded "is a male person who by an act of casual sexual intercourse impregnates a woman and shows no sense of responsibility for the natural consequences of the act of sexual intercourse." The Divisional Court determined that mother and father, in such cases, were not "similarly situated. The mother because of physical necessity has shown responsibility to the child ... It is thus apparent that the different statutory treatment of the two persons is based on their respective demonstrated responsibility to the child, not upon their different sexes."[20] The adoption was allowed to proceed. This case acknowledged both that most men who were not attached to the mothers of their children did not want to be social fathers, and that biological mothers and fathers were not similarly situated at the time of birth. Yet there was little consistency or predictability in Ontario law with regard to the rights of uninvolved unwed fathers in newborn adoption cases into the twenty-first century.

A new emphasis on the rights of biological fathers, however, was entrenched in Canadian law in *Trociuk v. British Columbia (Attorney General)* (2003),[21] in which an uninvolved father was deemed to have been discriminated against in being denied the right to participate in the naming of his children. In *Trociuk*, the Supreme Court of Canada found that "differential treatment of [unwed] mothers and fathers [in birth registration and naming] ... withholds a benefit from fathers in a manner which has the effect of signaling to them and to society as a whole that fathers are less capable or less worthy of recognition or value than mothers."[22] Feminist legal scholars were critical of this decision, asserting that it relied on a formal equality analysis that decontextualized the positions of an unwed (and largely uninvolved) father and a custodial mother. Hester Lessard, for example, in a trenchant critique of the case, asserted that the *Trociuk* court failed to recognize that "distinctions between mothers and fathers at the time of birth are based, not on stereotypes that mothers are superior nurturers, but on the realities of pregnancy."[23]

The impact of *Trociuk* was immediately apparent in adoption cases. In 2003 prospective adoptive parents were confronted by an uninvolved father who sought custody of his child and, to this end, brought a motion before the Ontario Court of Justice contesting legislative provisions mandating that only the mother must consent to adoption. The father had been told of the pregnancy, but he responded with anger, not support. He denied responsibility, bad-mouthed the mother, and shut her out of his life. He provided no emotional or financial support during the pregnancy. She decided to place the child for adoption. After the birth, and after giving a medical history for adoption, the father asserted that he and his parents wanted to raise the baby. The mother told him to seek his rights through the Children's Aid Society by admitting his paternity, which he failed to do within the prescribed time frame. The mother had not cohabited with the father, did not name him on the birth certificate, and he had not claimed paternity. She therefore asserted that he did not have standing as a parent under the Children's Law Reform Act to challenge her decision.

Despite acknowledging that the man did not meet the criteria for fatherhood as set out in the Children's Law Reform Act, the court determined that it "must consider whether the decision in *Trociuk v. Attorney General for British Columbia* has any bearing on this court's decision whether to declare the mother to be the only parent as defined in the legislation or whether this court should find that the biological father should be notified." The court found that the father "is in fact the biological father of the child," and because *Trociuk* required a mechanism to allow the father to appear on the birth registration, it followed that "the failure to notify the biological father of this proceeding and the failure to give him an opportunity to respond to a motion to dispense with his consent, on the basis that he is statutorily excluded as a biological parent, similarly violates his rights under subsection 15(1) of the *Charter*." The adoption agency was ordered to obtain the father's consent. If they could not do so, a hearing would be held to determine whether his consent could be dispensed with. If his consent was found to be required, the wardship order would be set aside and he could claim custody.[24]

A.L. v. S.M., 2009, heard in the Ontario Superior Court, in which a father opposed the mother's decision to relinquish a child for adoption, further illustrates the conflicts between the rights of the mother and the rights of the putative father created by the ruling in *Trociuk*. The mother in this case had hidden the birth from the father and then claimed that he was not the father. His application was allowed in part because he had been deceived. The mother was determined to have given up her rights, but a hearing was to be held to determine custody/access as between the father and the adoptive parents.[25] Although the mother in this case was castigated by the court for being dishonest, the underlying facts of the case were complicated.

The father had been informed of the pregnancy. The parents had agreed upon an abortion, but the mother decided that she could not follow through with this decision. The father knew that she had not aborted but did not show interest in her pregnancy or provide her with financial or emotional support. Because the mother also did not feel ready to be a parent (she was a university student at the time at which she became pregnant), and because the father had not been supportive, she told him that the child had been stillborn when in fact the child had been released for adoption. The father learned through a third party (the maternal grandmother) that the child had been adopted. The mother then revealed to the father that she had been sexually assaulted at the time of conception and that she was not sure about paternity.[26]

The court found that "the essence of the father's case is established, namely that she did deceive him by telling him the child was stillborn and in this way prevented him from asserting his paternity," but did not contextualize the fact that the father had been adamant that the mother should abort. The court admitted that the father did not fall within the strict definition of a father as set out in the Children's Law Reform Act: he was not married to the mother; he had not lived with her during the pregnancy in any relationship of permanence; he had not signed vital-statistics documents; and he had not been found to be the father by a court of competent jurisdiction.[27] However, despite his own failure to assert the rights available to him at law, the father argued that the strict definition should be avoided "by reference to principles of fundamental justice, including *Charter* values." He relied expressly on the reasoning in *Trociuk* to assert that the definition of "father" "may be ripe for reconsideration." Without an explicit constitutional challenge, the court did not decide the Charter issue. The mother asserted that, if the adoption were to fail, she would prefer to seek custody herself rather than have the father obtain custody. But the court determined that she had no such right: "the adoption placement is vulnerable as to the father only and not as to the mother." A new hearing was ordered in which the adoptive parents' petition to dispense with consent and the father's custody claim would be heard on the same evidentiary basis to save time and money; the mother would not have standing.[28]

Feminist scholars in the United States have noted the conflict between decisions such as this one and recognition of women's reproductive autonomy. The father had harassed and failed to support the mother. She had chosen adoption on the assumption that he could not interfere. She might well have chosen either abortion or custody herself had she been able to predict the outcome of these court proceedings. The biological father had also failed to take any positive steps to assert his paternity by the means available to him at law. While he was allowed to intervene in the adoption, her consent was considered irrevocable. As Karen Czapanskiy argues with regard to similar U.S. cases, fathers have been allowed to misbehave, including denying paternity to friends and family, and these facts "have [had] no legal impact on his opportunity for fatherhood, symbolic or otherwise."[29] The mother, however, despite investment in the child and her demonstrated concern for the child's best interest through her decision not to terminate the pregnancy, was denied such second chances in this case.[30]

The Supreme Court of Canada has upheld that "the right to liberty guaranteed under s.7 of the *Charter* gives a woman the right to decide for herself whether or not to terminate her pregnancy."[31] The fact that men do not have any right to intervene in the decision to abort was confirmed by the Supreme Court of Canada in 1989. The argument of Guy Tremblay (himself an abusive man)[32] that he had an interest in the fetus and could prevent his girlfriend's abortion was based, like arguments regarding adoption notification, "on the proposition that the potential father's contribution to the act of conception gives him an equal say in what happens to the fetus."[33] This argument, however, was rejected by the Court, which held that women were not obligated to tell men that they were pregnant, and could abort without interference. Nonetheless, decisions such as *Trociuk* and *A.L. v. S.M.* have created a conflict between new rights accorded to biological but uninvolved fathers and the reproductive autonomy granted to mothers.

Feminist legal scholars have argued that vesting putative, uninvolved fathers with rights "does not sufficiently acknowledge the asymmetry created by men's and women's different biological roles in reproduction."[34] They point out that pregnancy is uncomfortable and involves weight gain, tiredness, and, for some, nausea and an increased risk of "medical problems like high blood pressure and diabetes."[35] Despite medical advances, pregnancy continues to create risk not only to the mother's health but also to her life. The risks incurred by a woman during childbirth are significantly greater than those incurred during an abortion, with the risk of maternal mortality estimated in Canada to be approximately 1 in 8,333 while first-trimester abortion, properly performed, has almost no health risks and is a quick, office-based, procedure.[36] In this context, feminist critics maintain that there is simply no comparison with "men who have ejaculated their sperm."[37] DNA can identify the progenitor of a child, but contributing genetic material does not make a man a father. The mother who has provided life, care, and economic support for a child for nine months is not similarly situated to the genetic father of her child. Critics of the law insist that this assertion is not a retreat into essentialism.[38] Instead, "ignoring the different biological positioning of birth mothers and fathers gives rise to the risk of reinforcing a cruder genetic essentialism, which suggests that genes are central to, and the most important part of, identity."[39] Nor is this acknowledgment of difference based on "false and pejorative associations" with regard to (potential) fathers;[40] instead, formal equality analysis erases the history of discrimination against single mothers demonstrated in the previous chapter.[41] As Nancy Erickson asserts in the U.S. context, the "pregnant woman needs to know that if she foregoes ... her right to abort, the state will enforce her plans for the child's future."[42] In Ontario, however, the conflict of law created by the Supreme Court of Canada rulings in *Tremblay v. Daigle* and *Trociuk* has yet to be resolved.

The initial inclusion of involved, often formerly cohabiting, fathers in decisions about adoption was both a response to wider gender neutrality in family law in the 1970s and a specific recognition of social fathers. More recent developments emphasize legal equality between fathers and mothers on the basis of biological connection alone. Such constructions of fathers' rights conflict with the rights accorded to women in the context of abortion and reproductive autonomy. Questions about the relative importance of biology, gestation, and social connection in parenting have yet to be resolved at law, a problem to which we will return in the context of assisted reproduction and the rights of donors.

4
Child Apprehension

Most histories of adoption have focused on babies, which is not surprising since they have long been the preferred children for adoption.[1] Older children are also sometimes adopted but most become available for placement through apprehension. Questions as to when and under what conditions children have been removed from parental care are important to this story. The prospect of adoption has been central to the rhetoric of apprehension (and the creation of mechanisms for such action by the state). Children must be deemed to be at risk of harm for apprehension to occur, but harm has been interpreted differently under changing legislation and social conditions. The earliest child-apprehension legislation "was mainly designed to keep neglected children away from the streets."[2] Apprehension remained uncommon and children came into the care of the state when they had already been abandoned by their parents, were homeless, or had been orphaned.[3] In a context of rising apprehension rates in the post-Second World War period, adoption was consolidated with other child-welfare provisions in Ontario in the Child Welfare Act of 1954.[4] Contemporaneously, a series of Supreme Court of Canada cases asserted that a high threshold had to be met in order for removal to occur.[5] In the 1960s, with a new medical emphasis on physical child abuse, provisions established mandatory reporting of suspected abuse and the apprehension of children increased dramatically.[6] By the 1980s, evidence illustrated that children who were apprehended too often lingered in foster care and that long-term social, psychological, and economic outcomes for such children were very poor.[7] The new Child and Family Services Act of 1984 placed emphasis on keeping the child in the family of origin and providing supports for family healing to prevent the harms of family disruption.[8] Apprehensions decreased, but funding was not adequate to the task of prevention and a series of child deaths in the 1990s swung the pendulum back to removal from parental care.[9] Amendments to Ontario legislation in 1999 reduced protections for parents and broadened grounds for apprehension, resulting in a huge increase in the number of children in care.[10] Current critics of child welfare assert that Ontario is again grappling with the consequences of over-apprehension and poor outcomes for children who age out of foster care.[11] Moreover, from the 1980s onwards, child-welfare provisions have been subject to Charter challenges. High-profile Supreme Court of Canada cases confirmed the right of the state to apprehend children, but also, by 1999, found that parents had a right to state-funded legal counsel when challenging the apprehension of their children.[12] Throughout the twentieth century, despite the high level of publicity accorded to cases involving violence against children, the majority of apprehensions have been on the basis of neglect.[13] Critics argue that neglect has been a nebulous, ill-defined concept, subject to interpretation by social workers and judges, and which "may tend to operate in a classist and racist way."[14] Child apprehension has therefore had a disproportionate impact on poor, racialized, and disadvantaged mothers.

Historically, children were the exclusive property of their legal fathers and the state was loath to intervene in the family or to limit the legitimate father's rights over his offspring. One of the first challenges to this authority was the English Poor Laws, "which enabled the state, or its agents, to destroy poor families through the removal and institutional placement of their children, for purposes of education, training, and apprenticeship. These laws provided no legal recourse for parents."[15] While the Poor Laws were unprecedented in their interventionist stance, apprehension was based on poverty and the inability to feed and house a child, not abuse. Although Upper Canada excluded England's Poor Laws from reception, in 1799 the authority of public officials to indenture children was clarified by legislation.[16] However, the state did not have the authority to take a child away from his or her parents or to intervene on behalf of children who were mistreated.

In the late nineteenth century, in a context in which child poverty was increasingly visible in growing urban centres and the unruly behaviour of "street urchins" was considered a threat to middle-class values, child savers advocated the removal of children from poor parental influence.[17] In 1892 the Children's Aid Society was established and in 1893 it was empowered to enforce new legislation, An Act for the Prevention of Cruelty to and Better Protection of Children. Under the act, as we have seen, anyone "having the care, custody, control or charge of a child" who "wilfully ill-treats, neglects, abandons, or exposes such child, or causes or procures such child to be ill-treated, neglected, abandoned, or exposed, in a manner likely to cause such child unnecessary suffering or serious injury to its health" could be charged with a summary offence. The act provided for the removal of abused and neglected children from their parents' custody and control.[18] Wilful mistreatment and neglect, however, were not clearly defined, leaving considerable scope for agency and judicial discretion.

Although this legislation empowered the Children's Aid Society to apprehend children, in practice this was done only rarely into the 1950s. Children came into state care primarily when abandoned by their parents, or orphaned, and child-welfare workers hesitated to remove children from parental care for fear that placements for such children simply did not exist. Money for foster care was limited, institutionalization was frowned upon, and child-welfare organizations were profoundly underfunded. Nonetheless, by the 1950s, the welfare of children was the subject of wide public discussion. Internationally, rights doctrines for children were under discussion at the United Nations. The Declaration of the Rights of the Child, 1959, articulated the right of the child "to protection against all forms of neglect, cruelty and exploitation."[19] Domestically, in the context of the Cold War and a fear of a perceived increase in juvenile delinquency, wide-ranging moral reforms with regard to adolescents, gangs, and drugs were the subject of parliamentary debate. Mary Louise Adams describes the post-war fear of delinquency as a "moral panic" in which "bad home life was a catchall that could refer to the moral atmosphere of the home, to its physical condition, or to the structure of a particular family unit."[20] Concern about the family as the bastion of democracy and a growing belief that all children were adoptable led to a renewed emphasis on apprehension and adoption placement for older children. In 1954, as a reflection of these changes, the Adoption Act was repealed and instead adoption provisions were incorporated into a comprehensive Child Welfare Act, suggesting an emphasis on the use of adoption not only to meet the needs of infertile couples for infants but also as a response to concerns about a wider range of children.

Simultaneously, however, a series of Supreme Court of Canada decisions, discussed previously in chapter 2, established a strong presumption in favour of biological parents' rights to custody of their children in disputes against other caregivers. In *Martin v. Duffell*, 1950, an unwed mother changed her mind about revocation, but the adoptive parents and the adoption agency refused to return the child. It was found that "at any time prior to the making of the [final] order of adoption the wishes of the mother of an illegitimate child as to its custody must be given effect unless very serious and important reasons require that, having regard to the child's welfare, they must be disregarded."[21] In *Hepton v. Maat*, 1957, a young couple had initially given up their twin children because the husband was unemployed and they faced considerable financial challenges; they quickly regretted the decision but the potential adoptive parents contested their right to reclaim their twins. Justice Ivan Rand found that "as *parens patriae* the Sovereign is the constitutional guardian of children, but that power arises in a community in which the family is the social unit. No one would, for a moment, suggest that the power ever extended to the disruption of that unity by seizing any of its children at the whim or for any public or private purpose of the Sovereign ... the welfare of the child can never be determined as an isolated fact, that is, as if the child were free from natural parental bonds entailing moral responsibility – as if, for example, he were a homeless orphan wandering at large."[22] In the final case of the trilogy, *Agar v. McNeilly*, 1958, the Court confirmed that the natural parent, unless he or she were grossly negligent, "is entitled to the custody of that child notwithstanding that other persons who wish to do so could provide more advantageously for its upbringing and future."[23] These cases did not involve disputes between parents and the state, but, in the absence of decisions specific to the apprehension context, the precedents set in this trilogy were considered determinative in the child-welfare context.

The parental-right standard, however, was challenged in the 1960s by the medical discovery of physical child abuse. New data on child abuse presented at a symposium at the American Academy of Pediatrics in 1960 by C.H. Kempe and his co-researchers documented physical assaults of children.[24] Evidence about violence against children had existed in pediatric literature since the 1940s, but the extent of abuse claimed by Kempe and his colleagues was shocking. In 1965 reporting of child abuse was made mandatory in Ontario.[25] In the 1970s, "shaken baby syndrome" was likewise publicized.[26] A massive study of the physical abuse of children in Ontario was completed in 1972[27] and in the same year Mary Van Stolk's best-selling book, *The Battered Child in Canada*, was published.[28] In 1977 Ralph Garber headed the Ontario Task Force on Child Abuse[29] and Benjamin Schlesinger wrote *Child Abuse in Canada*.[30]

Tragic cases of physical abuse also riveted public attention and resulted in investigations such as that into the 1976 death of Kim Anne Popen.[31] Popen, who died at nineteen months of multiple contusions and abrasions, had been the subject of Children's Aid Society attention and even an apprehension order, but had been returned to her family. Her mother pled guilty and was sentenced to seven years in prison; her father's conviction was ultimately overturned. The report into the little girl's death, however, largely ignored the systemic disadvantage to which Jennifer Popen (the mother) had been subjected: only sixteen years old at the time of Kim's birth, Jennifer was a Black Jamaican immigrant who had been abandoned by her birth parents and abused by her extended family; pregnant for the first time at age eleven, at thirteen she was forced to marry an older man, Kim's father, who was only intermittently employed; she then immigrated to Canada where she was isolated and marginalized. But, as Sally Mennill and Veronica Strong-Boag assert, the four-volume report detailing the case "effectively crucifie[d] the bad mother in the first pages ... and never really acknowledge[d] the desperate situation of an isolated young Black immigrant." The inquiry "concentrated on the failings of the child welfare system. The larger picture remained out of focus."[32]

The medical discovery of "battered child syndrome," and publicity surrounding cases such as that of Kim Popen, increased public concern about child abuse and justified the apprehension of ever-increasing numbers of children believed to be at risk of harm. Apprehension rates were also increased by the creation of voluntary-surrender provisions in 1978. Such agreements, still an option under current child-welfare legislation, could be terminated by the parents and could last six to twelve months but could not be renewed beyond twenty-four months. Parents who released their children under voluntary surrender had to undertake improvement courses and the social worker accordingly had "the possibility of turning to the coercive means of attaining his goal. The parents [were] aware of this fact and the coercive measures [were] a powerful tool for negotiating a voluntary acceptance of supervision or a voluntary custody agreement."[33] Under the voluntary-surrender provisions of 1978, many child-welfare interventions resulted in "consent" orders but it is unclear whether parents were truly consenting or instead felt coerced or pressured. Throughout the process, the state had access to unlimited funds, but parents did not, and voluntary surrenders, critics have argued, were [and are] "frequently secured in circumstances which raise questions about the nature of 'consent': lack of counsel; differences in sophistication; fear of the authorities; and the use of subtle forms of coercion."[34] The amendments of 1978 also eliminated the presumption that evidence from earlier cases could not be used to re-try parents, instead establishing that "the court may consider the past conduct of a person toward any child who is or has been at any time in that person's care; and any statement or report, whether oral or written, including in a transcript or finding in an earlier proceeding," thus reinforcing the obligation of parents to prove that they were fit. This, too, contributed to increasing apprehension rates.[35]

In the context of rising apprehension rates in the late 1970s and into the 1980s, critiques of child apprehension emerged. Michael Wald's work was internationally influential in asserting that the interests of children themselves should be at the centre of all apprehension and placement decisions. Did removing children from families create better outcomes for such children or could apprehension itself cause harm? Critics asserted that often apprehension did not serve children's interests or, tangentially, those of their parents.[36] Despite the belief that all children were adoptable that had been promoted so optimistically in the 1960s, in practice social workers experienced significant difficulties in finding permanent homes for older children, particularly those with behavioural issues as a result of long periods of instability of care. If apprehended children were floundering in foster care, as study after study in the 1970s and 1980s illustrated was the case, what was the purpose of apprehension?[37] What could be done instead to promote the improvement of homes so that children could remain with their families of birth?

In 1984 the provincial government responded to critiques of the apprehension regime, and to reports of the harm inflicted on children by long stays in the foster-care system, with the new Child and Family Services Act.[38] This act emphasized keeping the child in the family of birth and supporting the family in its healing journey through the provision of counselling and educational services. The government, however, did not invest in other support mechanisms which were necessary for the well-being of children; in particular, no extra money was invested in poverty-reduction strategies, mental-health supports, treatment for addictions, or services for women as victims of violence, limiting the ability of child-protection workers to promote the familial transformation envisaged by reformers. Although the federal government passed a resolution in 1989 to end child poverty by the new century,[39] as Strong-Boag notes, "any serious tackling of inequality required some redistribution of wealth, which few in power or sufficient numbers of voters were willing to consider."[40]

Despite a rhetorical commitment to children, in the 1990s governments withdrew further from the post-Second World War promise of social security and children were deeply affected. In Ontario, Premier Mike Harris's Common Sense Revolution slashed social assistance and other services. The emphasis on individual responsibility resulted in a 21.6 per cent reduction in social-assistance rates,[41] and the poor, particularly single mothers, were highly vulnerable to being cast as deficient parents. Another round of high-profile deaths of children also contributed to a renewed emphasis on preventive apprehensions. The deaths of Jennifer Kovalsky-England in 1990,[42] Shanay Johnson[43] and Tiffany Coville[44] in 1993, and Afua Boateng[45] and Margaret and Wilson Kasonde in 1995[46] led to calls for investigation of the Children's Aid Society. Following the example of the Gove inquest into the death of Matthew John Vaudreuil in British Columbia,[47] in 1996 the Ontario Child Mortality Task Force was constituted with a mandate to study all deaths of children in care in Ontario between 1 January 1994 and 31 December 1995. Further child deaths, of Sara Podniewicz,[48] Angela and David Dombroskie, Jamie Lee and Devin Burns in 1996,[49] Jordan Heikamp in 1997,[50] and Randall Dooley in 1998,[51] further fuelled community outrage. In 1998 the Report of the Panel of Experts on Child Protection recommended legislative reform, including a less onerous test for substantial harm and apprehension, an expanded definition of neglect, and adoption with contact to encourage voluntary relinquishment.[52] The report excoriated the CAS, as well as individual parents, but some social workers fought back, asserting that "inquiries have become prominent and powerful institutions ... the public attention becomes focused on a phenomenon of child deaths which is not necessarily driven by an increase in incidence, but instead by a surge in attention" and that this "diverts attention from societal causation and societal solutions."[53] Nicholas Bala, an established expert on child welfare, also warned that the Panel of Experts was a "quick, low budget study" and that proposals seeking increased apprehension risked "creating a child welfare system that is overly intrusive and ultimately harmful to children and their families."[54] He also expressed fear that

"Ontario's Conservative government [would] act quickly to legislate reform but [would] be unwilling to provide adequate services or funding or even to restore the funding cuts it ha[d] made in the child welfare field since coming into office."[55]

Despite such warnings, but in response to the high-profile child deaths and scathing inquiries into the operation of the Children's Aid Society, the Child and Family Services Amendment Act, 1999, introduced a shift away from considering the family as a whole. The revisions extended the reasons for which a child could be determined to need protection, expanded the duty to report abuse and neglect, gave CAS workers access to new kinds of information about children and their families, and reduced the maximum time for society wardship.[56] As Bala had warned, however, funding remained low. Not surprisingly, apprehension rates increased. But this did not stop child deaths. In fact, the deaths of three children in various forms of alternative care approved by the CAS – Stephanie Jobin in 1998,[57] William Edgar in 1999,[58] and Jeffrey Baldwin in 2002[59] – should have highlighted the fact that apprehension can have very negative outcomes and that the care of the state is not guaranteed to be safe and nurturing.

Problems in the process of apprehension were recognized in a 1999 decision of the Supreme Court of Canada. While the decision originated outside Ontario, it had implications for child-welfare practice in the province. *New Brunswick (Minister of Health and Community Services) v. G. (J.)* raised, for the first time, "the issue of whether indigent parents have a constitutional right to be provided with state-funded counsel when a government seeks a judicial order suspending such parents' custody of their children."[60] The appellant, a poor single mother, was accompanied in the initial hearings by a friend but did not have legal representation. Her children were taken into custody for six months; she sought and was denied legal aid when the state sought another six-month order; with pro bono representation she challenged the apprehension order, which was reversed, but her application for representation was still dismissed by all provincial courts. In dismissing the case, the court of first instance concluded that there was no general right to paid counsel in a custody hearing because "it could not be said that parents can never adequately state their case in the absence of counsel." In dissent at the Court of Appeal, Justice Michel Bastarache "retorted that 'the trial judge erred in finding that Ms. G could assume her own defense in the given proceedings without sacrificing her right to a fair trial.' In reaching this conclusion, he noted that the proceedings were adversarial in nature, the appellant's conduct was being examined and the findings of the court would create a stigma similar to that of a finding of guilt in some criminal prosecutions. The appellant was destitute, receiving welfare, and 'not seen to be very rational.' All other parties were represented by counsel."

Concurring with Bastarache, the Supreme Court of Canada found that state-funded counsel must be provided. The majority concluded that the failure to provide counsel "constitutes a violation of security of the person because ... direct state interference with the parent-child relationship ... is a gross intrusion into a private and intimate sphere."[61] In separate reasons, Justices Claire L'Heureux-Dube, Charles Gonthier, and Beverley McLachlin asserted that the case was of particular importance with regard to gender equality "because women, and especially single mothers, members of other disadvantaged and vulnerable groups, particularly visible minorities, Aboriginal people, and the disabled, are disproportionately and particularly affected by child protection proceedings."[62] They accepted the argument of the Legal Education and Action Fund (LEAF), an intervener in the case, that legal representation was necessary because "to the care-giving parent, the wardship hearing takes place in an institutional environment subject to rules and regulations that are often unintelligible." The parent faced with the potential loss of a child "must be able to cross-examine experts, dispel many of the myths and stereotypes underlying the state's evidence, address any judicial assumptions based on cultural or class bias and put forward her own perspective as to what is in her child's best interest, all of which must be done at the very worst period of her life,"[63] and all of which require confidence, public-speaking skills, and legal acumen. As Mary Jane Mossman asked rhetorically with regard to this case, if we provide legal aid for an individual charged with theft, but not for a mother facing the loss of her child, "what are the unstated values of society?"[64] The decision of the Supreme Court in *New Brunswick (Minister of Health and Community Services) v. G. (J.)* represented what Dale Blenner-Hassett has referred to as its "boldest statement regarding the protection offered by the *Charter* in the child protection context."[65]

As this case revealed, historically it has been very difficult for parents to contest the power of the Children's Aid Society. Children who have been apprehended have come almost exclusively from poor and marginalized communities with a particular predominance of Indigenous children in the child-welfare system, a subject that is explored in much greater detail in a later chapter. While marginalized parents are subject to intervention, often such intervention has been based on stereotypes and misconceptions. A large Canadian study found that "poverty, ethnicity, race and immigrant status were not risk factors for physical abuse ... Most incidents involved white parents with steady income and home life."[66] In 2003 Health Canada and the governments of Quebec, Ontario, British Columbia, and Newfoundland released an incidence study of child abuse intended to describe the nature and severity of physical harm caused by child abuse and neglect and to estimate national rates of physical abuse.[67] The authors concluded that the scope and severity of this public-health issue remain poorly understood.[68] Instead of emphasizing risk assessment and the prevention of violence, the authors argued, preventive services should focus on poverty-reduction strategies and the improvement of mental-health and addictions services. The most recent official provincial report on child abuse, published in 2008, likewise concluded that incident rates are difficult to verify, that 93 per cent of cases do not involve physical harm to children and 74 per cent do not involve emotional harm, that investigations are most likely to be triggered by accusations of neglect and intimate-partner violence, and that more should be invested in preventive measures rather than in apprehension and/or prosecution of parents.[69]

According to this study, the system is triggered by complaints or the attempts of impoverished parents to obtain assistance with child care (and child support) from helping agencies. Investigations have been primarily driven by concerns about "neglect," which was and is strongly linked to "factors including poverty, poor housing, domestic violence and substance abuse."[70] As contemporary critics note, only the most marginalized in our society "lack access to resources to help them through difficult times – babysitters, relatives, bank loans, jobs, washing machines, a car, decent clothes, a cleaning person, occasional holidays, counseling, and therapy." Mothers have been particularly subject to blame.[71] Physical violence by the father towards the mother has been a reason for the mother to lose custody, even when there was no evidence that children were directly in physical danger. In a study of women who were involved with child welfare as a result of partner violence, the majority reported that they found the involvement "intrusive and demeaning" and that apprehension of their children caused further harm to both mothers and their children.[72] The current approach to child protection has been criticized for providing little "recognition of the need for support to be provided to the child's caregiver."[73] In a context of underfunding and overwork, however, such problems have not necessarily reflected the choice of social workers. As one researcher has put it, "current funding frameworks create an incentive to bring children into care."[74]

Children who have been apprehended, particularly Indigenous children, often have not been adopted but instead have drifted in the foster-care system, frequently experiencing multiple placements and abuse under the care of the state. The history of state care provides "ample tragic examples of the fact that children are not necessarily better off when apprehended."[75] Apprehension and removal from the family of birth were not and are not the norm in our society, and, even when placements have been consistent and loving, any child forced to "live in foster placement lives through an experience pregnant with pain and terror ... placement is a shocking and bewildering calamity."[76] While apprehension has historically been justified on the basis that, when removed from risk of harm, children will bond with foster or adoptive parents,[77] such bonding has been impossible when children are in and out of care and/or are transferred frequently between placements. Too often, moreover, children have experienced harm at the hands of those charged by the state to care for them, a fact that has resulted in the recent certification of a class-action suit against the provincial government on behalf of children who experienced sexual and physical abuse while crown wards.[78] The reality has been – and remains – that there were not and are not enough loving homes to which to send apprehended children. Despite this fact, the myth of adoption has continued to be used as a justification for apprehension.

Historically, the state has intervened "more aggressively to take children into care than to support disadvantaged parents,"[79] resulting in unwarranted and damaging apprehensions. Undoubtedly, this has been driven by highly publicized cases of extreme neglect and violence against children, by the precautionary principle itself (and fear of liability), and by the financial constraints faced by child-welfare agencies; in the short term, apprehension was and is less costly than the myriad social supports necessary for preventive child welfare. Successful child-protection services would ultimately mean that far fewer children would be available for adoption. Ironically, however, this might not have much impact on adoption rates; sadly, apprehended children continue to languish in foster care since they are viewed as "damaged" and undesirable for adoption by many prospective adoptive parents.

5

Secrecy and Disclosure in Adoption

From the mid-twentieth century, questions with regard to secrecy in adoption and potential adoption reunions have captivated the public imagination. As Veronica Strong-Boag illustrates,[1] the rise of a vocal adoption-rights movement led to myriad challenges to the closed adoption-records regime. Advocates of open records relied in part upon the 1989 United Nations Convention on the Rights of the Child[2] to articulate claims for the right to access information about birth parents.[3] But such demands for identifying information came into direct conflict with the expectation of privacy of some adopted children as well as birth and adoptive parents. In responding to controversies about adoption records, governments have had to balance these interests. Disclosure laws can be structured to allow access only to non-identifying information; reunion registries can be passive or active, either requiring mutual consent or allowing unilateral disclosure at the request of either party to the adoption; and changes to laws can be retroactive or prospective. Ontario has experimented with variations of all of these options and has recently passed compromise legislation which resolves many of the controversies involved.

Initially, Ontario, like other provinces and states, worked with a closed adoption system. In slow stages, however, adoption agencies and the Ontario legislature moved to provide means by which birth mothers and adopted children could obtain non-identifying information about each other and initiate searches for the purposes of reunion.[4]

First, adoption agencies responded informally to requests from mothers and adopted children for non-identifying information about other parties to adoption. Some individuals sought access to identifying information through proceedings in court, but overwhelmingly such requests were denied. In 1978 a voluntary registry, for birth parents and adoptees aged eighteen and up, was created; if both the birth parent and the child registered, registry workers would initiate contact between the parties and provide counselling.[5] In 1987 this passive registry was made active.[6] In 2005 the Ontario legislature passed the Adoption Information Disclosure Act,[7] which would have given all adult adoptees and birth parents an absolute right to information about adoption. However, the legislation was challenged by adopted children and a putative father and, in the controversial *Cheskes* decision,[8] it was determined to violate privacy rights. The province has subsequently established a registry system which allows those involved in adoptions before 2008 to file disclosure vetoes. For adoptions completed after 2008, a disclosure veto is available only on application to a board; the default position of legislation is openness, upon the age of maturity of the adopted person, unless a disclosure veto has been registered.[9] This represents a compromise between the demands of some adoptees and birth parents for greater openness, and respect for the privacy of those who oppose retroactive exposure of their personal lives.

From 1921, an adoption order in Ontario divested "the natural parent, guardian or person in whose custody the child ha[d] been of all legal rights in respect of such child."[10] The ties between the child and his or her natural parents were irrevocably severed and the relinquishing parent had no right to information about the child. The adopted child could not obtain information about his or her natural parents and birth parents were not informed about details with regard to child placement.[11] Although there was some ambiguity in this regard in the legislation of 1921, a 1927 amendment confirmed that records would be sealed and provided that "an application for an adoption order may be heard and determined in chambers, and if the child was born out of wedlock this fact shall not appear upon the face of the adoption order."[12] As one commentator on adoption in *Chatelaine* magazine asserted approvingly in 1932, many adopted children knew nothing about their ancestry because "a good deal of trouble and expense" had been employed to "cover up the fact" of adoption.[13]

Birth parents were and are required to register the births of children with provincial authorities, and a registration of birth contained the child's name, the date and place of birth, and the birth mother's name, age, marital status, and residence at the date of the child's birth. In cases in which the mother was married, or when an unmarried father acknowledged paternity, the father's information was also recorded. An adoption order contained the pre-adoption surname of the adopted child, the names of the adoptive parents, and the adopted child's post-adoption surname. New birth certificates were often issued for adopted children and it is estimated that, for about 60 per cent of those in Ontario who have been adopted, two registrations of birth exist: "a sealed original birth registration ... and a substituted birth registration containing the post-adoption name and the particulars of the adoptive parents."[14] Even when adopted persons were able to obtain original birth certificates, however, such records were sparse and personal detail was primarily to be found in the adoption files created by agencies facilitating the transfer of children. The Adoption Act of 1927 stipulated that "the papers used upon an adoption application shall be sealed up and shall not be open for inspection save upon the direction of a Judge or the Provincial Officer."[15] The circumstances under which an adoption file might be opened by a judge or provincial officer were not detailed and much was left to the discretion of both adoption agencies and courts. Closed adoption records were "rooted in the perceived need to obliterate the stigma of illegitimacy for the child and birth mother and to protect the rights of possible adoptive parents." The secrecy provisions in Ontario adoption law were not unusual and similar systems existed in all the Canadian provinces as well as the United States, New Zealand, the United Kingdom, and Australia.[16]

In this context, as Wayne Carp argues with regard to the United States, social workers "had the power to provide or deny access to adoption records." In a context of agency discretion, Carp argues that U.S. social workers often revealed non-identifying information.[17] Evidence from the Children of Unmarried Parents Act files illustrates that some workers at the Children's Aid Society in Ontario behaved similarly. Social workers seem to have been willing to reassure mothers that children had been placed in loving homes and that they were healthy and thriving, but to have routinely refused to release any information which might have identified the child's whereabouts or adoptive name. For many mothers, in Ontario and elsewhere, particularly in a context in which adoption was chosen under significant pressure, perhaps even harassment, lack of knowledge about children released for adoption caused distress. In revealing autobiographical stories, birth mothers have eloquently described being "haunted by fear for their child's welfare, [and of] guilt both for abandoning their child and for continuing to love and long for him."[18] Those who mourn children relinquished for adoption assert that not knowing how they have fared is the most painful aspect of the loss of the child. These emotions are evident in CAS adoption files. One mother, seeking information about the welfare of a child she had relinquished, stated that "there are things that go on in your mind. You think about it. Sometimes you wonder if the child is alright."[19] Several described yearning to "know that she was ok, that she was happy, that my decision was good for her."[20] Although women who sought information from the CAS were usually reassured that their children had been placed in good homes and were thriving, they were told to get on with their lives, that they had no right to any identifying information, and that their relationships with the children had been permanently and irrevocably severed.

Children also informally approached the Children's Aid Society for information and adoption case files reveal that relinquishment could raise subtle questions about belonging for some adoptees. For example, one child, born and adopted in 1960, started writing letters to the CAS in 1971 requesting information about her biological parents. She wrote eleven letters of inquiry between 1971 and 1977.[21] As was the case when mothers sought information, it seems that social workers were unwilling to provide identifying information about birth parents to adopted children. These inquiries, however, did not advance to court. The number of such cases was also limited and, for many birth parents, adoptive children, and adoptive parents, the closed system may have worked well. Those who opposed secrecy, however, became increasingly vocal as the twentieth century progressed.

In the United States, public discussion of closed adoption files began as early as 1949. Jean M. Paton, who had been adopted twice, attempted to publish an article calling for a mutual-consent registry to allow adoptees and birth parents to contact each other when both sides wanted such contact, but the article was rejected.[22] She then wrote the first book of the adoption-rights movement, *The Adopted Break Silence*.[23] She did not, however, garner much public support, although her suggestion that mutual-consent registries be created has proven to be prescient. In her comprehensive review of the searching movement in Canada, Strong-Boag highlights the work of Paton's lesser known Canadian counterpart, Clare Marcus.[24] Marcus was born to an unwed mother in Winnipeg in 1924 and adopted privately from the hospital.

She wrote two books, *Adopted? A Canadian Guide for Adopted Adults in Search of Their Origins* and *Who Is My Mother?* She advocated the creation of an adoption registry and provided advice for searching adoptees as to how to find their biological parents. She was also a founding member of Parent Finders, a group that originated in British Columbia and remains the leading organization assisting adoptees and birth parents in the reunion process in Canada.[25]

Simultaneously, social-science research was asking important questions about outcomes in adoption. David Kirk, a Canadian sociologist and adoptive parent, in a provocative book published in 1964,[26] argued that more openness was necessary in adoption. As Strong-Boag notes, he hypothesized that adoptive children were like first-generation immigrants, and this theory was described as "complacency-shattering" for those involved in adoption.[27] He "stressed the need to acknowledge that adoptive families are different from biological ones."[28] He did not, however, denigrate adoption itself, and emphasized that with acknowledgment of difference adoptive families could be very happy. Other researchers advanced much more controversial findings, in particular Annette Sorosky, Reuben Baran, and Arthur Pannor,[29] who claimed that for all members of the adoption triad feelings of loss, pain, and mourning were permanent. As Wayne Carp illustrates, much of the research on adoption outcomes contained "serious design flaws that discredit its propositions." In particular, Carp points to the work of Sorosky, Baran, and Pannor as "laughable."[30] Their work, however, did not represent the worst of the genre and the "most insidious adoption myth" is "adopted child syndrome."[31] David Kirschner claimed that adopted children were so damaged that they were "prone to lying, stealing, defiance of authority and setting fires, among other anti-social behaviours."[32] While he later admitted that he did not have any evidence to support this theory, "this has not stopped others, including members of the search movement who oppose all adoption, from using it to support their claims."[33]

Beyond the obvious problems in unsubstantiated assertions such as those of Kirschner, and the overt hostility to adoption in the works of Sorosky, Baran, and Pannor, much adoption psychology research was inherently biased by selective sampling. Very few studies exist with regard to the impact of relinquishment on mothers. While those who have suffered have offered individual stories, "birth parents who do not want their identities revealed are perhaps the least studied members of the adoption triangle since they do not come forward for interviews, and their desire for continued privacy is highly respected by researchers."[34] Studies of adopted children suffer from similar problems. As the Ontario Superior Court found in *Cheskes*: "There are few, if any, clinical studies [of adopted children who had happy placements and/or are opposed to disclosure] ... because the non-searching population prefers anonymity and is hence unorganized. Unlike the searching population, it does not have lobby groups working on its behalf."[35] To assert that the research is problematic is not, it should be noted, to disparage the very real feelings of some relinquishing parents and adoptees; however, the most vocal cannot be assumed to speak for all. Despite problems in this research, the search movement in the 1970s based its demands on the presumed psychological needs of adopted children.[36]

The search movement gained significant public attention in a context of increased concern about children's rights in general, in particular as articulated by the United Nations Convention on the Rights of the Child. Article 8 of the Convention explicitly articulated the child's "right to identity, including nationality, name and family relations."[37] Although such arguments were originally framed with regard to children subject to dislocation during wartime and other crises, the adoption-rights movement extrapolated from this a right to identity for adopted children and found considerable public support. Moreover, the emphasis on popular psychology and the demand for individual rights in adoption and reunion stories were "tailor-made for mass circulation magazines which were quick to exploit the melodrama inherent in adoptee searches,"[38] ensuring wide interest in adoption and secrecy. Public discourse about adoption outcomes and the harms of secrecy undoubtedly influenced the decision of the Ontario government to create a mutual-consent adoption registry in 1978.

In this year, by a 37–36 vote in the legislature, the Adoption Disclosure Registry was established through a revision to Ontario's Child Welfare Act.[39] The registry worked to match adult adoptees and biological parents who consented to reunite with one another. A series of forms had to be completed and then revised and verified in order to initiate a search. Next, a social worker would attempt to make a match. A match was possible only if both parties had applied. If this were not the case, the applicants were entered in the registry and they were told that the ministry would contact them in the case that the other party registered. Parties were explicitly granted veto powers.[40]

It was in this context that the first challenge to Ontario's closed-adoption regime reached the Ontario County Court, Middlesex in 1983.[41] The applicant wanted access to information about her birth parents and the court had to determine what would constitute "good cause" to order that files be opened. The applicant, Elizabeth Ferguson, had entered her name in the adoption registry, but her relinquishing parent had not. She had tried to convince the Children's Aid Society and the Department of Vital Statistics to release the information voluntarily and explained that she had "experienced a sense of incompleteness, as if missing a piece of the puzzle of my identity." Both Vital Statistics and the Ministry of Community and Social Services had refused to release the information on the basis that, absent the consent and registration of her birth mother, it could do so only "where some overriding compelling circumstances related to the health of the adoptee dictate the release of such information as a matter of policy." The court was very impressed by the applicant, who had "not attempted to colour or clog her application with dubious or tenuous medical materials aimed at establishing that she has a compelling need for the requested biological and related information. Rather, she grounds her application on the simple argument that she has a healthy and continuing 'natural curiosity' to know about her origins." Her lawyer asserted that the "best interests of the child" should override the concerns of birth parents, although he did recognize that "most birth parents – and especially birth mothers – have given up their children for adoption in the expectation that their particular role in the adoption process will be accorded some privacy and confidentiality." The ministry, however, asserted that the voluntary-adoption registry was sufficient and that the revisions of 1978 provided "a complete code on the disclosure of Ministry information about adoptees except for those rare cases – based on a 'compelling need' standard – where the court might order the release of information." The court chastised the government for failing to publicize the existence of the registry, lamented that "both counsel candidly admitted that their joint research disclosed no Ontario case, reported or unreported, which directly dealt with the scope of an adoption judge's jurisdiction under the subsection," and found that anonymity remained central to adoption. While the "best interests of the child" test should determine the adoption itself, this doctrine had "no place in a disclosure decision: after the adoption order has been signed, the shield of secrecy erected around the adoption process demands that equal prominence be given to the interests of each of the parties to the adoption triangle." While sympathetic to Elizabeth Ferguson, therefore, the court denied her request.[42] Ferguson appealed this decision, but was unsuccessful.[43]

In response to the *Ferguson* case, the Ontario government attempted, in 1985, to make the release of any information from adoption files illegal. The minister of community and social services, Frank Drea, asserted that any information could identify individuals in small communities and that therefore such information had to be carefully protected to ensure privacy. However, he was accused of wanting to reseal adoption records because his own adopted daughter was actively seeking her birth family. Public outcry "prevented the legislation from being enacted"[44] and, also in 1985, Dr Ralph Garber was appointed a special commissioner to make recommendations regarding the disclosure of adoption information.

While the legislature was awaiting the report of Garber's commission, another county court in Ontario denied access to information regarding adoption. This time the request came from a birth mother, not an adopted child, and the court was significantly less sympathetic than had been the case in *Ferguson*.[45] The mother had been provided with detailed, non-identifying information by the Children's Aid Society to reassure her that her child was thriving in his adoptive home, but this did not satisfy her. In her affidavit the applicant mother described eloquently the "social pressures to which she [had been] subject in 1964 at age 20 on her pregnancy being confirmed and complain[ed] of lack of counseling as to how she could keep her baby and thrive on her own." She claimed not only that a reunion with her son would be good for her but also, echoing the rhetoric of the adoption-rights movement, that contact would benefit her son. The court found otherwise: "The applicant appears to be obsessed with making contact with her son, but ... he is of university age, and may never have been curious about his natural mother, in which case any inquiry or communication will come to him as a brutal surprise. Indeed, if he is vulnerable, it could be a blow from which he might never recover. I consider that the best interests of the child come before those of the natural mother." The applicant had registered with the Adoption Disclosure Registry "and if the applicant's adopted son should develop any curiosity about his roots and his natural mother, he is free to register also, at which time appropriate meeting arrangements can be made."[46]

Shortly thereafter, Garber recommended that adult adoptees be permitted access to identifying information without the consent of the person identified, but this recommendation was not enacted by the legislature.[47] In the House, John Sweeney, the newly elected Liberal minister of community and social services, rejecting complete openness, "asserted that the adopted adult's 'right to know' had to be balanced against the birth parents' historic right to confidentiality and privacy."[48] As others have noted, achieving consensus about how to reform the adoption-disclosure provisions was and remains difficult because all approaches have limitations. While passive registries may mean that significant numbers of people are unaware of their right to register, or simply do not bother to do so, active registries create the risk that "adoptees and birth parents may be contacted by government or agency representatives in order to obtain consent to release information; this contact, by letter or phone, may be enough to breach their privacy rights and reveal their history to current family members and associates."[49]

As a compromise measure, in 1987, while still requiring consent, amendments to the Child Welfare Act and the provisions of the Adoption Disclosure Statute Law Amendment transformed the once passive Adoption Disclosure Registry into an active search system[50] "whereby adopted persons and certain categories of birth relatives [could] be located even in the absence of registration in the passive registry." Under this system, instead of waiting to match parents and children once both had registered, "the registrar [would] conduct an active search for a specified second party after the first party ha[d] registered with the registry ... [and] when a match [was] made on the registry, the two parties [were] contacted by a government social worker who determine[d] if the parties g[a]ve their 'mutual consent' for the identifying information to be released and/or for contact to be made." The registrar also retained the right to allow disclosure "of identifying information where required for the health, safety or welfare of any individual."[51] In the months after the implementation of the new provisions, more than 4,500 requests for information were submitted.[52]

Pressure for further reform continued to mount. The most vocal advocate of reform in Ontario was Marilyn Churley, an MPP and birth mother who introduced private member's bills to the legislature in 1998, 2000, 2001, and 2003.[53] She proposed a system that would allow a contact veto but not a disclosure veto.[54] But opposition to openness coexisted with pressure for reform. In Nova Scotia, for example, after an adopted child located his mother and, by revealing himself to her family, brought about its destruction, the provincial government passed legislation stipulating that adoption records could be opened only with ministerial or judicial approval.[55] It was asserted that the potential need of birth parents for privacy, while less vocally asserted, must be "remembered alongside the pain and loss of rights appropriately emphasized by activist birth mothers."[56] Despite mixed press and divided public opinion, advocates of reform were successful in Ontario in 2005.

After years of debate, Ontario passed the Adoption Information Disclosure Act.[57] The bill was introduced on 29 March 2005 by the then minister of community and social services, Sandra Pupatello. Adoptees over eighteen years of age and birth parents (once the children in question reached the age of nineteen) were to be able to obtain copies of original birth records and adoption orders. Birth parents and adoptees could file no-contact notices and a mechanism was created for denying disclosure altogether, but it required a determination by a board that the non-disclosure was necessary to prevent physical or sexual harm to the party seeking to prevent disclosure (a show cause procedure).[58] Reform, however, was controversial and faced serious opposition in the House. In particular, the information and privacy commissioner, Ann Cavoukian, "repeatedly criticized the retroactive nature of the bill and the consequent harmful social consequences – careers ruined, family life destroyed, privacy invaded – that she warned would occur as a result." In a context in which privacy was of increasing public concern owing to the development of new means of communication, particularly the Internet and the increasing use of large computer data sets by governments and other organizations, her arguments had some public support. Nonetheless, the bill passed by a vote of 68–19 and received royal assent on 3 November.[59] Implementation was delayed until 19 September 2006 in the interest of public education (to allow time for non-contact orders to be filed). In the interim, two Ontario court cases challenged adoption-disclosure provisions. In *Marchand*[60] an adoptee sought retroactive disclosure of her putative father's name and was denied access to this information. In *Cheskes*[61] four parties to the adoption triangle challenged the provisions of the Adoption Information Disclosure Act as violating their constitutional right to privacy and were successful.

The plaintiff in *Marchand* had been adopted as an infant in 1957. By the time she sought out her birth parents, her mother was long dead but adoption agency files contained the name of a man identified by her mother as her father. The man denied paternity, however, and when approached by the Children's Aid Society he refused to have his name released to the applicant. The CAS had released non-identifying information to her, as was permitted under legislation. She again contacted the Adoption Disclosure Registry and was given information about her mother's cause of death and place of burial.⁶² The applicant then had her lawyer approach the registrar seeking disclosure of her putative father's name and disclosure was again denied.⁶³

During her childhood the applicant had not been told of her adoption and had been subjected to severe physical, emotional, and sexual abuse. She claimed that her life had been seriously marred by secrecy and that denial of knowledge about her putative father had deprived her "of what she describe[d] as the fundamental right to know where she c[ame] from. She argue[d] that the closing of records is profoundly damaging to adoptees as it prevents them from achieving wholeness ... [and that the provisions were] in breach of ... her right to liberty, security of the person pursuant to s. 7 of the *Charter*, and ... her equality rights pursuant to s. 15 of the *Charter*." The attorney general countered that the Adoption Disclosure Registry was intended to balance the "competing demands of access to information and protection of privacy of those involved in an adoption."⁶⁴

The Ontario Superior Court of Justice found that the "information was refused ... because there was no match on the Adoption Disclosure Register and because the man denied his consent to disclosure." The court held that "while there is no question that the applicant is enormously frustrated by her inability to access the name of the person identified by her birth mother as being her birth father ... the evidence does not support her assertion that her life would have taken a fundamentally different course had she been allowed to openly access her birth and adoption records," and that "extensive sexual and physical abuse" and "the secrecy that informed her childhood" were problems created, not by the impugned legislation, "but rather [by] the attitude and approach of her adoptive parents."⁶⁵ The court rejected her expert evidence asserting that adopted children suffered harm because of secrecy⁶⁶ since it was deemed to be biased and to ignore "recent, large, representative and methodologically sophisticated studies ... that have found no significant differences between the behaviors and characteristics of matched groups of adopted children and non-adopted children." Her assertion that only the rights of the adopted child should be considered was also rejected: "While there may not be anything in writing confirming to birth parents that their privacy will not be breached, their understanding and expectation was that their confidentiality would be maintained." The court asserted that "there is no liberty right to obtain identifying information about a person who has expressly refused to consent to its disclosure." Her section 15 claim was denied because the legislation was intended to facilitate reunions and to ameliorate the condition of adopted children and "a reasonable person, in assessing whether the scheme treated the applicant as less worthy of respect and consideration than non-adopted persons, would take this into account."[67]

Marchand appealed, but in the interim the legal environment had changed because the Adoption Information Disclosure Act had been deemed unconstitutional in the Superior Court. On the first day of the appeal hearing, the Ontario government announced that it would not appeal the *Cheskes* decision but instead would "introduce new legislation that would let parents and children involved in past adoptions veto disclosure of information."[68] Because such an announcement was deemed likely to lead to the "return to something like the repealed *Child and Family Services Act* scheme," the court asserted that it was important to hear Marchand's appeal. The Court of Appeal accepted the judgment of the lower court in full: "In our view, this analysis is sound ... [and] the unconditional disclosure of identifying personal information of third parties, even if they are birth parents of the claimant, without regard to the privacy and confidentiality interests of the persons identified and without regard to any serious harm that might result from disclosure ... is not a principle that is vital or fundamental to our societal notion of justice." Leave to appeal to the Supreme Court of Canada was filed on 29 January 2008, submitted to the Court on 10 March 2008, and dismissed by Justices Beverley McLachlin, Morris Fish, and Marshall Rothstein on 24 April 2008.[69] The claim that adult adoptees have a right to information about their birth parents had failed.[70]

In the interim, moreover, the rights of parties who do not want reunions had been upheld in the Ontario Superior Court. In *Cheskes v. Ontario*, four applicants, three adult adopted children and a putative father, expressed fear and anxiety about the possible implications of the Adoption Information Disclosure Act for their families, and argued that disclosure of personal information without their consent would violate their section 7 rights to life, liberty, and security of the person. They did not oppose the idea of open adoption in the future but objected to "retroactive application of the legislation." They asserted that "the opening of confidential adoption records on a retroactive basis and the removal of the consent requirement violates the applicants' right to privacy under s 7 of the *Charter* in a manner that cannot be justified under s 1. On the other hand, the right of searching adoptees or birth parents to gain access to confidential adoption information, although important and heart-felt, is not a *Charter*-protected right." The personal reasons for opposition to the opening of records varied.

Joy Cheskes had a happy adoptive family life and did not want this life disrupted by contact from birth parents. She also maintained that the proposal that a disclosure veto be obtained via a hearing violated her right to make autonomous decisions: "I do not see why I should be forced to reveal this information or go through the stress and emotional turmoil of having to divulge these feelings to a board in the hope of then being allowed to keep my personal information private." Moreover, she asserted that providing identifying information to a birth parent would have an enormous, and unwanted, impact on her family: "By disclosing my identity, I am disclosing theirs, too."[71]

Denbigh Patton was concerned about the impact of contact with a birth parent on his elderly, and very loving, adoptive parents, and asserted that the "no-contact provision would not prevent the disclosure of his identity and with that identifying information." He spoke eloquently about the process by which he had come to the decision that he did not want to have contact with his birth parents: "I am not currently willing to risk trauma to my life as it is, to my family, to my loving aging parents, to my identity. This is a weighty decision that I have carried all my adult life and will continue to ponder. But it is for me to ponder and it is I who will suffer or benefit as a consequence of this decision." He also asserted that the prospect of being exposed against his will had caused him such anxiety that he had sought medical intervention.[72]

C.M. had also grown up in a happy adoptive home and for fourteen years had known that a birth parent was avidly searching for her. She had repeatedly told the social-work agency that she did not desire contact, but the searching continued and she feared that the release of identifying information would lead to an unwanted invasion of her privacy, since her birth parent had already disregarded her clear statement that she did not want contact: "The no contact order is totally irrelevant to me, because no contact will not mean that they cannot watch me, they can't drive past my house. This person could get my name and give this to children that she has, to other friends, to relatives. It ... does not provide me any comfort whatsoever ... I could be stalked." She described feeling "hunted" by her birth mother.[73]

The fourth applicant, D.S., had fathered a child who had subsequently been adopted. The child was the product of a brief sexual relationship and the putative father had heard about the birth itself only when contacted by the Children's Aid Society. He had denied paternity at the time, but his name was nonetheless included as the father of record. He married and had his own family, only to later be contacted by a social worker asking if he would be willing to have contact with his birth child. He declined, since his wife and family were and are unaware of the existence of the adopted child and he feared that knowledge of the adoption would tear his family apart. He asserted that "this exposure would render me even more powerless, humiliated, and vulnerable."[74]

The *Cheskes* court accepted the validity of the arguments and concerns of the applicants, noting that, while the interests of searching adopted children have been the subject of public discussion, "the feelings and the fears of the 'non-searching' adoptees and birth parents who do not want to be found are no less legitimate and no less compelling" and that "the impact on their lives and those of their families is just as significant ... Lives could be shattered." The violation imposed by the Adoption Information Disclosure Act was deemed not simply to involve documents or records but also to constitute an invasion "of the dignity and self-worth of the individual, who enjoys the right to privacy as an essential aspect of his or her liberty in a free and democratic society"; such liberty interests include the right to make fundamental life choices without interference from the state. The court asserted that "the protection of privacy is a fundamental value in modern democracies" and noted that personal information is for that person "to communicate or retain for himself as he sees fit." The no-contact provisions and the non-disclosure provisions were also found to be inadequate to protect the needs articulated by the applicants. The court affirmed the line of cases asserting that "the right to know one's past" is not a constitutionally protected right under Canadian law but that the right to privacy is such a protected interest: "Where a reasonable expectation of privacy has been established in the collection and storage of one's personal and confidential information, one should have the ability to control the dissemination of this information." Contrary to the arguments of the Ontario government, moreover, the legislation could not be saved by reference to section 1 of the Charter: "Opening adoption records on a retroactive basis is no doubt extremely important for many, but the new law cannot be said to fall within any of the extraordinary or emergency categories."[75] The court asserted that other provinces continued to endorse mutual-consent provisions with regard to adoption registries such as those in Ontario that had prevailed before the passage of the Adoption Information Disclosure Act.[76] Further, even the four provinces that had recently reformed their adoption-information disclosure provisions allowed for disclosure vetoes without show cause procedures.[77] In this context, the Adoption Information Disclosure Act was declared null and void and Ontario was ordered to amend its legislation.

In the wake of the *Cheskes* decision, the Ontario government announced that it would not appeal. Instead, Community and Social Services Minister Madeleine Meilleur stated that the government would introduce new compromise legislation.[78] As a result of these reforms, under current provisions, adopted adults and birth parents can file disclosure vetoes to protect their privacy if the adoption was finalized before 1 September 2008. The veto prevents the release of post-adoption information about the person who filed it. If the adoption was finalized after the specified date, a person can file only a no-contact notice and this requires an appearance before a board and proof of exceptional circumstances.[79] This legislation represents an acknowledgment that adoptive relationships are not identical to those based in biology and that the past cannot simply be wiped clean. It also respects the privacy of those who were adopted, or who released children for adoption, in an era in which secrecy was taken for granted. While the issue of secrecy with regard to adoption records appears to have been resolved through legislative reform that makes openness at maturity the default position for all adoptions from 2008 on, a closely related issue, the enforceability of open adoption, remains controversial. Why, with the right to identifying information about birth parents at maturity being the reality of modern adoption, do we continue to limit the ability of these same children to have knowledge about, and potentially contact with, birth parents and families during their minority?

6

Open Adoption

Open adoption – a variety of arrangements allowing knowledge of and/or contact between birth and adoptive families – "has generated a great deal of controversy."[1] Openness has gradually evolved from basic information sharing to the possibility of ongoing contact and close relationships between adoptive and birth families and can involve "information cleared through an intermediary, pictures, direct letters, phone calls, gifts and visits."[2] Although informal openness may have occurred in some cases, until 1990 the Child Welfare Act required termination of all access orders with regard to crown wards before an adoption could be undertaken.[3] Under section 58 of the Child and Family Services Act, 1990, orders for contact made before adoption could continue post-adoption under limited circumstances.[4] By the Child and Family Services Amendment Act, 2006, c. 5, birth parents who had lost children through crown-ward proceedings could apply for access orders even after adoption; such orders, because vetted by the court, were enforceable. Further reforms in 2011 eliminated the existence of an access order as an impediment to the adoption of a crown ward; the intention of this reform was to facilitate the adoption of more crown wards by foster parents.[5] These revisions, however, did not and do not apply to infant adoption or in other cases in which the surrender of the child is voluntary. While the reforms of 2006 allow openness agreements between birth and adoptive parents in the context of voluntary relinquishment, such agreements are not enforceable by the court. Birth parents in non-crown-ward situations, whatever the age of the child at the time of adoption, are dependent upon the goodwill of adoptive parents to ensure that the terms of adoptive agreements are respected. The growing acceptance of open adoption in the context of crown wards with established relationships with birth families illustrates an increased understanding that multiple individuals can be important in children's lives and that the past cannot simply be erased in adoption. Ironically, however, the distinction that those who release their children voluntarily can seek openness agreements, but not enforceable orders, seems to punish those who try to act voluntarily in the best interests of their children. Moreover, with regard to infants, society and adoptive parents seem less willing to embrace openness, despite its potential benefits for birth and adoptive parents.[6]

Open adoption emerged as a result of three interrelated changes in the adoption landscape. First, the open-records movement suggested that the secrecy of adoption created potential problems for adoptees and advocates of open records demanded change in future adoptions. Second, step-parent adoption, the subject of the next chapter, paved the way for exceptions to the closed adoption model. If natural fathers could be allowed to maintain contact with their children after divorce, even in the case of formal adoption of their children by step-fathers, why could other parties with existing relationships with children not also maintain such relationships post-adoption? Third, the emergence of the belief in the late 1960s that there was no such thing as an unadoptable child, and the push for the adoption of racial minority and older children, as well as those with special needs, meant that many adopted children, like children adopted by step-parents, entered adoption with long histories of relationships that might be important to their well-being. The net result of these changes was "the introduction of a continuum of open adoption possibilities into social work practice."[7] Only some of these open adoptions, however, were and are enforceable in court.

Open adoption received increased public attention and support in the context of the debates about secrecy in adoption.[8] As Cindy Baldassi asserts, despite the fact that releasing adoption records for adults is very different from maintaining openness throughout a child's life, the "history, theory and practice" of the open-records movement and open adoption were intimately interconnected and arguments in favour of opening adoption records have had a powerful impact on debates regarding open adoption.[9] As Strong-Boag illustrates, the first adoption researcher to discuss open adoption appears to have been David Kirk, a Canadian sociologist and adoptive parent who directed the Adoption Research Project at McGill University from 1951 to 1961. His work argued that secrecy was problematic and that knowledge about biological parents might be useful to adoptees.[10] Other researchers, including Annette Sorosky, Reuben Baran, and Arthur Pannor, the most widely cited of the adoption-outcome researchers of the 1970s, asserted that if adoption were to be allowed at all, it should always involve ongoing knowledge of, and contact with, birth families.[11] The concept of open adoption became much more widely known in the 1970s as a result of their work. Despite flaws in research design, as outlined in the previous chapter, critiques of closed adoption gained public traction because they coincided with the emergence of the adoption-rights movement and the public denunciation of the closed adoption system by some adoptees and birth mothers. The visibility of the searching movement undoubtedly influenced public opinion. Adoptive parents, moved by the rhetoric of searching and concerned that a lack of information about genetics might distress children later in life, became more accepting of the idea of sharing information about birth families with their children.

Developments in step-parent adoption also influenced attitudes towards open adoption.[12] Connections were drawn between the rights of fathers, the opening of adoption records, and the changing face of adoption more generally. In 1995 the Ontario Court of Justice considered a case in which a father who had voluntarily waived his parental rights by allowing a step-parent adoption had come to regret his choice and sought an order for access. While the court rejected the father's application, it was noted that access might be awarded, even after adoption, in any case in which a relationship had developed "between the child and the natural parents after an adoption order was made" or when "pre-adoption assurances by the adoptive parents [were] not respected."[13] This suggested that the court had some concern for the need of children to maintain pre-adoptive relationships. Similarly, in 1997 the Alberta Court of Appeal found that it was insufficient simply to recognize that "the adopting parents may permit either or both biological parents to have access to the child," stating unequivocally that there are circumstances "in which such access is in the child's best interests. Obvious examples are step-parent and relative adoptions. And there may be cases where the child has had a prior relationship with a biological parent, foster parent, grandparent, or sibling where the continuation or re-establishment of the contact is in the child's best interests." The court lamented that "there are no statutory provisions which address these situations."[14] Such arguments were particularly compelling with regard to older children who had established relationships with birth mothers, fathers, siblings, or grandparents.

Rising rates of apprehension and concern about the failure of foster placement for children also influenced the development of open adoption. Foster care emerged as an alternative to institutional care in the early twentieth century, but by mid-century it was clear that foster care was not meeting the needs of children.[15] Not only were large numbers of children in care, but also placements were unlikely to be stable. Children moved too often between homes, a fact that had negative implications for their health and well-being. Further, foster care, funded by the state, was expensive. It would be in the interest of the state, therefore, to encourage the adoption of foster children. However, large numbers of the children in care were considered unadoptable. It was widely believed that parents would have no interest in adopting children with health problems, children of mixed race, and children who were simply older and could no longer be seamlessly absorbed into families while preserving the myth of the normative household. In 1954, in the context of the consolidation of adoption, fostering, and child-welfare provisions in the new Child Welfare Act,[16] the Ontario government, while still noting that many children were not adoptable, tasked the Children's Aid Society with creating "innovative advertising campaigns geared to finding families for these children."[17] In 1955 the province established the office of the Provincial Adoption Coordinator and the Adoption Clearance Bureau. In 1959 the Ontario Department of Public Welfare began a three-year publicity campaign in which hard-to-place children were advertised, and it received responses from across the continent from parents seeking children to adopt.[18] "Today's Child," a column in the *Toronto Telegram*, was established in 1971. In it, Helen Allen, who later became the information officer for adoption in the Ministry of Community and Social Services, Ontario, created profiles or biographies of children who were available for adoption.[19] These programs were all intended to encourage the adoption of hard-to-place children and to reduce rates of institutionalization. Older children were predominant. Similarly, the federal Adoption Assistance and Child Welfare Act, passed in the United States in 1980, designated adoption as the desired outcome "for foster children who [could not] be reunited with their families." The act also provided financial support for adoption and "challenged the notion that older children [and other hard-to-place children] [were] not adoptable."[20]

While stable homes for children were clearly desirable, all of these efforts failed to take into account the fact that older children came to adoption with previous experiences, good and bad, of biological families, foster homes, and institutions, and that some of the relationships from their pasts might be important for their futures. Moreover, in a context of rising rates of adoption from foster care, and the promotion of such adoptions by the state, the issue of ongoing contact with former caregivers became more common and pressing. Openness in such cases might require more than simply the provision of information about the status and well-being of a child; parents and children might desire regular visitation. As clinicians argued, the adoption of an older child "may result from traumatic circumstances involving abuse, neglect or criminal conduct on the part of the birth parents and may involve a lengthy, adversarial court process ... [but] despite these concerns, multiple benefits can accrue from openness in special needs adoptions." Moreover, because many children have siblings with whom they cannot be adopted, "openness works to maintain and nurture the strong attachment between siblings who cannot be placed in the same adoptive home."[21] But, until 1990, an access order had to be terminated in order to allow a child to be eligible for adoption, creating a situation not conducive to the best interests of the child; children with access orders might not be able to return to their homes of birth, but neither could they find new permanent homes. When children were adopted, all contact with birth families was denied and important relationships were severed.

Legislation in Ontario allowed courts no option but to refuse access even in crown-ward situations in which children had established relationships with birth parents. For example, in a case in which a mother had given birth in 1973 and released her child in 1977, the child was subsequently adopted, but the mother later applied for access. Her request was denied at the court of first instance, but on appeal the case was sent back for a hearing on the merits based on her right to apply as an interested party; the adoptive parents, supported by the Children's Aid Society, appealed and succeeded. The mother then appealed and the Court of Appeal found that the adoption code was a complete code and no application for access was possible: "Once the final order of adoption has been made, with the natural parents having every opportunity to oppose the making of such order if they so desire, s. 80 makes it equally clear that there shall be no disclosure of information about the child or the natural parents." The court also noted that the Child Welfare Act, 1978, section 69(14), prohibited any interference with a child placed for adoption by visit, letter, or telephone. The court admitted that section 35(1) of the Family Law Reform Act, 1978, allowed any person with an established relationship with a child to apply for access, but found that the mother, despite having raised the child for four years, did not have such a relationship.[22]

In a 1989 case a birth mother who had had access during a period of wardship was denied contact after adoption. The children had been removed as a result of a scalding incident that had led to the permanent scarring of one daughter, but the children had retained contact with their mother while in foster care, a period of over seven years. Access had initially been allowed but on appeal it was held that "the primary purpose [of denying birth parent access] is family stability ... The granting of an access order after adoption would hamper the relationship between an adopted child and the adopting parents. It would put that relationship on an unequal basis with that of natural child-parent relationships, because a judicial or administrative official would determine who had access to the children, rather than having that determination made within the family unit." The court also found that the legislation required "that there be termination of access by the birth parents by the time the children are placed for adoption: the choice was between continued Crown wardship or adoption with no access for birth parents." The mother claimed that a denial of access violated her sections 2, 7, and 15 Charter rights (association, liberty, and equality) but, citing a Saskatchewan decision, this argument was dismissed: "When a child is taken into protective custody, it is because the officer has reasonable grounds to believe the health and welfare of the child is in immediate jeopardy. A deprivation of association is justified in the best interests of the child. Loss of the freedom of association in such circumstances is a reasonable limit prescribed by law as can be demonstrably justified in a free and democratic society."[23] This was the first case in which the Ontario Court of Appeal dealt "with the *Charter* in a child protection context."[24]

Critics argued, however, that denial of contact might have adverse consequences for children who had long-standing relationships with their parents, however troubled such relationships might have been. In this context, and explicitly acknowledging the importance of contingency planning and support for families of origin, the Ontario Child and Family Services Act of 1990 distinguished between crown wards, who are often older, and infants relinquished at birth, establishing a mechanism by which "any person" could bring an application for continued access to a child if there was a pre-existing relationship and an access order and it could be proven that access would be in the child's best interests.[25] This process could result in post-adoption access for members of the birth family. The relevant section of the act, however, did not apply to children released voluntarily for adoption.

In a 1993 case that challenged this contradiction, the birth parents had released their child to the Children's Aid Society voluntarily and the child had eventually been adopted by the former foster parents who had a long knowledge of and relationship with the birth parents. Although the adoptive parents had repeatedly guaranteed that they would allow the birth family to see the child after the adoption, and a home study had determined that continued contact would be in the best interests of the child, the adoptive parents terminated access immediately after adoption and unilaterally asserted that access was harmful to the child. This was patently unfair since the parents had released the child for adoption, believing that this was in the best interests of their child, rather than facing adversarial proceedings for wardship; ironically, they had thereby vitiated their right to insist upon visitation. The court questioned the distinction in the act between crown wards and children relinquished voluntarily whether at birth or later in life, and asserted that the provisions were not a complete code with regard to access to children: "This is one of the increasingly more common situations in which the secrecy provisions of the adoption statute are either meaningless or, at least, of considerably less significance and relevance than they might be in a more traditional adoption ... I find no philosophical or legal conflict between the two statutes that would prevent the determination of this issue on its merits. Nor do I find anything in the case law or the legislation that leads me to the conclusion that the adoption provisions of the *Child and Family Services Act* operate as an absolute bar to a subsequent application for access."[26] Access was allowed.

Similarly, in 1995 the Ontario Court of Justice held that access could be ordered for family members other than parents in the adoption context. In this case, an adoptive mother had brought two orphan children from Mexico. Conflict developed and she adopted only the girl, abandoning the boy to the Catholic Children's Aid Society. The boy sought visitation with his sister. The children were not and never had been crown wards, but nonetheless the court held that "the relationship of brother and sister is a basic human relationship. It existed between these two children long before Ms. V. became involved in their lives. They visited one another in the orphanage in which they resided and they lived as brother and sister in Ms. V.'s residence until her fateful decision was made. The effect of Ms. V.'s decision is that M. has been effectively deprived of his relationship with his sister."[27] Although this case did not involve the rights of a birth parent, it set the precedent that, even in the context of non-crown-ward adoption, the Child and Family Services Act provisions could be used to assert a right of access. Sadly, however, the mother eventually left the country with the girl, effectively vitiating the order; the boy committed juvenile offences and, since no effort had been made to make him a Canadian citizen, "the teenager was subject to deportation."[28]

In a 1998 case heard in the Ontario Court of Justice, adoptive parents had agreed to an open adoption with ongoing contact by the mother, but a dispute had arisen and, despite mediation, contact had been impossible for a significant period of time, although all assessments of the child found that access would be in his best interests. The adoptive parents sought an order terminating all contact on the basis that "the continued proceedings violate the s. 7, 12 and 15 *Charter* rights of A.R. [the child]. Specifically, the continued proceedings expose A.R. to the risk of irreparable harm and have, in fact, caused harm." The court, however, found that "there is no evidence the proceedings have caused harm to A.R. There is no evidence that he even has any knowledge of the proceedings. He will only be harmed by the proceedings if told of them in a fashion in which one party lays blame or fault on the other party. There is no evidence that any of the parties has done so to date. They all profess to love him and hold his best interests paramount." The Charter arguments were found to be without merit. The court asserted that, if there had been harm to the child, it was in part caused by the applicants' behaviour and that they could not therefore claim a remedy. It was also found that "it can only be in A.R.'s best interest to enjoy the love and attention of his birth mother through regular access visits."[29]

In an attempt to clarify the conditions under which openness would be allowed, in 2006 the provincial government passed An Act to Amend the Child and Family Services Act and Make Complementary Amendments to Other Acts. The amendments empowered the Children's Aid Society to apply for an openness order "at any time before an order for adoption of the child is made." Openness orders were to be allowed only when deemed to be "in the best interests of the child" and when the order would permit "the continuation of a relationship with a person that is beneficial and meaningful to the child." All parties – the CAS, the parties seeking contact, the adoptive parents, and, if over twelve years of age, the child – had to agree to the ongoing contact. Openness orders could be made with regard to birth parents, foster parents, extended family members, and siblings. Mechanisms for dispute resolution could be incorporated into the order to prevent recourse to the court; the court could, however, enforce such orders if mediation failed.[30] All of these provisions applied only to crown wards. With regard to children relinquished voluntarily, openness agreements could be entered into but they would not be enforced by the court.

In 2009 the Ontario Court of Justice (Toronto) had to consider the rights of birth parents and these new provisions in a poignant case in which a ten-year-old boy had been made a crown ward when his mother, and then his father, succumbed to mental illness.[31] The court found that "openness orders are a relatively recent addition ... and counsel were unable to find any jurisprudence to guide the interpretation of these particular provisions." Openness, it was asserted, applied only "to a specific class of children: crown wards in the care and custody of a Children's Aid Society."[32] The court noted that, while contact with the birth parents was in the child's best interests, the legislation did not guarantee such contact; concern was expressed that "there is no ability to reach to the court to try to set aside the adoption order if the adoptive parents do not comply with the openness order" since the revisions of 2006 were clear that the "validity of [an] adoption order [is] not affected by openness order or agreement."[33] The birth parents in this case were opposed to adoption and hoped to reclaim custody of their child, a possibility that the court (and other specialists) deemed remote: "Both parents were themselves in need of care. Both were residing in supportive housing in this city and recipients of services to help them to manage the tasks of daily life."[34] The child was a crown ward, and had been for several years, and the birth parents' consent to the adoption was not required. The child was present at the openness hearings and clearly wished to continue to have contact with his birth parents. The court found that, while "at first blush, it might be easy to find no real benefit to a child in continuation of a relationship with parents whose ability to engage in the relationship is clouded by dementia," the child had never been maltreated and evidence of an emotional bond between the child and his birth parents was strong. The adoptive parents, it was acknowledged, "bring into his adoptive life all sorts of experiences that are very new to him – private schooling, pets, camps, organized sport, music lessons, a trip to Europe, a residence that is not social housing," a dramatic contrast with the poverty in which he had lived with his birth parents. Despite the clear economic benefits of the adoption for the child, and the obvious affection between him and his adoptive parents, the court asserted that in this case adoption was a "particularly artificial construct. This boy cannot reasonably be expected to pretend his parents out of his life. They will always be his parents. His adoptive parents take over where his own parents left off." The court found that openness would be in the best interests of the child.[35] The biological parents themselves noted that the child had been healthier and happier since the involvement of the adoptive parents. The adoptive parents had created "other means of establishing contact for the boy and his birth parents; including cards, pictures and telephone. They have established an e-mail account so that he can get information to his parents through their caregivers." It was ordered that the boy would have "contact with his birth mother and birth father at the discretion of his adoptive parents, with their prior express consent."[36]

Further reform of the Child and Family Services Act in 2011 eliminated the existence of an access order as an impediment to adoption for crown wards. Often children had access orders, and whether or not access was actually ongoing, the order itself precluded adoption. In this context reform was driven by concern for the large numbers of older children who were (and are) languishing in foster care, without permanent homes, and often with problems integrating into society when they aged-out of the foster-care system. Reports by the Ontario Association of Children's Aid Societies pointed to these concerns.[37] Under the amendments of 2011, agencies are now required to plan for every crown ward to be eligible for adoption regardless of whether the child is subject to an access order. Where an access order exists, parents must be given thirty days' notice of a planned adoption; the parent then has the right to seek an openness order, but not to contest the adoption. While the legislation "opens the door slightly" for parents to continue contact after adoption, critics have asserted that the onus on parents remains high.[38]

Openness orders, moreover, were made available only in the crown-ward context. Under the 2006 amendments, the parents of children relinquished voluntarily could enter into adoption agreements with adoptive parents, but such agreements were not enforceable at law; the legislation of 2011 did not eliminate this distinction. In voluntary cases, recognition of openness still remains contingent on the willingness of the adoptive parents to facilitate such exchanges, irrespective of the age at which the child was adopted and the nature of the relationship between the child and his or her natural parents. Open adoption in the context of newborns is particularly controversial. In such cases, children are often placed directly from the hospital at birth and birth parents do not have established relationships with children on which to base claims for access, in part because the court does not recognize the relationship inherent in gestation itself. While a mechanism that has been used in infant adoption cases by adoption agencies is to incorporate the terms of the openness agreement into the adoption-consent order, such agreements are not legally enforceable.

Advocates of openness agreements with regard to infant adoption assert that selecting the adoptive family gives the birth mother reassurance that the child is doing well and that this "increases a birth mother's sense of control ... which assists with grief resolution."[39] Advocates also argue that "if a woman can make the monumental decision to relinquish a child for adoption then she is surely capable of deciding whether contact is beneficial to her well-being and that of the child."[40] Numerous studies of open adoption confirm that it allows the birth mother to be more honest about relinquishment.[41] Critics, however, posit that, while this argument is based in ideals of choice and female autonomy, openness "arrangements tacitly embody and reinforce a ... troubling assumption: that children are property."[42] To this, feminists might counter that such arrangements instead reflect the nurturing relationship inherent in gestation.

Advocates of open adoption also argue that it is good for adoptive parents and that in open adoption "adoptive parents do not fear the 'unknown,' have 'no secrets' and take comfort in the knowledge that their child will have access to information and communication links that may obviate unhealthy fantasizing about biological heritage."[43] While adoptive parents might initially express concern about open adoption and interference from birth parents, ultimately studies have consistently found that adoptive parents appreciate the ability to find out about "personalities, medical histories and health risks during pregnancy" to enable them "to answer more adequately their children's questions about their origins." For adoptive parents, the fact that they have been chosen by birth parents "alleviates their guilt about having someone else's child and alleviates fears that the birthmother would reappear to reclaim her child later."[44] Despite the long history of closed adoption, longitudinal studies have demonstrated that adoptive parents in open adoption benefit from openness and have "greater feelings of permanence in their parenting relationship."[45] Research suggests that a central issue in comfort with openness is a sense of control over contact with the birth mother for the adoptive parents,[46] an issue that illustrates the importance both of clear counselling for birth and adoptive parents and of strong communication between these parties. Perhaps surprisingly, clinicians have not studied the most important issue with regard to openness in the newborn context: whether or not it is good for babies themselves.

Critics of the state of the law assert that the status of openness in voluntary newborn adoptions is a pressing issue because many unenforceable agreements have been created. Since the 1970s, the number of adoptions arranged privately has grown steadily; most adoptions of infants are now finalized by private agencies while the Children's Aid Society places primarily older and special-needs children who have been crown wards. Currently in Ontario, all of the six private adoption agencies licensed to facilitate domestic adoptions advocate openness.[47] For example, Jewels for Jesus asserts that open adoptions create "kinship networks that link the two families through the child,"[48] and Children's Bridge defines birth and adoptive parents as "making a commitment to one another so that their child will be able to have meaningful relationships with all members of his/her family." All of the agencies allow the birth mother to view files of potential adoptive parents and to select the parents for her child; she may interview potential adoptive parents to make this selection. All of the agencies assert that agreements are negotiated individually between the parties to each adoption, and that "the nature of the relationship will vary from family to family." All recommend that written openness agreements be registered with the adoption itself, and that such agreements cover issues including the type and frequency of access, confidentiality, and methods of potential dispute resolution. All websites advertising the services of private adoption agencies make it clear that openness agreements are "morally but not legally binding ... [and] that the adoptive parents are the legal guardians of the child in the eyes of the law in Ontario."[49] Despite the acknowledged increase in the number of open adoptions negotiated by private agencies in Ontario in recent years, no case involving these issues has yet been reported by an Ontario court, perhaps because birth parents are explicitly warned that their rights exist at the discretion and goodwill of adoptive parents.

Openness was created to meet the needs of older children with established relationships with previous caregivers, relationships that have come to be acknowledged as important to the well-being of children adopted later in life. Openness agreements in the context of crown wards are enforceable in Ontario courts. However, children released voluntarily by parents do not have a similar right to maintain relationships with such parents, even in contexts in which children have long-standing relationships with parents by whom they have been relinquished, and despite an acknowledgment by the court that access is "a right that belongs to the child and not to the parents."[50] Agreements in the context of voluntary newborn relinquishment are also not enforceable in court. Hesitance in endorsing open adoption, particularly with regard to infants, is related to concerns about limiting the family to two legal parents, an issue that is also central to step-parent adoption and queer-family formation, the subjects of the next two chapters.

7

Step-Parent Adoption

Under the Ontario Adoption Act, an unmarried mother had sole right to relinquish a child for adoption and she could therefore allow the adoption of her child by a new husband; without an exemption, however, such an adoption would have required the mother to relinquish her own custody of the child. Legislators saw this as undesirable and created a mechanism which maintained maternal custody in the case of step-parent adoption and exempted such adoptions from the home studies normally required by the Children's Aid Society. In cases in which women were formerly married, however, such regulations did not apply and husbands had rights of access to children, and control over adoption, even when they had not maintained social or economic relationships with their children. Courts had the right to dispense with the consent of a parent "having regard to all the circumstances of the case, [if] the Court is satisfied that it is in the best interests of the child that the requirement be dispensed with";[1] mothers sought such exemptions so that new husbands could adopt their children. A decision to dispense with consent terminated any existing order of access. Step-parent adoptions involving formerly married mothers constituted an increasing share of adoptions from the post-war period onwards.[2] As one observer noted in 1981, in Canada, "step-parent adoption[s] account for a median of 42% of all adoptions completed."[3] As increasing numbers of married women sought exemptions with new husbands, courts had to strike a balance between the rights of married fathers, normally assumed to be of great importance, and the best interests of children when such fathers were largely absent from their lives. The question for courts was not whether fathers were deemed necessary for children – this was assumed to be true – but which father, biological or step, could better meet a particular child's needs.

It was widely recognized that the status of the relationship between the unadopted child and his or her step-parent was tenuous. Mothers and step-fathers repeatedly argued to the court that the objections of the marital father should be disregarded in the interest of the stability of children's lives, that children needed to have the same surname as step-parents, and that adoption would prevent difficulties with regard to succession and custody. Initially, courts were responsive. Biological fathers, however, asserted that their ties to their children deserved respect. Perhaps not surprisingly, given rising rates of divorce and the emphasis on gender neutrality in family law in the 1970s and 1980s, courts became increasingly solicitous of the rights of biological fathers, particularly marital fathers. Critics decried step-parent adoption as a means by which mothers could defraud biological fathers of their natural rights.[4] Debates about step-parents reflected tensions between the evolving recognition of social parenthood as expressed in the standard of the best interests of the child, on the one hand, and a continued emphasis on patriarchal rights and biological connection, on the other. Courts crafted exceptions to the severing of biological ties with adoption and allowed fathers to continue to have access to children adopted by step-parents, thereby creating the first open adoptions in Canada; they also came to hold a strict standard that allowed adoption by a step-parent only when a biological parent had either given permission or had so absented himself from the child's life that the original family tie was rendered meaningless.

In this context, step-parent adoptions have largely ceased. However, this has not solved the larger problem of defining the relationship between a child and his or her step-parent or former step-parent. Increasing numbers of children have multiple parental figures through step-parent relationships that do not involve formal adoption, yet the legislature has not clarified the legal status of such relationships. While the Divorce Acts of 1968 and 1985, the Family Law Reform Act of 1978, and the Family Law Act of 1986 included step-parents and other de facto parents as people potentially liable for child support, these acts did not clarify whether such status could be terminated unilaterally by a step-parent.[5] The *Chartier* decision of the Supreme Court of Canada established that a step-parent could not terminate an economic relationship with a child unilaterally after relationship breakdown.[6] A finding that an unmarried parent has status as a person *in loco parentis*,[7] however, is still necessary before child support can be ordered and current critics of the law assert that further reform is necessary.[8] Despite the statistical predominance and theoretical importance of this subset of adoption cases, the legal history of step-parent adoption has been completely ignored by previous authors who have written about the history of adoption.[9]

Re L. et al. and C., heard in 1972, was the first reported Ontario case of this kind. A mother and her new spouse sought to adopt a child against the wishes of the biological and marital father, and the court was asked to determine what constituted the best interests of the child. The father had never sought custody but had visited his son on a semi-regular basis and claimed that his reluctance to visit was based, not on a lack of love for his son, but on respect for the wishes of the mother and her husband. The Court of Appeal found that the father had

> not only done his duty according to his view of the matter but loves his son and wishes to care for him, even to the extent of abstaining from seeing him in his very early formative years. I have reached the conclusion, however, that there will be a positive benefit to the child in adoption and that, in fact, he needs to be incorporated as normally as possible in the family being raised by his mother and stepfather, to the extent that cannot be achieved by custody, disposition, change of name and the like. He needs to feel ... that he will have the stability, continuity and encouragement of such a home.

The biological father's tie with his child was severed.[10]

In a case heard in 1973, another step-father wanted to adopt the mother's child. The biological father was opposed, but his consent was deemed unnecessary and the adoption was allowed based on the doctrine of the best interests of the child. In this case the father had not abandoned the child after separation but visited, with permission, once or twice a month. He did not pay child support since he had no money or employment. When the mother limited access, asserting that it must take place away from her home, he stopped visiting. The step-father had been involved in the child's life from the age of six and the divorce had not been contested, or even attended, by the father. Full custody had been awarded to the mother and no provisions had been made for access. The father opposed the adoption proceedings but the mother and her new husband said that without an adoption "there would be a very negative effect" on the child. They asserted their willingness to allow visitation a few times a year. A pre-adoption report had recommended the adoption for the stability of the child. The child "was very adamant in her views. She very much want[ed] to be adopted." The court found that the absolute right of fathers to refuse consent should not be dogmatically applied and that "the 'child's best interests' [might] require a severance of parental rights even where the natural parent has arguably been rather consistently involved with the child and has appropriately conducted himself."[11]

In another case, also heard in 1973, the couple had married in 1954, separated in 1961, and divorced in 1965. Immediately after the separation, the children lived with the father and, although the mother claimed custody in the divorce, no order was made and the children remained with their father until 1969. Mrs Kennette then brought an application for custody that resulted in a consent order granting her custody of two of the children, with the third son remaining with his father. She gave up any claim for support. The third child decided soon thereafter to live with his mother and her husband. The mother and her husband applied for an order dispensing with the consent of the father for adoption, but the father was opposed. While the mother claimed that the marital father had been too physical in his punishment of the children, "the Children's Aid Society investigator in this case found them to be emotionally stable, mature for their age, with normal interests" and credited the father, in part, for this stability. Although the children expressed no desire to see their father, the court found that the father had "put the boys' wishes ahead of his own. Rather than fight out the custody application and have the boys be subjected to a Court appearance, he chose to let the boys go to their mother after they told him that was what they wanted to do. He should not be criticized for that." The court expressed concern that an adoption order would eliminate all legal connection between the father and his children as well as that of "all of the blood relatives from their grandparents to their most distant collaterals on the Munro side." In striking contrast to earlier decisions, the court found that there was no reason for an adoption to be necessary and that Mr Kennette "need only make a will to ensure their sharing in his estate." The court explicitly distinguished this case, in which the children had a long knowledge of and relationship with their father, from cases involving babies: "No stroke of the judicial pen can blot out of the boys' minds the knowledge of the existence of their natural father. At this stage of their lives, their preference is for Mr. Kennette as a father. But very often children who are at odds with a parent during their adolescence come to realize in their mature years the value of that parent and develop a new respect for that parent." The application to dispense with consent was denied.[12]

In *P.C.S. v. D.B.H.* (1975), the county court expressed discontent with the state of the law, interpreted to be that the rights of the biological father could be disrupted only in the most extreme of cases, and asserted instead "that where an effective end has been put to the relationship between a father and his children and his place has been taken by another it is desirable that the new relationship be confirmed by adoption."[13] Notwithstanding, the court found itself to be bound by the jurisprudence. The benefits of adoption – rights with regard to support for the child and access to the child for the step-parent in the case of the death of the mother – were clear. But how would these issues be resolved in a context in which non-custodial biological fathers also wanted to continue relationships with their children?

Judges in other jurisdictions also expressed their concern with the status of both adoptive families and non-custodial biological parents by recognizing existing visitation orders to which adoptive parents had agreed, or by imposing such orders themselves, despite the lacuna in legislation. In fact, the first of what we would now call open adoptions were orders in step-parent cases that allowed continued access to the child by a natural parent. For example, in *Kerr v. McWhannel*, the British Columbia Court of Appeal confirmed the right of access of a father after adoption: "I see nothing inconsistent in the child's being adopted by the respondents while at the same time the appellant retains his rights of access."[14] In *North v. North* (1978), the Supreme Court of British Columbia granted visitation to a mother after the adoption of her children by her ex-husband's new wife: "The rights of access of the respondent ... have not been terminated by the subsequent adoption order, and ... the welfare of the children is the paramount concern in determining what, if any, right of access ought now to be permitted to the natural mother."[15] Reversing previous decisions in the province, a county court in Manitoba found in 1979 that "an Adoption Order will not and cannot under the present law and legislation affect, or as I see it, remove those rights [of access]" awarded to the mother under a divorce decree.[16] Conversely, a Nova Scotia court found explicitly that the non-custodial parent's "legal right of visitation is terminated by an adoption order." This decision was made, however, in a context in which there appeared "to be no danger of a refusal of access to her, although it cannot be legally guaranteed."[17] While continued access to an involved parent made intuitive sense, these cases aroused opposition. Commentators concerned about the wider implications of precedent in non-step-parent circumstances considered decisions that formalized access after adoption to be "manifestly wrong ... they undermine the whole basis of the adoption laws, i.e., that the child becomes a stranger to his natural parent."[18] Such observers urged instead that guardianship provisions be created specifically to deal with the step-parent situation.

In Manitoba, legislation was passed in 1979 to deal with the issue of access to children by a natural father after a step-parent adoption.[19] As a Manitoba court confirmed, adoption completely severed the relationship between the adopted child and his or her biological parents and "this created injustices in the matter of step-parent adoption ... The 1979 amendment is an attempt in this province to remedy this intolerable situation." New Brunswick passed similar legislation in 1980 which allowed the court discretion to maintain visitation orders after a step-parent adoption.[20]

Similar legislation was not passed in Ontario. The question of when and whether step-parent adoptions should be granted remained contested, as did the rights of non-custodial parents after such adoptions. Decisions of the courts were inconsistent throughout the 1980s. In the most extreme cases, it was recognized that the rights of the natural father did not survive. For example, in a case in which the parents had lived together at the time of the pregnancy (and had gone through a marriage which the mother then found out was bigamous), the father's consent to the adoption was dispensed with since he had ignored the child and initially had denied paternity altogether: "I infer that, but for this application, he would never have enquired about the child or his circumstances. He conceded as much in cross-examination."[21]

Despite the line of authority that the rights of the natural father could be disrupted under only the most extreme of circumstances, in 1981 a county court held that an involved father's consent could be dispensed with under the doctrine of the best interests of the child. In this case the parents had separated two months after the child's birth and the child had known only her step-father as a father. There was considerable hostility between the biological parents and the father's access was limited, on average, to twice a year. The mother made no effort to collect child support, and the biological father did not pay it voluntarily. The court noted that the child viewed her father as a friend and wished to continue to see him and his extended family, but she also "wanted her step-father to be her real father and her half-brother to be a real brother." The adoption also offered important stability to the child: "If the natural mother were to die, for example, her husband would, in the present circumstances, have no *prima facie* right to custody of the child of whom he is to all psychological and emotional interests and purposes the father. There are very many other normal and naturally desirable consequences which flow out of the establishment of permanent relationships through adoption." The court allowed the motion to dispense with consent while also advising strongly that the child continue to see her natural father; no order to such effect, however, was made.[22]

In a similar case, heard in 1982, the father had exercised access a couple of times a year and the child expressed a desire to continue to see him, but the court found that "adoption would strengthen the bonds which the child had developed with her step-father and half-brother." The father had not mistreated the child and the court admitted that it was likely "continued access would be beneficial to the child." It held that "these considerations did not outweigh the benefits of the adoption" but recommended that the adoptive parents permit "reasonable visitation" by both the father and the child's grandmother.[23]

As another county court asserted in 1982, in such decisions the best interests of the child were held to outweigh any rights of the non-custodial parent: "Parental rights remained an important factor, but only one factor, in the assessment of the child's best interests ... But this was an entirely different proposition from one that urged that a parent only lost his rights as a result of abandonment or other misconduct. The child's best interests could require a severance of parental rights even where the natural parent had arguably been rather consistently involved with the child and had appropriately conducted himself." The application to dispense with consent was granted because the father in this case had maintained only a tenuous relationship with his natural daughter.[24] But at what point was a relationship with a non-custodial biological parent strong enough and important enough to prevent the severance of ties through adoption? And what measures could be taken to strengthen the custodial family that would not exclude the biological father?

As one county court judge asserted in 1983 in a case in which he dispensed with the consent of the father, the determination was a weighing exercise: "Are there any benefits to the child from the relationship with the natural parent? Is the child's right to know and be loved by his birth-parent outweighed by the benefits to be derived from the adopting parents, which of course includes the relationship with the other natural parent?" The respondent in this case had never had any meaningful relationship with his daughter and had been nothing more than a visitor on infrequent and sporadic occasions. This was "a result of his own actions and not by any fault of the Applicants," and the adoptive parents were willing to continue to allow the child to see paternal grandparents and an aunt whose support they appreciated.[25] However, the best interests of the child were not well defined and left considerable room for judicial discretion and disparity of outcomes.

Although there seemed to be a trend towards recognizing the adoptive family in the interest of the stability of the child's home environment, some courts questioned the severance of the rights of the biological father and asserted that custodial families could be stable and supportive without excluding the natural father. For example, in a case heard in 1980, a county court found that "the fact that a second marriage has occurred, bringing about a step-parent situation, is not *prima facie* sufficient to warrant the removal of the right to parenthood of a natural parent. Just as a natural parent has the right to know and interact with a child, so has the child a reciprocal right. There is no reason why mature adults cannot integrate the role of a natural parent into the raising of a child in the presence of a step-parent." The judge believed that the father in this case had been particularly cooperative, since he had allowed his daughter to change her name to that of the custodial step-father in order to "avoid embarrassment." The application to dispense with consent was denied.[26]

Similarly, in a case heard in 1984 in which the father had never paid support and had had no contact with the child (but claimed that contact had been prevented by the mother), the court found that "it is not enough to show that the interests of the child are enhanced by the new family relationship. Happy family relationships between step-parents and step-children are not uncommon. The emotional security of a child is not so fragile that it needs to be isolated from the knowledge that the *de facto* parent is not the natural parent." The application was refused because of the failure of the mother to provide conclusive evidence that the child would be harmed by denial of adoption.[27]

In a context in which decisions in applications to dispense with consent were unpredictable, Justice Virginia Mendes de Costas of the Hamilton Unified Family Court, in a widely cited case heard in 1985, summarized the considerations before the court in step-parent adoption cases, finding that "the onus is on the applicant who seeks an order of dispensation, and the applicant must satisfy the court that it would be in the child's best interests to grant the order. The court should be ever conscious of the awful finality of an adoption order and of the fact such an order severs the relationship that formally existed between the child and the child's natural parents. While the court should intervene with caution, these issues, as well as all others, must be perceived through the eyes of the child."[28] Echoing such sentiments, a county court found in 1986, that while all other orders under child welfare proceedings are ultimately variable should circumstances change, "an adoption order is not ... and therefore the test is conservatively applied," and dispensing with consent should occur only in the rarest of cases. Further, no step-parent adoption case had yet engaged Charter interests, which would add "another picture on the seriousness of a determination which has the effect of cutting off the child's rights to his natural family and cutting off the natural family – in this case the father's rights – to the child. If there is any effect or impact ... it will only be to raise the threshold even higher." Commenting on other developments in adoption law, and the push for the opening of adoption records, the court noted that the idea that "one should never make an order dispensing with consent" was too extreme and "perhaps is a faddish response to the present current emphasis on roots, background and culture." The request to dispense with consent was denied.[29]

Abruptly, by the end of the 1980s, step-parent adoption cases became less common, probably as a joint result of a strict interpretation of consent and the increasing visibility of step-families in the wider culture and therefore a lessening sense that such families had to be "normalized" through adoption and name changes. Legal controversy about step-parents, however, did not cease. This was because most step-parents did not and do not adopt their step-children (and many no longer marry the parent of such step-children), leading to uncertainty about the obligations of step-parents to their step-children. Surprisingly, step-families have not been widely studied. The few studies that have been undertaken confirm that "when biological fathers were deeply involved with children adoption was not considered appropriate," and that parents "expressed fear of losing child support payments in case of adoption." This led both social scientists and legal commentators to suggest that social-policy and legislative mechanisms should be developed to allow the legal recognition of "ties between the step-parent and step-child without relinquishing the biological parent's ties," which would clarify the legal and financial obligations of step-parents who do not adopt their step-children.[30]

The legislature, however, failed to act comprehensively in response to such critiques and the legal obligations of step-parents to step-children, and their right to see such children in the case of marital or quasi-marital relationship breakdown, remained unclear into the twenty-first century. When children were not formally adopted, the question, as one commentator put it in 2001, became "whether an intention similar to that which informs adoption has been expressed through the step-parent's actions."[31] Could an adoption-like relationship, similar to a marriage-like relationship in the context of cohabitation, be presumed from the de facto support that a step-parent provided while living with children the step-parent did not adopt? Did a step-parent who lived with and supported a child for the duration of a marriage or quasi-marriage therefore have an ongoing obligation of child support? Did such a parent have a right to access to the child post-separation?

Under divorce legislation of 1968 and 1985, the Family Law Reform Act of 1978, and the Family Law Act of 1986, statutory provisions for child support covered de facto parents, such as step-parents, who could be held liable for child support post-relationship.[32] In 1997 the Federal Child Support Guidelines, intended to ensure that all children would receive adequate support from separated parents, established that discretion in the quantum of child support was possible with regard to biological parents only in the context of very high incomes (over $150,000 per annum), status of a step-parent, shared/joint custody, and undue hardship. With regard to non-biological or step-parents, the tables do not apply and discretion is always available.[33] Moreover, while the biological parent who has never been responsible for a child can nonetheless always be held liable for child support, liability for a step-parent remains contingent on a threshold determination that a person stands *in loco parentis*. But the threshold that must be reached for such relationships to be recognized at law has not been clearly defined. As contemporary critics assert, "many step-parents who cease contact with the child after separation will argue that they assumed an obligation to support the child only as long as their relationship with the child's biological parent lasted," and, even if actions are indicative of intent, "the actions of a step-parent are often socially ambiguous ... When are we justified in inferring that a step-parent has permanently assumed the role of a parent?"[34]

In practice, under the interpretation of successive courts, until 1999 in Canada the responsibilities of step-parents who did not adopt their children were quite limited and could often be revoked unilaterally by the step-parent in the event of relationship breakdown. When there was no ongoing relationship between the step-parent and the child post-separation, courts were loath to impose a financial obligation on a former step-father. The most extreme version of such a doctrine was adopted by the Manitoba Court of Appeal in *Carignan v. Carignan*. This case, heard in 1989, confirmed the unilateral right of a step-father to withdraw his financial support and *in loco parentis* status after separation from the mother of the child. Justice Charles Huband asserted that "it would seem appropriate that one would lose the status of being *in loco parentis* in the same manner as it is gained, by knowingly intending to terminate the relationship, and thus end the financial obligation. It is surely not a status that, once acquired, can never be shed."[35]

Such decisions, however, were explicitly overturned by the Supreme Court of Canada in 1999 in *Chartier v. Chartier*.[36] The parties to the dispute had lived common law from 1989 and married in 1991; a child was born to them in 1990 and the wife had a child from a previous relationship; they separated in 1992. During the period of cohabitation the husband acted as a father to both children and falsely changed the stepchild's birth certificate to include his name;[37] thus, as Nicholas Bala and Meaghan Thomas assert, "along a spectrum of step-parent relations [*Chartier* was] one that can be characterized as 'near adoption'" despite the brevity of the relationship.[38] In 1994, under a consent judgment, the father/step-father recognized both children but agreed to pay maintenance only for his natural daughter, and in 1995 he initiated divorce proceedings and expressed his wish to discontinue support for both the wife and his step-daughter. No mention was made during the trial of the girl's natural father, who had never played a role in her life. The court of first instance applied *Carignan* and held that the husband had repudiated the child and was not obligated to pay support for her. The Court of Appeal allowed the wife's appeal with regard to reduced support for the child of the marriage, but dismissed her appeal for support for the step-daughter, finding that "modern marriages and other forms of cohabitation were often fragile and time-limited relationships and wondered how many obligations divorced or separated parties must carry with them as they travel from relationship to relationship." The Supreme Court of Canada, however, unanimously allowed the wife's appeal, noting that while *Carignan* was a leading case, a contrasting body of law, insisting that step-parent responsibilities cannot simply be shed, also existed.[39] Justice Michel Bastarache held that "until Mr. Chartier's unilateral withdrawal from the relationship, Jessica saw the respondent as her father in every way. He was the only father she knew ... Jessica was as much a part of the family unit as Jeena and should not be treated differently from her because the spouses separated."[40]

This case articulated a functional test with regard to parenthood and "endorse[d] a basis for familial obligation that is based on the reality of relationships and the needs of children over time." The *Chartier* decision established that the obligation of a parent towards a step-child is not "contingent on the continued existence of the relationship between the adult partners."[41] Nor is the link between step-parent and child dependent upon legal formalities such as adoption; in determining whether or not a parental link has been established, the court is to consider holistically a number of issues, in particular "whether the child participates in the extended family in the same way as a biological child would; whether the person provides financially for the child; whether the person disciplines the child as a parent; whether the person holds themselves out in the world as a parent to the child; and what the child's relationship is with the absent biological parent." Each of these issues is open to significant judicial discretion in interpretation. In her review of post-*Chartier* cases, Carol Rogerson asserts that additional factors that have been considered by courts at all levels include the involvement of the biological parent, references to the step-father as "Dad," name changes, a decent relationship between step-parent and child, and siblings born to the family subsequent to the step-child.[42] Apart from the birth of siblings, these factors are discretionary. Critics assert that, while *Chartier* established that a step-parent cannot simply unilaterally terminate a relationship with a step-child, it "provided only limited direction about how judges are to determine whether a person has stood in the place of a parent."[43]

Perhaps not surprisingly, the *Chartier* decision has been controversial. Marie Gordon notes that Justice Bastarache did not explore the importance of either the length of the relationship or the requirement that a parent "substantially replace a natural parent" in order to be considered *in loco parentis*. She asserts that it is therefore likely that "there will continue to be two lines of jurisprudence after *Chartier*." The clear judicial intent in *Chartier* was to eliminate a problem that had long been evident in the courts, the "financial incentive for a step-parent to terminate a relationship with a child," but it may simply be that step-parents who refrain from investing either emotionally or financially in children with whom they cohabit can thereby avoid incurring the obligations of a person who is *in loco parentis*.[44] Commentators have also questioned whether this decision has gone too far in excluding post-separation relationships between the parties from consideration: "A lack of desire for contact post-separation may reveal something about the nature of the relationship between the step-parent and step-child that formed prior to separation."[45] While de facto parents do not, by reason of being found liable to provide child support, have an automatic right of access to children, a support order would be seen as evidence of connection to a child that could justify an order for access on the grounds of the child's best interests; yet such visitation may not be desired, or desirable, for children.[46] Moreover, while recognition of step-parents represents an important acknowledgment of social parenting and evolving definitions of the family, as Wanda Wiegers argues, "a conjugal (or former conjugal) relationship with the biological mother is usually a condition of a social father's liability for child support," a fact that dramatically reduces the radical potential of the reconstituted family.[47]

Step-parent cases raise important questions about the assumption that a sexual relationship with the mother is a proxy for a relationship with a child and about "the complex and contentious question of what is the role of a father in contemporary Canadian society."[48] Neither legislation nor court decisions have fully clarified how many fathers or parents one child can have and how rights and responsibilities will be divided between multiple parents. These questions, of course, are also raised in the context of same-sex adoption and new reproductive technologies, the subjects of the next chapter.

8

Same-Sex Parents, Assisted Reproduction, and Adoption

Surprisingly, legal issues in same-sex adoption have been dealt with only superficially in the historical literature in Canada, although legal scholars have devoted significant attention to issues related to assisted reproduction and legal parenthood.[1] Despite the fact that equality-of-relationship status, not the issue of recognition of alternative families, was at the forefront of gay and lesbian legal struggles in the 1990s,[2] victory with regard to adoption preceded relationship recognition. In 1995 four lesbian couples,[3] all of whom had conceived using anonymous sperm donation, succeeded in *K (Re)*[4] in convincing a provincial court judge that second-parent adoption was in the child's best interests and that denial of such recognition constituted discrimination against both same-sex parents and their children. Although the second-parent adoption case was a significant victory for lesbian couples, it was based in part on an analogy with step-parent adoption that elided the specificity of lesbian families. Step-parents normally join families already in existence, but it is more likely that lesbian co-parents (and gay men seeking custody of children born of surrogacy arrangements) have planned for children together from the time of conception. In this context, lesbian couples sought access to other mechanisms to recognize parent-child relationships. In 2006 lesbian couples challenged the vital statistics regime in *M.D.R. v. Ontario (Deputy Registrar General)* and achieved the right to include both partners on a child's statement of live birth in cases of anonymous sperm donation.[5] Statements of live birth, however, create only a presumption of parentage. This can be overturned by the use of DNA evidence with regard to paternity and the contradictions between lesbian parental rights and, as current critics assert, "the Supreme Court of Canada's affirmation of the rights of genetic fathers in the *Trociuk* case [discussed in the previous chapter on the rights of unwed fathers in adoption] is far from being sorted out."[6] Surrogacy raises analogous concerns. The two-parent model may be inadequate to meet the needs of queer families (as well as step-families). As a recent Ontario case, *A.A. v. B.B.*, confirmed, some children can and do have more than two involved parents. Critics of current law assert that open adoptions could be used to solve some of these problems.[7] However, as was illustrated in an earlier chapter, open-adoption agreements with regard to children relinquished voluntarily are not enforceable in Ontario. Legal scholars argue that such problems should be resolved through new uniform parentage provisions, such as those recently introduced in British Columbia.[8]

Historically, adoption statutes terminated all rights of the biological parent on adoption, but step-parent exception clauses allowed a mother to maintain her own legal connection to her child while facilitating the adoption of her child or children by a new husband. The questions that dominated discussion of step-parent adoption, as illustrated in the previous chapter, involved the issue of dispensation of the consent of the biological father and his right to ongoing contact with his children. In the second-parent adoption cases that challenged lesbian exclusion, however, couples had employed anonymous sperm donation and dispensation of consent was therefore a moot issue. The barrier to adoption by the same-sex parent was not the claim of a third party but the prejudice of a wider society with little sympathy for same-sex families. In *K (Re)* (1995), Justice James Nevins had to consider the right of the same-sex parent to adopt her partner's biological child.[9]

In this case four lesbian couples presented seven joint applications for adoption. In each case the decision to have children had been undertaken jointly and "all of the couples ha[d] shared in, and committed themselves equally to, the care of the children." The court determined that all of the non-biological parents met the statutory definition for *in loco parentis*[10] and could therefore be held liable for child support. One couple had also obtained an order for joint custody but still sought the further security of an adoption order. However, while these women might be recognized as parents under the Family Law Act, they were not spouses under provincial legislation and the non-biological mother therefore could not adopt and secure her long-term connection to her child. Adoption legislation in place in Ontario in 1995 allowed adoption by a single person, by the spouse of a parent in cases of step-parent adoption, or by a couple jointly, in which case the birth mother (and any known father) would have to relinquish rights to the child before adoption could take place. Same-sex couples could not apply as spouses and birth mothers did not wish to relinquish their own rights and responsibilities to their children in order to facilitate partner adoption. The four couples asserted that the definition of spouse, by excluding same-sex couples who were co-parents, was discriminatory because it denied the equality rights protected in the Charter under section 15(1).[11]

Justice Nevins asserted that he had to consider the wider best interests of children in same-sex families and addressed the issue as to whether there is evidence "to indicate that children raised in a family structure in which both parents are homosexual persons, and particularly lesbian couples, exhibit symptoms or indicia of inadequate care significantly more often than one would see in the general population" which would justify treating same-sex families differently from other families. He explicitly rejected this argument, asserting that he could not "imagine a more blatant example of discrimination." He found that it was in the best interests of the child to be raised in a "stable, secure and caring family environment" and that the purpose of adoption is to provide such families for children. Since there was no rational connection between the purpose of the legislation and the exclusion of lesbian couples, the legislation was unconstitutional. Further, he asserted that the "limitless parade of neglected, abandoned and abused children who appear before our courts in protection cases daily, all of whom have been in the care of heterosexual parents," illustrated that the "suggestion that it might not ever be in the best interests of these children to be raised by loving, caring and committed parents, who might happen to be lesbian or gay, is nothing short of ludicrous." The definition of "spouse" in section 136(1) of Part VII of the Child and Family Services Act was henceforth to be read, interpreted, and applied so that spouse meant "the person to whom a person of the opposite sex is married or with whom a person of the same or opposite sex is living in a conjugal relationship outside marriage."[12] From this date forward, same-sex couples who had conceived through anonymous sperm donation could apply for adoption of children by the social parent without sacrificing the parental rights of the birth mother.

Since 1995 same-sex second-parent adoption has also been endorsed by courts or legislatures in the other provinces of Canada.[13] This has meant that couples who use anonymous sperm donation can protect the relationship between the child and the non-biological parent through adoption. Critics have argued, however, that the facts involved in same-sex second-parent adoption and step-parent adoption were (and are) often very different. Fiona Kelly notes that "unlike most heterosexual step-parents, non-biological lesbian mothers are typically present at conception and raise the child from birth. Put simply, non-biological mothers are not step-parents; they are usually equal co-parents from the outset."[14] While second-parent adoption solved many practical problems by confirming parenthood, it was expensive and cumbersome. And the closest analogy to same-sex second-parent adoption was not step-parent adoption but the situation of an infertile husband whose wife conceived with donor sperm. Such a husband was not required to adopt his child.

Early discussions of artificial insemination asserted that "the basic purpose of artificial insemination demands complete secrecy," and queried whether "when a wife permits herself to be artificially impregnated with the seed of a man not her husband, has she committed adultery" and would her child therefore be illegitimate? As early as 1949, an article in *Maclean's* reassured heterosexual parents and potential users of artificial insemination that a married woman in Ontario was required to enter only the name of her husband on registration documents, not that of a donor, and that "all children born to married mothers rate as legitimate."[15] But such presumptions of parenthood did not apply to lesbian co-parents who asserted that it was particularly galling that a heterosexual male whose partner became pregnant using sperm donation in Ontario did not have to undergo adoption proceedings but could simply sign registration of live birth forms, while this opportunity was explicitly denied to a same-sex partner.[16]

In this context, in *M.D.R. v. Ontario [Deputy Registrar General]*, 2006, lesbian co-parents, citing the equality provisions of section 15 of the Charter, asserted that excluding the non-biological mother from registration on the statement of live birth constituted discrimination on the basis of both sex and sexual orientation.[17] They argued that this exclusion violated their dignity by forcing them to undertake adoption proceedings at considerable time and expense. All the birth mothers in the case had become pregnant with the use of anonymous sperm and all had raised their children together with social parents from the time of birth. They had sought registration of their families under the Vital Statistics Act but had been denied such registration by the deputy registrar general because the language of the act determined that each child could have only one mother and one father. While the right to register had been granted to one couple by Justice Nancy Backhouse in an emergency case conference owing to exceptional circumstances (the birth mother had been diagnosed with breast cancer), the deputy registrar general asserted that lesbian co-mothers were not denied dignity, or recognition of their parenthood, since they could seek declarations of parentage under the Children's Law Reform Act. The parents, however, responded that having to pay approximately $4,000 for a declaration of parentage was itself a form of discrimination. They also argued that they felt "marginalized, dehumanized and vulnerable because they were required to commence these proceedings to secure parental status." Finally, they pointed to the many practical problems that are encountered by families in which parentage is not clearly specified:

Birth registration provides an important means for parents to participate in their child's life. The inclusion of a parent's particulars on a child's birth registration document ensures that consent is required for an application for the child's adoption and that the parent is entitled to participate in determining the child's surname. It allows the named parent(s) to obtain a birth certificate, an OHIP card, a social insurance number, register the child for school, and assert his or her rights under various laws. It facilitates cross-border travel by the named parent(s) with the child. It is a marker of the parent-child relationship and the composition of the child's family.

As well as alleging a constitutional violation, the applicants asserted that the failure of legislation to address the circumstances involved in assisted reproductive technologies constituted a gap in vital-statistics legislation that could be addressed via the *parens patriae* jurisdiction of the court.[18]

Justice Paul Rivard of the Ontario Superior Court agreed that a gap in legislation existed and could be addressed by the court and held that "if there was not a legislative gap because the government intentionally excluded lesbian co-mothers from a social parentage scheme, this is clearly discriminatory." He rejected the assertion of the deputy registrar general that the primary purpose of vital-statistics regimes was to obtain biological information about children and noted that the "birth registration scheme has tracked the particulars of parentage differently depending on the government's and society's views in a given historical period," citing in particular changes that had been intended to eliminate distinctions between legitimate and illegitimate children. In assessing the discrimination claim, he limited the comparator group to heterosexual couples who had reproduced using donor sperm, noting that fathers in such cases could readily sign registration of live birth documents without attracting attention and that the registrar's office "only makes an effort to verify a genetic or biological connection between a child and listed parents in the case of lesbian parents." He rejected the possibility that only the individual litigants in the case be offered a remedy, asserting that "only through enabling other parents to register under the *Vital Statistics Act* without having to go to court will the applicants be successful in establishing that lesbian co-mothers are parents as of right." He found that the legislation violated the parents' section 15 equality rights by discriminating against them on the basis of sex and sexual orientation and that such discrimination could not be saved under section 1. He ordered that the legislation be suspended for twelve months pending revision but, referencing *Trociuk*, explicitly rejected the applicants' suggestion that a birth mother could simply name a co-parent, asserting that "birth fathers have rights to be registered that must be protected" and limiting his findings to the context of assisted reproduction involving the use of anonymous sperm donation. Nonetheless, he clearly asserted that, in revising the statute, one option that was not available to the legislature was to establish DNA procedures to test all parents, thereby creating a system that was founded entirely on biology.[19]

In August 2006 the provincial government responded to this case by amending the Vital Statistics Act so that a statement of live birth could be signed by the mother, father, or other parent. The other parent was defined explicitly as "a person whom a child's mother acknowledges as the other parent, who wishes to be acknowledged as the other parent, and who agrees to certify the statement with respect to the child where the father is unknown and conception occurred through assisted conception."[20] Even the gender-neutral birth certificate, however, provides only presumptive proof of parentage and is thus contestable; while it is an improvement over adoption since it is far less expensive and can be utilized at the time of birth, it is rebuttable. In Ontario, because only couples who have conceived with anonymous sperm can utilize these provisions, gender-neutral birth certificates "are limited in their effect as well as their applicability."[21]

In cases involving known donors, apart from illegal registration, the only option available to the non-biological mother is to undertake a second-parent adoption, but this can occur only when the donor consents to the process. This requires the services of a lawyer and cannot take place immediately at birth, which leaves the mother and the child in a state of legal limbo,[22] particularly since this gives a donor an extended opportunity to change his mind about adoption. Further, Fiona Kelly argues that by the *Trociuk* decision "the Supreme Court held that certain rights attach to the status of biological fatherhood and that those rights are operational even in the absence of a relationship between the father and child."[23] Such rights are potentially directly in conflict with the parenting rights of the social, but non-biological, parent in lesbian known donor cases.

To reduce this conflict in law, Alberta, Prince Edward Island, Manitoba, Quebec, and British Columbia have revised legal parentage to deal with situations involving assisted reproduction; in all cases, the language regarding the presumptive parent has been rendered gender-neutral, such that the partner of a woman who gives birth via anonymous sperm donation, whether the partner is male or female, is the parent of the child as long as the partner has agreed to conception. Moreover, donors of gametes are explicitly not legal parents.[24] As critics have asserted, however, even reformed parentage laws do not necessarily resolve all the questions that emerge in the context of new reproductive technologies. What happens if all three parents, the two mothers as well as the sperm donor/biological father, intend to parent the child?[25] Or in cases involving surrogacy services provided to gay men in which neither male partner is in a relationship with the birth mother and presumptive legal parenthood therefore belongs to the mother and her spouse, even when sperm has been donated by one of the intending gay fathers?

As legal critics have repeatedly noted, but historians of adoption have largely ignored, these gaps in legislation have particular implications for the queer community and alternative family formation. Gay men are disproportionately likely to serve as known donors in lesbian known donor cases and are vulnerable in that their own options for family creation are very limited. Gay men are dependent upon women, either female (often lesbian) friends with whom they will co-parent, or surrogacy arrangements, to create their families. In a context in which many known donor situations involve informal arrangements between parties, or contracts that are drawn up by lawyers but that are not clearly enforceable in court, the potential for disputes is enormous. In a context in which parentage has not been clarified by law reform, the competing interests of lesbian co-parents and sperm donors are dealt with on a case-by-case basis in the courts in Ontario. The problems that thus arise are clearly evident in a second-parent adoption case heard by Justice Marion Cohen in 2009.

In *M.A.C. et al. v. M.K.* the birth mother and her partner sought an order dispensing with the consent of the biological father. The respondent was a gay man who was "a known and involved father." Mr M.K. was required to give his consent to the adoption and refused to do so. The applicants wanted to adopt B. to resolve the conflict that had developed between the parties. The respondent had exercised regular access with the child (one night per week and one weekend per month) from the time of her birth and for several years this arrangement had worked for all parties. The donor father wanted to increase the time spent with the child, but the applicants refused and argued "that an order for adoption is the only way to resolve this ongoing conflict." The donor father, however, asserted that an adoption order would "enable the applicants to marginalize his role in the child's life – that he would become 'little more than a friendly uncle.'" Ironically, earlier, when relations between the parties had been amicable, they had considered attempting to proceed with a three-parent adoption and had also attempted to conceive a second child.[26]

Justice Cohen held that "the concerns that the applicants raise are commonly expressed by heterosexual step-parents who resent the ongoing presence of the child's access parent" but differentiated that "the applicants, as lesbians, belong to a historically oppressed group whose achievement of social acceptance is an ongoing project." She recognized that the social mother felt herself to be invisible in many social contexts and noted that the applicants felt threatened by the instant recognition accorded to B.'s biological father. Simultaneously, however, she asserted that "the applicants discount the fact that Mr. M.K., who also belongs to a historically oppressed group, might likewise feel some fragility in his position." Cohen determined that adoption was not necessary, since the social mother could pursue a custody order and had been recognized, in practical terms, as a parent. She also asserted that it was in the best interests of the child to maintain an existing relationship with her father since "she knows where her primary home is and who her primary caregivers are. She also knows that she belongs to a second family." Cohen noted that the mothers had deliberately chosen to have a known sperm donor and wanted their child to have a known and involved father, "but now they want to turn back the clock and make a different choice. If this was ever possible, it is not possible after six years." Given the respondent's relationship with the child, this decision had many parallels in post-divorce scenarios in which fathers have established and positive relationships with children. Cohen cited the fact that open adoptions are increasingly recognized by the courts and argued that "the introduction of openness provisions suggests that a child's best interests may lie in knowing and maintaining a connection to a biological parent." She also clearly stated that, whatever the private agreement between the parties, "a court is not bound by the provisions of domestic contracts."[27]

A contrasting decision, in which relations were amicable between the parties and in which an openness agreement was recognized, was recorded in *Ss.M (Re)* in 2007. In this case the lesbian mothers had planned a pregnancy with a known donor, a long-term friend, and had executed an agreement that he would have an ongoing relationship with the child who would nonetheless be adopted by the social mother. The agreement also stipulated that he would be the guardian for the child should the mothers both die. At the initial hearing, Justice Robert Spence rejected the application for adoption, finding that it contradicted the agreement which suggested that the donor did not intend to give up all parental rights. After extended discussion with all parties, Spence accepted that the child's best interests were being met by the two women, that the donor understood the agreement fully, that the revisions to section 153(6) of the Child and Family Services Act allowing open adoption were remedial and therefore could be retroactive (the agreement had been signed before the act was passed), and that the "fostering of the relationship" between the biological father and child (which had been ongoing throughout the proceedings) could "be construed as an openness agreement." He advised the parties, however, that openness agreements did not and could not cover guardianship and that they should deal with this via "a testamentary guardianship clause."[28] Being voluntary, moreover, the agreement could be recognized, but not enforced, by the courts. Parentage legislation, as recommended by Fiona Kelly and as enacted in British Columbia, could prevent such litigation by allowing the parties to agree to terms in writing – recognizing a third parent or quasi-parent – before the birth of the child.

While the parties to litigation in *M.A.C. et al. v. M.K.* had considered a three-parent adoption while they were still amicable, and *Ss.M (Re)* effectively created a three-parent open adoption, an explicit challenge to the two-parent limitation in parentage laws was raised in *A.A. v. B.B.*, first heard in 2003 and reversed on appeal in 2007. As an alternative to adoption which would have required the father of the child to relinquish his parental rights, the applicant, A.A., asked the court "to declare that she is a 'parent' (specifically a 'mother') of the two-year-old child D.D." The respondents, the biological mother and father of the child, consented to the order being sought but did not relinquish their own claims to parenthood. The court of first instance asserted that the central issue in the case was whether or not the court had jurisdiction under the Children's Law Reform Act to acknowledge three individuals as equal co-parents to a child and found that the child was "thriving in a loving family that meets his every need" and that the "applicant has been a daily and consistent presence in his life." It was acknowledged that the non-biological mother met the definition of having shown a "settled intention to treat a child as a child of his or her family" and therefore could be held liable to support the child. While it was clear that she was eligible to adopt the child with her partner, such an adoption would have required that the father relinquish his rights to the child, a possibility rejected by all parties to the application. The court held that Part II of the Children's Law Reform Act contemplated only one mother of a child and that "the court also must be concerned about the best interests of other children" and expressed a fear that allowing three people to be equal parents to a child would open the door "to step-parents, extended family and others to claim parental status in less harmonious circumstances." The court queried, "If a child can have three parents, why not four or six or a dozen? What about all the adults in a commune or a religious organization or sect? Quite apart from social policy implications, the potential to create or exacerbate custody and access litigation should not be ignored."[29]

On appeal, however, the applicant was successful. Justice Marc Rosenberg asserted that the three-parent adoption would reflect the reality of D.D.'s life. Despite the one-man, one-woman language of legislation, the Children's Law Reform Act had been "intended to remove disabilities suffered by children born outside of marriage" and "was progressive legislation, but it was a product of its time." The Law Reform Commission, whose report had led to the passage of the act, did not consider the "possibility of legally and socially recognized same-sex unions and the implications of advances in reproductive technology ... or the disadvantages that a child born into a relationship of two mothers, two fathers or as in this case two mothers and one father might suffer." Rosenberg held that the court's *parens patriae* jurisdiction could therefore be applied to "bridge a legislative gap." Since the purpose of the legislation was to "declare that all children should have equal status" and because "advances in our appreciation of the value of other types of relationships and in the science of reproductive technology ha[d] created gaps" in the legislation, the court had to bridge the gap in order to meet the best interests of the child.[30]

Reactions to the decision in *A.A. v. B.B.* were mixed. While *A.A. v. B.B.* expands recognition of alternative families, critics assert that it also reinforces ideas about the importance of fathers in children's lives. For D.D., his father is an important and loving presence in his life, but critics argue that it is ironic that "in seeking to expand the traditional two-parent model of the family, A and C were simultaneously trying to hold on to the more traditional role of B as the father in D's life."[31] The most unpredictable implication of the decision of the Court of Appeal is the question of what will happen in a contested application when not all parties are in agreement about what is in the child's best interests. It is in this context that reform of parentage legislation has been advocated by critics. Such reform would provide gender-neutral language making the spouse of the birth mother a presumptive parent and explicitly exclude donors as parents, unless the parties had entered into a written agreement, acknowledging a third parent, before the birth of the child. This is precisely the model which has been adopted in British Columbia.

Critics also assert that revision of parentage laws could reduce some of the problems that emerge in the context of surrogacy. Parentage laws give presumptive status to the mother and her partner, but in surrogacy arrangements the mother intends to relinquish the child and her husband or partner has no genetic connection to the child and no intention to parent him or her. Moreover, while in traditional surrogacy the gestational mother is also the genetic mother, in gestational surrogacy, which is increasingly common, the gestational mother is not genetically related to the child and donor eggs (or the eggs of the commissioning mother) have been used to create the embryo, creating multiple potential parental claims. Rules clarifying the parental status of gamete donors would reduce the contradictions in such circumstances. Surrogacy is particularly important in the queer community. Gay men have very limited options for creating families. They remain discriminated against in the international adoption market and they cannot simply reproduce through gamete donation, as can lesbians: "Gay men face a different set of concerns and limitations in accessing reproductive technologies. While lesbians require only sperm to become biological parents (a commodity that may be relatively easy to procure outside of the purview of the regulatory agency), gay men require a womb and potentially eggs."[32] Surrogacy, however, is a grey area in Canadian law. Under the Assisted Human Reproduction Act, surrogacy is legal but payments to surrogates for anything other than reasonable expenses are not.[33] Perhaps as a result, few surrogacy cases have been litigated in Canada. In a B.C. case in which the intended parents were the biological parents of the child, the gestational mother agreed to relinquish the child at birth and the social parents were granted the right to include their names on the registration of birth as "presumptive proof of their relationship to the child."[34] The outcome of this case might have been different, however, had the parents not both been the genetic parents of the child, or had the gestational mother opposed the registration. In another case, heard in Ontario in 2004, a gay father was declared to be the sole parent of a little girl created by anonymous egg donation and his sperm and gestated by a surrogate who did not wish to have custody.[35] Without parentage legislation, the potential for unpredictability in such cases is considerable. As was noted by an Ontario court in 2002, "gestational carriage agreements [are] an emerging matter of public policy ... a roadmap is necessary so that the genetic parents and the birth mother and her spouse, if there is one, know what to expect at the conclusion of the legal process."[36] The model of reform that has been adopted in British Columbia legislates that, whatever the genetic relationship of the surrogate to the child she is carrying, and whatever the agreement she has entered into with the intended parents, she has choice about relinquishment at the time of birth. Yet, once she has signed a written agreement after the birth, and once she hands over the child, parentage is established for the intended parents; as long as a period of time is allowed in which revocation would be legal, such legislation is analogous to best adoptive practice.[37]

Adoption has been essential in providing the means for same-sex couples to create families of choice. Open adoption provisions may provide a model for same-sex couples seeking to maintain a relationship with gamete donors, but critics assert that Ontario should undertake revisions to the law of parentage on the model provided by British Columbia. While for queer families open adoption and reforms to parentage laws could be used to recognize the complexity of multi-parent families, for Indigenous children, who are the subject of the next chapter, open adoption and multiple parentage could be used to facilitate access to culture and heritage.

9

Indigenous Children and Adoption

The sad history of out-of-community adoption and the treatment of Indigenous children in general in Canada "is part of a longer story of massive social upheaval caused by colonial imposition, dispossession and oppression."[1] Before the 1960s, while Indigenous children were sent to residential schools, formal adoption[2] by non-Indigenous people was rare. The exclusive reliance on residential schools began to change in the post-Second World War period and "child welfare law has provided a new modality of colonialist regulation of First Nations." As provincial governments slowly moved onto reserves, prejudice against Indigenous people, widespread poverty in Indigenous communities, and a failure to understand and value communal responsibility for children ensured high apprehension rates of Indigenous children. From the 1960s onwards, the proportion of First Nations children in care increased dramatically across the country.[3] Adopt Indian Metis (AIM) was created in 1967 and worked explicitly to place Indigenous children in white homes.[4] While some placements were successful at an individual level, Indigenous communities soon targeted what came to be known as the "sixties scoop."[5] Indigenous individuals and communities protested not only that adoption into white homes created identity confusion for individual children, but also that removing children from reserves undermined the future of Indigenous nations.

The "sixties scoop" raised profound questions for (settler) law.[6] If adoption represented an absolute severance of the relationship between birth parent(s) and child, did children lose Indian status on adoption? If so, was formal adoption possible under the Indian Act? The legality of formal adoption (at least in the eyes of settler society and the government) was confirmed by the Supreme Court of Canada in 1976; Indigenous children would maintain status after adoption by non-status people, but they could claim such status only on reaching maturity. Further cases, however, continued to challenge the legitimacy of adoption. Ultimately, Indigenous opposition to non-Indigenous adoption placements led, in 1984, to an amendment to child-welfare provisions in Ontario which required that courts considering the best interests of Indigenous children acknowledge "the uniqueness of Indian and native culture, heritage and traditions" and the goal of "preserving the child's cultural identity."[7] Bands were to be informed of, and participate in, decisions regarding child placement. Indigenous social-service agencies were established in areas with significant Indigenous populations and were "charged with the difficult task of supporting First Nations children and families with complex needs."[8] While these reforms were positive, resources remained inadequate to meet needs and "devolution of services ... [did] not ... address ... material conditions of poverty."[9] Moreover, non-status children, whatever their cultural affiliations, were not protected under such provisions.[10]

The story of adoption did not end with the amendments of 1984. Courts were hesitant to enforce fully the new provisions and adoptions outside communities declined only slowly, in part as the result of further legal challenges by individuals and bands. The power of bands to control adoption also conflicted directly with the rights of individual Indigenous mothers who sometimes wished to place their children outside their communities of origin. Further, the reduction in out-placements did not solve the wider problem of child welfare and Indigenous children continue to be institutionalized through long-term foster care.[11] Currently, a class-action suit alleges that the federal government failed in its fiduciary duty to care for Indigenous children by allowing them to be adopted out of their communities, thereby causing them to lose connections to their families, communities, and cultures.[12]

The unequal and differential treatment of Indigenous children and Indigenous people more generally is enshrined in the legal foundations of Canada. Under the British North America Act of 1867, all "Indians and lands reserved for Indians" were placed under federal jurisdiction;[13] social services, however, were made provincial responsibilities. This division of power produced an ongoing jurisdictional nightmare in regards to the delivery of key services to those living on reserve. The federal government was committed more to the elimination of the "Indian problem," via enfranchisement and assimilation, than to the welfare of Indigenous people or social services for communities.[14] Assimilation was encouraged primarily through religious day schools, attendance at which became mandatory for children age seven to fifteen in 1920.[15] Mandatory English-language instruction, religious indoctrination, often harsh punishment, and sometimes violence and sexual abuse have made the residential schools infamous. In 2008 the federal government belatedly, but officially, apologized for the residential-school debacle and its long-term negative impact on Indigenous communities and individuals.[16] For children too young for residential schools, and those who escaped the residential-school sweep, the provinces provided no social-welfare services on reserve into the 1950s.[17]

Despite clear disparity in services available on and off reserve, the fate of First Nations, Metis, and Inuit children was rarely the topic of public or government concern in the years before the Second World War. However, in the wake of the Universal Declaration of Human Rights, the Canadian government began to rethink Indian policy.[18] As Veronica Strong-Boag illustrates, for the first time "Aboriginal peoples became the subject of 'equality talk.'"[19] In 1950 responsibility for Indian Affairs was moved from the Department of Mines and Resources to the Department of Immigration and Citizenship.[20] In 1951 revisions to the Indian Act provided that "all laws of general application ... in force in any province are applicable ... except to the extent that such laws are inconsistent with this *Act*";[21] this measure was explicitly intended to facilitate the extension of provincial social-welfare services onto reserves. In 1954 the Ontario government endorsed the ideal of service agreements between Ottawa and provincial Children's Aid Societies, but the federal government provided only minimal funding through Aboriginal Affairs and Northern Development Canada throughout the 1950s.[22] Only with the introduction of the Canada Assistance Plan did the federal government allocate substantial money to provincial social-service agencies.[23]

The arrival of white social workers from provincial agencies represented a new mode of intrusion in reserve and family life, rendering communities vulnerable to child apprehension. As was illustrated in the earlier chapter on apprehension, social workers brought with them middle-class, white notions of the proper family. A belief that children needed to be rescued from "poor" parenting and the "disadvantages" of Indigenous heritage was prevalent.[24] Many social workers failed to recognize wider communal responsibility with regard to child rearing in Indigenous communities, a lack of cultural understanding that may be "the greatest failing of the child protection system."[25] While individual social workers may have struggled with the reality of poverty on reserve and the lack of funding provided for supporting extended families, the net result of their interventions was dramatically increasing numbers of First Nations children in care.[26]

As it became clear that large numbers of First Nations, Metis, and Inuit children were in limbo in foster care, Adopt Indian Metis was created in Saskatchewan in 1967, originally as a pilot project, and worked explicitly to place Indigenous children for adoption in white homes.[27] Other provinces, including Ontario, followed suit, and the number of Indigenous children adopted by non-Indigenous parents increased fivefold from the early 1960s to the late 1970s.[28] AIM was modelled on the Indian Adoption Project, a program that ran in the United States between 1958 and 1967 and was "designed to remove Indian children from their families on reservations in an effort to assimilate them into mainstream society."[29] Likewise, AIM placed Indigenous children in white homes, often across provincial and national borders. As one social worker and advocate of AIM (and affiliated efforts) asserted: "A concentrated educational program must be developed in order that the community no longer turns its back on the Metis and Indian child. The 32.3 per cent of children in care who are of Metis or Indian extraction have proven that they are no different from the other 67.7 per cent except for the color of their skin. All children have one common denominator, they need secure homes. These children are being denied that basic human right."[30] As this quotation reveals, not only were Indigenous children disproportionately likely to be in care, but also the motives behind the push for formal adoption were mixed. The parenting skills of Indigenous peoples were denigrated, but the adoption of First Nations, Metis, and Inuit children was simultaneously motivated by a liberal, naive belief that ethnicity and race were irrelevant if children were raised with love.

Neither social workers nor adoptive parents, many of whom acted in good faith,[31] recognized that "denigration of Aboriginal cultures and racism abound in both subtle and blatant ways for Aboriginal people. For Aboriginal adoptees, in particular, these experiences may be a harsh contrast to their experience of a safe, privileged non-Aboriginal environment."[32] Such contrasts could, and did, create identity confusion and anomie for many adoptees. Too often, these adopted children grew up "being so dislocated in terms of their race, their family, that they have no clear sense of their identity and no home to which they can return: the circle has been broken."[33] As Suzanne Fournier and Ernie Crey, prominent critics of the Indigenous child-welfare regime, recognized in 1997, foster care and adoption may have been even more harmful than residential schools: "Residential schools incarcerated children for 10 months of the year, but at least the children stayed in an Aboriginal peer group; they always knew their First Nation of origin and who their parents were and they knew that eventually they would be going home. In the foster and adoptive system, Aboriginal children typically vanished with scarcely a trace, the vast majority of them placed until they were adults in non-Aboriginal homes where their cultural identity and legal Indian status, their knowledge of their own First Nation and even their birth names were erased, often forever."[34] These problems, however, were not immediately evident in the 1960s, and numerically AIM and other efforts to promote the adoption of Indigenous children had some success. Yet more First Nations, Metis, and Inuit children remained in foster care than were adopted. Ironically, in part this was (and is) because the racism that AIM advocates were optimistic could be overcome has proven intransigent. The numbers in foster care were also high because of disproportionate apprehension rates. By the 1970s, "1 in 3 Aboriginal children in Canada were separated from their families of birth through adoption or fostering."[35]

In this context of rapidly rising rates of apprehension and adoption of Indigenous children by white families, the first issue that the courts had to consider was whether or not, under the Indian Act, the adoption of a status Indian child by any non-status family was legally possible. Adoption orders in all provinces divested "the natural parent, guardian or person in whose custody the child has been of all legal rights in respect of such child." The child became, instead, "for the purposes of custody of the person and rights of obedience, to all intents and purposes the child of the adopting parents."[36] But white parents could not bestow Indian status on their offspring. Status was determined under the Indian Act. As noted, under the revisions to the act enacted in 1951, "all laws of general application ... in force in any province are applicable ... except to the extent such laws are inconsistent with this *Act*."[37] Were adoption laws as articulated by provincial legislatures inconsistent with the Indian Act? Did such laws deny children Indian status? Was adoption legislation therefore inapplicable with regard to First Nations and Inuit children?

In the 1976 case of *Natural Parents v. British Columbia (Superintendent of Child Welfare)*, the Supreme Court of Canada found that the adoption of a status Indian child was legal and that the child did not lose his or her status as a result of adoption.[38] By the time the case advanced to the Supreme Court, the child in question had been with the adoptive parents for six years. He had been removed from parental custody as an infant as the result of abuse which had led to his hospitalization. A nurse at the hospital had become the child's foster/potential adoptive mother. The natural parents, supported by their band, contested the application for adoption, asserting that adoption would be illegal since it would deny the boy his Indian status. The judge at first instance held that there was an inconsistency between the Adoption Act and the Indian Act and refused to approve the adoption, despite believing that it was in the best interest of the child. In overturning this decision, the British Columbia Court of Appeal was unanimously of the opinion that Indian status survived despite adoption; "since the *Indian Act* made no mention of adoption, the provincial adoption statute was not in conflict with the *Indian Act* and was therefore valid." The Supreme Court of Canada, with the majority opinion delivered by Justice Bora Laskin, confirmed the B.C. Court of Appeal's finding in favour of the adoptive parents, asserting that it would be undesirable to exclude "Indian children from possible adoption ... outside of the Indian community, a result to which I would not come unless clearly compelled to do so by unambiguous legislation." He cited the doctrine of the best interests in asserting that the boy had to "be considered as an individual," which required thinking of him as "not part of a race or culture."[39] He did not discuss whether or not in-community options had been considered at the time of the child's apprehension, although it was clear that at the time of the hearing a family in the community was willing to adopt the child. This conception of best interests, adopted by many subsequent courts, emphasized bonding with the adoptive parents and minimized the importance of culture and heritage in a child's well-being. While bonding is important and reflected, as described in the earlier chapter on apprehension, a desire of the court to recognize the right of children to consistent care, the bonding had been facilitated by the long proceedings of the court. By this decision, the adoption would proceed and the child could claim Indian status upon reaching the age of majority.

The obvious question that emerged from this case was: If a child retained his or her status, but had no knowledge of, or contact with, his or her birth parents or his or her Indigenous community, how would this status be recognized? If adoption law created the "statutory death of the biological parents and the rebirth of the adoptee,"[40] and parents were not required to tell children about adoption, how was the child to know that he or she had rights as a status Indian that could be claimed at maturity? Would the child therefore be involuntarily enfranchised? In the wake of the *Natural Parents* decision, the federal government acted to encourage parents who had adopted status Indian children to apprise the children of their right to claim status. In a guidebook for adoptive parents, the government provided a very basic, condescending, and homogenizing history of First Nations and Inuit peoples in Canada pre- and post-contact and urged parents to be aware of the status rights of their adopted children. The pamphlet explained that the adopted child remained registered on his or her band list of birth, but reassured parents that identifying information with regard to the birth parents was excised from the band records to ensure confidentiality. At the age of majority the child could claim his or her status.[41] The Department of Indian and Northern Affairs took the position that its "'lawful obligations under treaty' to status children adopted by non-status parents [were] met by the adoption itself" because the adoption was intended to meet the material and developmental needs of the child. However, "the Department took no action to inform the child of his status or his rights" and critics argued that this was a form of cultural genocide since it "may represent involuntary enfranchisement. The child who is unaware that he has status cannot apply for status recognition and is effectively enfranchised without choice."[42] As Ovide Mercredi and Clem Chartier,[43] prominent Indigenous leaders in Canada, subsequently asserted, "the increase in adoption has been viewed by Indian people as a form of assimilation and genocide; however, the courts have attempted to negate them by ruling that an Indian child does not lose his-her status upon adoption."[44]

Despite, or perhaps because of, the finding of the Supreme Court of Canada that out-of-community adoption was legal, First Nations, Metis, and Inuit communities took aim at what came to be known as the "sixties scoop." The out-placement of Indigenous children in Canada was first labelled the "sixties scoop" by Patrick Johnston in 1983. He took this name from the remorseful words of a British Columbian child-protection worker who admitted that workers had "scoop[ed] children from reserves on the slightest pretext."[45] The name reflected both "notable increases in Aboriginal child apprehensions" and the fact that the children were "literally apprehended without the knowledge or consent of families and bands."[46] Surprisingly, however, particularly in comparison with autobiographical and other works outlining the suffering created by residential schools, "there is a relative dearth of literature relating Aboriginal children and youth's experiences of the 'sixties scoop.'"[47] Yet, even without stories directly from children or their mothers, the assertion that "removing First Nations children from their culture and placing them in a foreign culture [through adoption] is an act of genocide"[48] is now widely accepted.

In the United States, Indigenous opposition to adoption and other child-welfare policies led to the promulgation of the Indian Child Welfare Act in 1978. This act was intended to rectify decades of "inadequate and insensitive treatment ... to promote the best interests of Indian children and to protect the stability and integrity of Indian tribal communities."[49] The act strictly limited out-of-community adoption. In combination, the decision of the Supreme Court of Canada in *Natural Parents v. British Columbia (Superintendent of Child Welfare)* enraged Indigenous leaders, statistics published by Patrick Johnston "shocked the public and the government," and the U.S. Indian Child Welfare Act provided Indigenous leaders in Canada with "a framework for articulating a position on child welfare jurisdiction."[50]

Despite pressure for reform, however, the apprehension of Indigenous children in Canada continued unabated. For example, by 1980, 85 per cent of the children in care with the Kenora District Children's Aid Society were of First Nations descent.[51] As Strong-Boag notes, a 1979 report for Indian Affairs and Northern Development admitted that services to Indigenous families were woefully inadequate and that Children's Aid Society offices did not receive adequate funding to deal with the challenges created by "geography, caseloads or cultural differences."[52] Some efforts were made at the local level to reduce apprehensions, but such programs were always constrained by finances: in 1977 a Children's Aid Society office was opened in Ohsweken to improve communications with Six Nations people;[53] and in 1978 the Children's Aid Society in Fort Frances hired Moses Tom of Big Grassy to work with First Nations families to prevent apprehension and to repatriate children.[54] Against this backdrop of large numbers of children in care, growing Indigenous protest, and some public recognition of the profound mistreatment to which First Nations, Metis, and Inuit children had been subjected, individual adoption cases were challenged in (settler) courts.

Although the issue of the legality of the adoption of status Indian and Inuit children by non-Indigenous families had ostensibly been decided, at least for the moment and from the perspective of non-Indigenous society, courts soon confronted questions about the desirability of such placements and the importance of culture in children's development. The Supreme Court of Canada case that set the tone for many decisions to come, *Racine v. Woods*, heard in 1982 and discussed earlier in the context of the rights of mothers, denigrated the importance of cultural connection in favour of the bonding that had occurred between the adoptive parents and the child. At the level of the Court of Appeal, Justice Roy Joseph Matas had expressed concern that the white foster mother could never provide the modelling necessary for the child.[55] He asserted that the foster father was Metis and had an understanding of racism; however, he did not explore "whether the adoptive father would be able to provide [the child] with any exposure to the Ojibway language and culture that were her heritage."[56] While Matas was more sensitive to the issues of culture and ethnicity than the Supreme Court would prove to be, he nonetheless relied on an image of the homogenized Indian in failing to differentiate between a person of Metis descent and an Ojibwa person.[57] The Supreme Court of Canada, in a judgment delivered by Madame Justice Bertha Wilson, deemed that the best interests of the child would be served by leaving her with the parents with whom she had bonded.[58] Beyond ignoring mounting evidence of the harm inflicted on Indigenous children by severing cultural connections, this decision denigrated the intense healing work that the mother had undertaken, ridding herself of addictions, obtaining an education, and finding employment, all with the intention of reclaiming her child. The birth mother explicitly asserted that the adoption of her child outside of her First Nations community reflected "systemic political oppression of native peoples."[59] The Court acknowledged that "consideration of bonding might effectively enshrine possessory rights for the parent who had obtained interim custody," but did not discuss the length of the proceedings as a problem. Nor did the Court further consider the issue of Indigenous culture, although the fact that the little girl would not lose her Indian status through adoption was cited as essential to the decision.[60] It should be noted that the Supreme Court refused to consider the possibility, raised at the Court of Appeal, that the adoption be open and that the mother be granted access.

Not all judges accepted the findings in *Racine v. Woods* uncritically. In a case heard in the Ontario Provincial Court – Family Division (York) in

1984, Justice A.P. Nasmith recognized the problems inherent in placing First Nations children in non-First Nations families. He found that the first child had been placed briefly with an aunt and uncle in Moosonee, but the aunt became ill and the child and mother could no longer reside in her home. They returned to Toronto but faced poverty and racism and by the time the mother was again before the court she had no fixed address, no plan for the child, and a second child had been born. The mother had left the children in the care of another resident of the Victor Home (a home for unwed, impoverished mothers) and they were apprehended. The court noted that she had two other children, aged seven and nine, who were also in care, and that she had herself been a very neglected and abused child. There was no discussion of why, as a Cree woman, and someone who had been abused, she might be intimidated both by the Catholic Children's Aid Society and by the court and therefore not appear. Her counsel asserted that a temporary wardship order would allow the mother a period to "be given the opportunity to get herself together ... and accept primary responsibility for the two children." Counsel also recommended that "the mother should stay involved in the lives of her girls if there was to be long term care by substitute parents." A social worker/expert witness for the mother asserted that "there is generally serious alienation where native children are raised in non-native homes," but acknowledged that there were very few Indigenous homes available for placement. This was the case, she argued, not because such homes were inadequate or inappropriate, but "due to the serious alienation between the native community and the C.C.A.S." Justice Nasmith found that the "least harmful choice" would be an order for Catholic CAS wardship for both children for a period of six months and he ordered the agency to seek "substitute parenting in the native community where the mother could continue to have access."[61] No record exists regarding the placement of the children at the termination of the wardship order.

This case was prescient of legislative changes to come. Indigenous opposition to child apprehension and out-of-community adoption was mounting. Most notably, in December 1983 Chief Dave Ahenakew, speaking on behalf of the Assembly of First Nations (AFN), announced that the AFN planned to inform all adopted children of their Indian status and, if necessary, to challenge the confidentiality provisions regarding adoption under the Charter. In this context, and perhaps fearing the consequences of such a challenge for adoptions not involving Indigenous children, the Ontario government took action.[62] In 1984 an amendment to Ontario adoption regulations for the first time required that courts undertaking a best-interests analysis with regard to First Nations children consider "the uniqueness of Indian and native culture, heritage and traditions" and the goal of "preserving the child's cultural identity."[63] Further, the Ontario Child and Family Services Act, which replaced the Child Welfare Act in 1985, explicitly set out under section 1(e) to "respect cultural, religious and regional differences" and in section 1(f) acknowledged that First Nations people are "entitled to provide their own child and family services." Independent First Nations child-welfare services were established in communities with large First Nations populations, such as northwestern Ontario. Priority was given to family and community placements under section 53(5) and bands were given a thirty-day window in which to contest any agency plan for child placement and to come up with an alternative proposal. One author has described these clauses of the act as "the most extensive provisions that recognize the special case of the Aboriginal child" in any of the Canadian provinces.[64] As critics have noted, however, problems remained. The provisions applied only to status Indian children. Moreover, the reforms "delegated authority given by the provincial government ... and tie[d] First Nations people to the child protection standards of the provincial *Child Welfare Act* instead of letting them establish their own standards."[65]

Additionally, despite the clear implications of the legislation, in the years immediately afterwards courts frequently limited the influence of Indigenous culture in the determination of best interests in adoption cases. For example, Provincial Court Justice John Gammell, while sympathizing with the Indigenous concern that adopted children "do not know what they are, neither white nor Indian," granted an adoption to white foster parents. Though he conceded that the girl was attached to her natural mother, Gammell asserted that the prospective parents were not "naive intended adoptive parents" because they worked and taught on reserve, had wider family members who had inter-married with "Natives," had already adopted two First Nations boys who seemed to be thriving, were "cognizant of and ha[d] discussed interracial relationships," and were committed to exposing the child to her First Nations culture. He determined that the need "to feel secure and happy outweighs her exposure to her culture and the danger is that if visits are continued while she is still young, she will not feel adopted." Moreover, he castigated the mother for her relationship with a white man, her failure to overcome her parenting problems, and what he believed to be her lack of connection to her own culture, claiming that "she has not really been able to expose the child to the Indian culture in a very meaningful way."[66] He did not contextualize this comment with any discussion of the challenges that the natural mother had faced as a First Nations woman, from an impoverished background, in a society rife with racism. It is also striking that, while the adoptive parents were praised for their knowledge of "Indian" culture, the mother was chastised for sharing her life with a white man. Open adoption, which might have allowed the mother to teach the child about her culture, was explicitly dismissed as harmful to the child's sense of belonging in her adoptive home.

In another such case, *C.J.K. v. Children's Aid Society of Metropolitan Toronto*, 1989, a grandmother was denied custody of her three grandchildren. She had left her reserve at the age of fifteen and the court deemed that "there was no evidence that she would ensure the [children's] retention and respect for the Indian culture."[67] The court assumed that "Indian" culture disappears in an urban environment,[68] minimized the importance of Indigenous culture to an Indigenous child's well-being, and claimed that the provisions regarding culture in the Child and Family Services Act, 1985, were not particularly about First Nations children but "underscored the recognized importance to any individual of familial roots, heritage and tradition." The grandmother had a serious drinking problem and had lost custody of four of her own children; she nonetheless had an extended history of caring for other children, including the children in this case, for lengthy periods of time and reasonably successfully. The court did not propose supports to help her to improve her parenting skills, or to reduce her dependence on alcohol, nor did they consider placements that might allow the children to continue to have contact with the grandmother while being cared for by someone who was healthy. Instead, the grandmother was castigated for even trying to retain custody and for claiming that the children needed her cultural guidance: "The benefits of retention of the children in the native culture lose significance when the proposed custodian herself ... caused their removal in the first place."[69]

Despite such resistance, over time, and largely because of the involvement of First Nations communities in decision making, courts increasingly accepted the limitations on placement outside of communities and refused adoptions when parents wanted to retain contact with their children. For example, in a 2003 case heard in the Ontario Court of Justice in Kenora, the court recognized the rehabilitation efforts of a mother and awarded her access to her children who were in long-term foster care. The mother had been sober for five years and was raising two younger children satisfactorily, but the older three children had been in a stable foster placement for several years. The foster parents wished to adopt the children and opposed access. The court found that "the children are attached to their foster parents, but they are Indian children placed in non-Native foster homes. As the children age, they will become curious about their Native heritage and roots" and "they should have the opportunity to forge links with their home community." Although the mother sought custody, this was denied since she was found not to "have a psychological relationship" with the children. While the court had initially advocated adoption of the children when they had first been apprehended, it was acknowledged that she had shown perseverance and succeeded in maintaining sobriety. In this context, despite the desire of the foster parents, adoption of the children was no longer tenable.[70] What was not considered, however, was an open adoption, a solution that might better have met the interests of all parties by providing the children with security of placement in the home that they had known for several years but also allowing them ongoing connection with their birth mother and her community.

Bands, as well as individual parents, contested the adoption regime. Although the 1976 decision in *Natural Parents* had confirmed that adoption by non-First Nations families was legal, and despite the reforms of 1984, in 2004 the Algonquins of Pikwakanagan First Nation challenged out-of-community adoptions as a violation of the Charter.[71] Pikwakanagan First Nation also asserted that the child-rearing practices of First Nations peoples "are distinctive characteristics of their society and are entitled to the protection afforded by sections 25 and 35 of the *Constitution Act, 1982.*" Justice Ruth Mesbur of the Ontario Superior Court rejected the assertion that distinctive child-rearing practices constituted a protected aspect of First Nations societies: "First, I have no evidence of any particular, or even general, child rearing practices of the band, or of first nations in general ... [the applicant provides] studies that support the proposition that Native children raised in non-Native homes have difficulty integrating into Native society as adults and that many suffer from behavioral and psychological problems. These reports and studies are not evidence and, even if they were, say nothing about the traditional rights the band seeks to protect. They also cannot determine if these difficulties are caused by the Native children being adopted by non-Natives, or have other or additional causes." The court also had to consider the question as to whether or not the placement of First Nations children for adoption outside their reserve violated their section 7 rights to liberty and security of the person.

The band wanted the court to exercise its *parens patriae* powers and place the children in question with a couple it had selected. Each of the siblings had been apprehended at birth, starting in 2000, and the Children's Aid Society had presented the band with its plans for the children in a timely manner, according to the requirements of legislation. These plans included the adoption of one of the children by an aunt who was First Nations and another child by a long-term foster parent. The band did not respond. Although the parents had initially consented to the children becoming crown wards, the father later opposed the placement of the children in white homes. He communicated his concerns to the band but was informed that "the band had no available homes for the children." It was in this context that the Children's Aid Society went forward with the proposed adoptions. The court asserted that "the band [had] received appropriate notice throughout. It was free to exercise any or all of these rights, within the same time constraints as a natural parent. That they chose not to is hardly a breach of any *Charter* right." The court dismissed the assertion that the children's liberty interests included a right to be raised in a First Nations home: "If that were so, then Native children could only be adopted by Native families or bands. The facts of this case highlight the lack of such homes for Native children. The applicant's interpretation would leave Native children in adoption limbo, waiting for Native placement ... and would be contrary to the requirement that all Crown wards be placed for adoption within a reasonable period of time."

The court emphasized that, despite his concern, the father had not registered the children; instead, the Children's Aid Society had done so. Further, the children's mother was Chinese, so even if the children were to live with a natural parent, there was no guarantee that they would be raised in a First Nations milieu. Justice Mesbur summarized that "even if there were a *Charter* breach ... children's emotional well-being always trumps concerns regarding the importance of nurturing their Native heritage." The band had not presented a plan for the children in a timely manner and its initial response indicated an inability to assist because of a shortage of foster homes on reserve. However, the assertion that "children's emotional well-being always trumps concerns regarding the importance of nurturing their Native heritage" denied the reality that often nurturing children's First Nations heritage will itself be essential to "children's emotional well-being."[72] The language of the decision dichotomized these issues when in practice it is possible to provide children with loving and stable homes through fostering or adoption and still guarantee a connection with community and cultural roots. Open adoption, which allows for continuing contact between children, their biological families, and communities, is probably the best solution when on-reserve placements, or placements with First Nations families off reserve, are not possible.[73] The case was also complicated by the mixed heritage of the children and by the fact that the mother was not a member of the band. Although the release of the children had been involuntary, the potential for a band to override the wishes of a non-Indigenous (or even an Indigenous) mother in a voluntary relinquishment case raises significant concerns from a liberty perspective.

As noted in the Garber Report on adoption disclosure in 1985, the rights of individual mothers themselves are not subsumed completely in the rights of bands: "As individuals, birth parents (or more typically birth mothers) have recourse to the *Charter* to affirm their rights ... [and] she may have left the band to live elsewhere and prefer, for her own reasons, that the child not be cared for by the band."[74] As both Veronica Strong-Boag and Karen Dubinsky remind us, "for some young women, the bonds of the Aboriginal community felt closed and restrictive" and out-placement was desirable.[75] In communities plagued by lateral violence resulting from racism, colonialist policies, and the community and family disruption caused by residential schools, women can have intensely personal reasons for wishing to release their children for adoption outside their communities of birth.[76] Further, First Nations women have been critical of male leadership in Aboriginal affairs in Canada and have asserted that "political considerations [have] outweighed concern about child welfare" and about mothers and their relations with their children.[77] As Val Napoleon argues, "in colonial aboriginal communities, rights characterized as collective (usually those rights held by males) have been held to override rights characterized as individual (usually those rights claimed by females) to the detriment of aboriginal women collectively."[78] While this issue has attracted limited attention in the Canadian context, commentators in the United States have noted that "some parents, especially birth mothers ... distrust the rhetoric of tribal preservation and want their children's destiny linked to mainstream American society."[79] Questions that have not yet been addressed in litigation in Ontario include: whether a child born to an unwed mother who is herself not Indigenous, but who reproduced with an Indigenous man, should be subject to Indigenous regulation; and whether or not women living off reserve can be forced to name their Indian status when they give birth and wish to relinquish children for adoption. This is a potentially acute problem for individual Indigenous women and for law because Indigenous women are disproportionately vulnerable to child apprehension, both at the time of birth directly from the hospital and as children age and mature.[80]

Children's Aid Society complaints against First Nations families occur at a rate over four times higher than that for non-Aboriginal children (140.6 per 1000, vs. 33.5).[81] Child-welfare experts note that First Nations children "are not removed from their parents because of higher rates of physical, sexual or emotional forms of abuse"; instead, it is "the persistent systemic and structural factors of poverty" and colonization that put Indigenous children at risk.[82] In Ontario, 21 per cent of children in care are Indigenous, but Indigenous children constitute only 3 per cent of the child population.[83] Such children are often not adopted but instead experience the revolving door of foster care. Indigenous children in the foster-care system are not guaranteed access to their home communities or cultures. Ironically, we are in much the same situation, with high rates of apprehension and an over-representation of Indigenous children in foster care, that prompted the creation of AIM and the promotion of the adoption of Indigenous children into white homes in the 1960s. It is in this context that the Assembly of First Nations and the First Nations Child and Family Caring Society of Canada (FNCFCS) filed a complaint with the Canadian Human Rights Commission over the lack of funding for Aboriginal child welfare in 2007; owing to delays by the government, this case was not heard until 2015. In a 2016 decision, the Canadian Human Rights Tribunal found in favour of the FNCFCS, admitting that services for First Nations children have been inadequately funded for decades.[84]

While the complaint of the FNCFCS is not directly related to adoption, another recent court challenge is. In *Brown v. Attorney General (Canada)*, Marcia Brown (now Martel) and Robert Commanda have initiated a class-action suit against the federal government on behalf of all First Nations children in Ontario who were adopted out of their communities and thereby lost their connections not only to their biological families but also to their cultures and languages. Brown and Commanda are of Ojibwa ancestry and were "scooped." In their application for certification to file a class-action suit, they "accuse the

Federal Crown of a systemic assimilation policy purposely designed to destroy First Nations families and communities." They are bringing their action on behalf of approximately sixteen thousand individuals who were scooped and who were therefore, they allege, "victims of a deliberate program of 'identity genocide of children' that occurred in Ontario." They assert that their loss and suffering, and that of other class litigants, is worth $50,000 a person, and also that the government owes fostered and adopted children an apology, much like that given to the victims of the residential-school fiasco. The applicants allege that the federal government failed in its fiduciary duty to care for First Nations people and "wrongfully delegated its exclusive responsibility as guardian, trustee, protector, and fiduciary of aboriginal persons by entering into an agreement with Ontario that authorized a child welfare program that systemically eradicated the aboriginal culture, society, language, customs, traditions, and spirituality of the children." Not only do Brown and Commanda assert that the federal government failed in its fiduciary duty and deprived them of connection with their First Nations heritage, but they also argue that the crown did not provide them with any information or documentation with regard to their Indigenous heritage and their right to claim status under the Indian Act.[85] Their application is supported by a resolution from the Chiefs of Ontario.

Both Brown and Commanda had unhappy childhoods with significant instability with their foster and adoptive parents; both tried, but found it very difficult, to reintegrate into First Nations society and their reserves of origin; and both suffered depression and anxiety as a result, they believe, of cultural dislocation.[86] Such reactions to repatriation are not uncommon, as is clearly illustrated in Veronica Strong-Boag's extended discussion of the problems that have emerged in the repatriation movement. For adopted First Nations children who have suffered identity confusion and anomie, repatriation efforts are challenging beyond the issues inherent in an ordinary adoptive search for roots. Attempts to return to reserves of birth "have been handicapped by limited resources and mixed feelings about those long absent from First Nations communities," ensuring that adoptees feel at home neither in white society nor on reserve.[87] In this context, Justice Paul Perell in the Ontario Superior Court of Justice found that, while the pleadings as presented were flawed, there was a fundamental issue amenable to a class-action decision, specifically, the question: "In Ontario, between December 1, 1965 and December 31, 1984, when an aboriginal child was placed in the care of non-aboriginal foster or adoptive parents who did not raise the child in accordance with the child's aboriginal customs, traditions, and practices, did the federal Crown have and breach a fiduciary or common law duty of care to take reasonable steps to prevent the aboriginal child from losing his or her aboriginal identity?" He accepted the temporal limitations for the class action as proposed, 1965–84, the period during which the federal government funded provincial welfare measures which facilitated apprehension, foster care, and adoption, and before the provincial government officially recognized the importance of maintaining the First Nations identity of children.[88] Perell also found, despite the assertion of the federal government that the case should be a test case only,[89] that there is common ground and that the action could be certified as a class-action suit under the requirements of the Class Proceedings Act.[90] The pleadings were to be limited to issues of failure of protection and negligence on the part of the federal government.[91] Similar pleadings were subsequently initiated in British Columbia, Saskatchewan, Alberta, and New Brunswick.[92]

In January 2012, however, the federal government won an appeal in Divisional Court; the ruling ordered Brown and Commanda to pay $25,000 in costs.[93] The costs awarded against Brown and Commanda were then set aside by the Court of Appeal (Justices Marc Rosenberg, Eileen Gillese, and Michael Tulloch) on 17 January 2013; the court found not only that costs were unfair because the case "raises novel points of law" and that "the treatment of Aboriginal children in Ontario's child welfare system and Canada's responsibility for what occurred are matters of public interest," but also that the plaintiffs should have another opportunity to certify their pleadings.[94] Justice Edward Belobaba of the Ontario Superior Court of Justice certified the class action on terms very similar to those of Perell on 27 September 2013.[95] The government was granted leave to appeal this certification by Justice Wendy Matheson on 11 March 2014,[96] but the appeal was dismissed. Justice Ian Nordheimer determined that while the pleadings with regard to fiduciary duty might not be perfect they were "sufficient to get the respondents over the relatively low threshold for defeating a motion [to dismiss]."[97] Hearing of substantive evidence began in 2015.

Brown v. Attorney General (Canada) provides a powerful reminder that Indigenous peoples suffered serious harms in the adoption context, but neither compensation nor an apology will satisfactorily address the current problems that plague Indigenous child welfare. While the dramatic decline in the adoption of Indigenous children by white families has not solved the problems faced by Indigenous children who remain, in disproportionate numbers, in the limbo of foster care, it has fuelled the rise of international adoption, a system that is also the product of profound economic and social inequalities, and that is the subject of the next, and final, chapter of this book.

10

International Adoption

International adoption, which is common in Canada and throughout the Western world, was initially promoted as humanitarian in the context of the post-Second World War refugee crisis and the desire to prove the superiority of the West during the Cold War.[1] The most vocal academic supporter of this ongoing vision of international adoption as rescue is Elizabeth Bartholet, herself a lawyer and an international adoptive parent, who asserts that international adoptions illustrate love across difference and are "a positive force for good." She laments that "almost no laws or policies ... focus on the devastating damage to children's life prospects that comes from spending months and years on the streets or in the kinds of institutions that typify the world's orphanages."[2] But she pays little attention to the inequalities that underlie adoption; in particular, she ignores the fact that the problem of ensuring the fully informed consent of relinquishing parents can be exacerbated in the international context. In a trenchant critique of Bartholet and others who adopt the rescue narrative, Karen Dubinsky asserts that this celebratory framework erases "unequal relations, between races, nations ... adults and children."[3] As Dubinsky, herself also an international adoptive parent, admits, adoption of foreign babies was and is about meeting the needs of infertile couples (and later same-sex couples and single mothers) and only became popular when the supply of domestic babies declined from the 1960s onwards;[4] the history of international adoption reveals graphically the inequalities that underlie the adoption system as a whole.

As international adoption became increasingly common, scandals revealed the exploitation possible in this process. In response, international efforts were made to regulate cross-border adoption, including most importantly the Hague Convention on the Protection of Children and Cooperation in Respect of Inter-Country Adoptions,[5] which was intended to encourage cooperation between nations in order to reduce disparities between relinquishing and receiving parents. Such efforts, however, have had limited overall success and new scandals continue to emerge. In this context, it is perhaps not surprising that "supply" nations "have come to define [international adoption] as imperialistic, self-serving, and a return to a form of colonialism in which whites exploit and steal natural resources," the resources in this case being children.[6] It is also not surprising that relinquishing nations have responded by increasing their own regulation of international adoption, reducing the number of infants and children available to the West. While in 1993 it was estimated that international adoptions outnumbered domestic adoptions in Canada,[7] and that, during the period 1993 to 2002, 6,573 international adoptions took place in Ontario alone,[8] thereafter numbers began to decline. In 2012 only 1,162 internationally adopted children entered Canada and were granted either citizenship or permanent residency status.[9] International law reform and increasing regulation in receiving countries have reduced the numbers of children available for international adoption and mitigated, but not eliminated, the unethical practices involved. As cases litigated in Ontario and described in this chapter illustrate, however, once children are landed in Canada, courts can do little to address problems with regard to relinquishment.

Formal, large-scale international adoption was initially led by "rescue" advocates in the United States; Canada did not develop legislation or agencies for international adoption until the late 1960s and beyond. Before the Second World War, unaccompanied children who immigrated to Canada were not infants and they were brought here not for the purposes of adoption but instead to supplement the youthful workforce. In the late nineteenth and early twentieth centuries, children were removed from impoverished families and communities in Britain in the hope that their economic and social prospects would be better on farms in the new world. But they were expected to improve themselves through hard work, not familial love.[10] During the Second World War, evacuee children from Britain were placed in Canadian homes, but only for the duration of the conflict.[11] More challenging to the public was the placement of Jewish refugee children after the war, since their ethnic background was considered undesirable for permanent citizenship.¹² All of the British and Jewish children who were brought to Canada as evacuees or refugees were admitted under exceptional conditions and rules that bypassed normal immigration procedures. During and after the experience with the Jewish refugee children, "the federal government was wary about setting precedents regarding Canada's obligation to the world's children" since bringing unaccompanied children into the country was viewed as "a potentially expensive proposition."¹³

In the United States, in 1948 the Displaced Persons Act included a provision for the immigration of "displaced orphans" from Eastern European countries who would be "admitted regardless of whether the quotas for their national origin had already been filled and without being charged to the quotas." In 1950 the definition of displaced orphan was broadened "to include children who had been abandoned, or had one remaining parent who was incapable of caring for the child and had agreed to relinquish the child for emigration and adoption or guardianship."¹⁴ The Korean War, and the birth of large numbers of illegitimate children sired by U.S. servicemen, led to demands that mixed-race, non-European children also be accepted as displaced orphans and in response an emergency measure was passed to admit Korean children.¹⁵ This allocation was small (5,000) and applied only to United States military and government personnel, but it was paradigm shifting in that "for the first time the path for immigration of adoptable children was open to children of any nation."¹⁶ In 1957 new legislation that lifted all numerical restrictions on the issuance of visas to orphan children for adoption was passed. It was renewed each year and made permanent in 1961 with changes to the Immigration and Nationality Act.¹⁷

International adoption emerged later in Canada.¹⁸ Canadian legislation with regard to displaced persons did not mention orphans and unaccompanied children were not welcome in Canada for adoption. Criticism of this limitation in the displaced-persons regime mounted in the 1950s. Major Coldwell, leader of the Co-operative Commonwealth Federation (CCF), the forerunner of the New Democratic Party (NDP), spoke for the liberal left in 1954 when he asserted that while it was good to send money to support orphans in Europe, it was better to "bring a child into this country, and place that child in a good Canadian home, because there are homes that are seeking children for adoption. The child could be brought up in a Canadian home, in a Canadian environment and then would become a first class citizen of our country."¹⁹ As

Sidney Katz asserted in a critique of adoption law published in *Chatelaine* magazine in 1957, adoption of foreign children was "possible but ... not easy. There are a few instances of Canadian couples going overseas and coming back with an adopted child. Arrangements have to be made in advance with immigration and citizenship doesn't necessarily follow a legal adoption completed in a foreign country."[20] Only in 1962 did the government of John Diefenbaker introduce tentative policies for the adoption of individual children from abroad. Diefenbaker's measure allowed adoption only of full orphans with refugee status and prospective adopters had to illustrate that no suitable Canadian child was available for them to adopt.[21]

The conditions under which individual foreign adoption would be made more accessible were created by increasing acceptance of interracial adoption, immigration reforms enacted in 1965, and the efforts of a handful of determined adoption activists. In the same period during which the "sixties scoop" was ensuring the removal of unprecedented numbers of First Nations, Metis, and Inuit children from their homes and communities, experiments in interracial adoption were also being undertaken in Montreal and Toronto. As Veronica Strong-Boag, Karen Dubinsky, and Karen Balcom have all illustrated, Montreal's Open Door Society worked to popularize the placement of Black children in white families.[22] The first Black child to be formally adopted by white parents in Toronto was placed by the Children's Aid Society in 1952; in 1954, 7 Black children were so placed; and between 1959 and 1961, 32 Black children were placed in white homes.[23] In 1962, with 150 Black children in care in the city, Toronto's Committee for the Adoption of Coloured Youngsters was created.[24] In a manner that parallels First Nations' reactions to child apprehensions, however, interracial placements were soon decried as damaging to the Black community and in 1972 in the United States the National Association of Black Social Workers officially opposed cross-racial placement.[25] Although the adoption of Black and mixed-race children did not end in Canada, the pronouncements from the United States did put a damper on the positive publicity surrounding such practices. While the "colour-blind" approach of the 1960s was undoubtedly naive, "the shift in public discourse"[26] helped to set the stage for international, interracial adoption.

The immigration reforms of 1965 also reflected more inclusive attitudes towards race, but these were not intended to facilitate foreign adoptions. The reformed criteria for immigration established a point system for entry into Canada which ostensibly eliminated racial discrimination in the selection of immigrants.[27] Family reunification was a central component of immigration reform and allowed women and children to be admitted as the dependants of men who were accepted as primary immigrants.[28] Adopted children were included in the list of family members eligible for immigration for family reunification. Immigration officials, however, foresaw adopted children arriving simultaneously with other family members, as part of immigrant families, not as individual immigrants joining new families.

In a context of civil-rights protest and reforms in the United States, experiments with cross-racial adoption, and the supposedly race-neutral revisions to immigration, public pressure for international adoption escalated during the Vietnam War. As Karen Dubinsky asserts, many adoption activists were motivated by religious beliefs, and transnational adoption grew "thanks to the sheer personal will of grassroots activists, most of them adoptive parents, many of them with staggering numbers of adopted children."[29] The movement for international adoption from Asia in Ontario was led by Helkie Ferrie who, in response to the ongoing Vietnamese orphan crisis and the visibility of orphans in Bangladesh as a result of the Pakistani civil war, went on a three-and-a-half-day hunger strike. Stephen Lewis, the provincial leader of the NDP, "rallied support for Ferrie's cause in the Ontario legislature" and the government slowly began to accept adoptions from Vietnam.[30] Child-placement networks in Canada succeeded in placing approximately 700 Asian children with Canadian families between 1968 and 1975. The most sensational moment in the promotion of international adoption was Operation Babylift. In 1975, just before the fall of Saigon, airplanes were dispatched to remove all children already screened to come to Canada (and other Western countries) in what has been dramatically described as "a last-ditch attempt to protect children from the supposed dangers of communism."[31] While Operation Babylift received very positive public attention at the time, it subsequently became symbolic of the problems inherent in international adoption.[32] In Canada, a reunion of the Babylift children led to the revelation that at least one airlifted child had not been an orphan. Thanh Campbell was reunited with his father and two brothers after pictures from the reunion went public. He had been placed temporarily in an orphanage and airlifted out of Vietnam without parental consent; his biological father had searched for him ever since.[33]

From the mid-1970s onwards, international adoption expanded dramatically in Canada. The decriminalization of birth control, the partial decriminalization of abortion, and the expansion of welfare benefits combined to reduce the number of domestic infants available for adoption, and, when opposition arose to the adoption of Indigenous children, international adoption became an alternative source of babies for infertile (and later same-sex and single-parent) families. In this context, the first agencies were established to assist families in finding children outside of Canada and in negotiating the immigration process.[34] Between 1978 and 1988, 2,642 children were adopted from overseas in Canada, 64.5 per cent of these from Asian countries.[35] In Ontario, such adoptions were outside the system of the Children's Aid Society, with services provided entirely by for-profit agencies, unregulated "humanitarian" charities, and private lawyers. Babies were drawn from a number of countries, all of which faced internal problems that facilitated the out-placement of children but also ultimately led to controversy and increasing calls for international cooperation in the regulation of adoption.

Although its impact in Canada was initially limited, the first large wave of international adoption involved Korean children. Adoption became an industry in Korea, and, while Korean adoptions were and are orderly, the Korean example nonetheless illustrates many of the problems inherent in regulating the international exchange of children. By the 1960s, biracial babies born of liaisons between U.S. GIs and Korean women during the war had been adopted and the adoption agencies that had been established in the country had to look elsewhere for infants. In a context of extremely rigid control of women's sexuality, unwed mothers provided this source; adoption agencies built homes for unwed mothers on the model that had been so extensive in North America in the immediate post-war period.[36] In 1986, 6,150 Korean children were adopted into the United States, a number that represented 59 per cent of all international adoptions to the United States in that year.[37] Throughout the 1980s, international adoption brought $15–20 million in foreign currency into the Korean economy.[38] The extent of foreign adoption in Korea was revealed to the world during the Seoul Olympics in 1988 when a "feature story on adoption of Korean children was broadcast internationally." It was reported that 909,579 Korean children had been adopted internationally between 1954 and 1988. Fewer than 25,000 had been adopted within South Korea and "Korea was portrayed as a third world country unable to care for the needs of its own children." Despite the fact that the South Korean government has worked hard to promote domestic adoption, and despite the negative publicity created in 1988, each year more than 2,000 Korean children continue to be adopted internationally, in part because domestic adoption and unwed motherhood remain stigmatized.[39]

International controversy also emerged with regard to adoptions from Romania. The illegality of abortion under the reign of Nicolae Ceausescu led to large numbers of impoverished children being dependent upon state care. As Karen Dubinsky asserts, journalists provided "footage of malnourished, despondent institutionalized children" and rates of adoption from Romania "sky-rocketed."[40] Horrific stories about the conditions in Romanian orphanages were documented by Human Rights Watch and other non-governmental organizations (NGOs).[41] With the fall of the Berlin Wall in 1989, Eastern European countries were abruptly open to Western intervention. A profitable black market in babies developed and "intermediaries were used by foreign parents to locate children and then the 'consent' of the parent(s) [was] induced through the payment of large sums."[42] Demand for babies was so high that the Canadian government posted a visa officer in Bucharest to expedite the transfer of children[43] and 663 Romanian children entered Canada between 1989 and 1991.[44] In the latter year the Romanian government strictly limited adoption to government agencies and imposed restrictions with regard to the relinquishment of children. Sadly, demand for Romanian children also declined as evidence mounted that many had suffered physical and psychological damage as a result of long periods in institutions.[45]

In response to the international traffic in children, and highly publicized scandals such as that in Romania, the United Nations began to debate the merits, and problems, of international adoption and proposed inter-country regulation of this practice. In 1991 Canada ratified the United Nations Convention on the Rights of the Child, which advocated international adoption only when children could not be cared for by families or institutions in their countries of birth.[46] However, pressure from Western countries, where demand for international infants was high and adoptive parents were (and still are) wealthy and powerful, led to further changes in 1993. The Hague Convention on the Protection of Children and Cooperation in Respect of Inter-Country Adoptions stressed the benefits for children of permanent families, first domestically and then internationally. In 1994 Canada became a signatory to this convention, which has been described as "GATT for kids."[47] The Hague Convention created common procedures to be followed by outgoing and incoming nations participating in inter-country adoption: it specified standards for consent, mandated background reports on both children and adoptive parents, required adoption agencies to be accredited and monitored, mandated mutual recognition of legal proceedings, and imposed limits on the payment of fees in the adoption context.[48] The Convention entered into force in Canada in 1996 and the Child, Family and Community Division of Human Resources Development was designated the federal agency responsible for international adoption, although most regulation of adoption still takes place at the provincial level. Ontario ratified the Convention in 2000 and all international adoptions in the province thereafter had to comply with its regulations.[49] From 2000 onwards, therefore, foreign adoptions in Ontario could be undertaken only by licensed adoptive agencies overseen by the government. International adoptions were also made subject to the regulations already in place for domestic adoptions with regard to the selection of parents.[50]

The Convention "allocate[d] to the nation of origin the responsibility for determining the child's adoptability." The nation of origin must ensure that the birth mother (and, if named, the birth father) give "an informed, counseled, and written consent conforming to local law, and that the consent was not induced by payment or other compensation." But it is difficult to determine the degree to which particular countries respect the rights of birth mothers and comply with these regulations. The market value of babies creates conditions in which corruption can thrive, particularly in countries disrupted by war, natural disaster, or poverty. Receiving countries are responsible for "investigating the prospective adopters' suitability to adopt," but relinquishing countries may also "set criteria for acceptable parents,"[51] a fact that can exacerbate other forms of inequality in adoption since sexual orientation, age, and other factors can exclude particular parents from adoption in a given country.[52] Moreover, not all countries supplying babies ratified the Convention and eliminating corruption is extremely difficult in poor, distressed, and war-torn countries without bureaucratic means for regulation.

Despite scandals in Korea, Romania, Guatemala,[53] Brazil,[54] and other countries, throughout the 1990s the number of children adopted from foreign countries into Canada averaged about 2,000 a year, with the ranking of surrendering nations varying, sometimes dramatically, based on shifts in policy in home countries and the emergence of international crises.[55] International adoption, always expensive, may have become even more exclusive as a result of closer regulation. Between

1993 and 2002, the greatest number of foreign babies adopted in Canada were from China (6,245), followed by: India (1,868); Russia (1,398); Haiti (1,372); the Philippines (984); the United States (786); Jamaica (713); Vietnam (697); Romania (693); Guatemala (640); Thailand (356); and Korea (303).

China has been the prime source of babies for international adoption in Canada and elsewhere in the West. By 2005, over one hundred adoption agencies in the United States were working with Chinese orphanages to facilitate international adoption, "with an average price [of] between $12,000 and $20,000 to adopt a child from China, not including airfare and hotel accommodations in China."[56] The one-child policy in China, in place since 1979, produced a surfeit of abandoned children, "95% of whom [were] baby girls" who were also perceived as more likely to be healthy than infants from other nations beset by war and famine.[57] Since 1992 China has treated all foreigners in the same manner as they would Chinese couples applying for adoption. In 1993 the government suspended all international adoptions for ten months to eliminate illegal adoptions. This "streamlined the process of international adoption in China, [but] ... barred many families and individuals from adopting" as age and sexual orientation restrictions were imposed on would-be adopters.[58] Despite these limitations, eligible parents have flocked to China and "readily accepted the terms the Chinese government set for these adoptions," including the requirement that they travel to China, complete the adoption locally, and make a significant cash donation to the orphanage providing them with a child. Unlike the situation in South Korea, however, transnational adoptions from China did not receive much coverage in the Chinese press or in the West throughout the 1990s. In 2002 the publication of *The Good Women of China – Hidden Voices* provided some insight into the "difficulties Chinese women often face" and chronicled "the stories of many Chinese women who spoke frankly and anonymously" about their reasons for relinquishing their children.[59] Although China is a signatory to the Hague Convention on Inter-Country Adoption, and does a better job of regulating relinquishment than many other countries, it is nonetheless possible that international adoption may have aggravated the problem of child abandonment in China: "People may [have been] more likely to abandon a baby girl in the hopes of having a son because of the high number of foreigners who wish to adopt such children."[60] In Canada, 6,245 of 19,576 children transferred for international adoption between 1993 and 2002 came from China, about 98 per cent of such children being baby girls.[61] In 2007 China introduced stringent new regulations with regard to the eligibility of adopters, refusing to allow adoption by single women or by couples over fifty. In 2011 single women were once again made eligible, but only for the adoption of special-needs children, and they are required to sign an affidavit that they are not homosexual. Strict health and economic criteria have also been instituted.[62] In recent years, moreover, with the elimination of the one-child policy and an upsurge in domestic adoption as a result of improved economic conditions, fewer Chinese babies are available for adoption, wait times for prospective international parents approach ten years, and Ontario agencies working with Chinese orphanages have suspended the acceptance of new applications from potential adoptive parents.

The second most common country of origin for international adoptions in Canada during the period until 2002 was India, but the contrast with China is illustrative of the complexity and variability of international adoption and its regulation. Statutory adoption does not exist in India, and adoption is instead regulated under various religious laws. Parents can be granted guardianship rights, but not status as adoptive parents, by local courts. In a country marked by desperate poverty and without traditions of non-relative adoption, orphanages welcomed the deluge of Western adoptive parents who sought infants and young children. Orphanages, however, were not regulated and the death of an Indian child in transit to an adoptive home abroad led to litigation which resulted in a Supreme Court declaration of principles to guide international adoption in 1984.[63] Sadly, many orphanages could not afford to, or did not care to, abide by these principles, in particular the need to give preference to domestic adoptions. The creation of the Central Adoption Resource Agency (CARA) in 1988 ensured that only authorized international adoption agencies could undertake placements; these organizations must work in coordination with agencies in India which are overseen by CARA. At the local level, agencies under CARA scrutinize both the adoption applicants and the background of the child and make recommendations to the court with regard to guardianship. Since 2000, however, under the Hague Convention and Ontario regulations, children are to be adopted in the country of origin before coming to Canada, not merely placed under guardianship orders, ensuring that there is a conflict of law inherent in all adoptions from India. Because domestic adoption has become more acceptable in India, CARA suspended international adoption as of 1 December 2012 and only special-needs children are now available for international placement.[64]

Russia was also, until recently, a leading relinquishing country for Western international adoption. After the fall of the Berlin Wall, in the wake of exposés about horrific conditions in Russian orphanages by Human Rights Watch and other NGOs,[65] Westerners flocked to rescue infants and young children from institutionalization; not all such adoptions, however, had happy endings. In 2007 a U.S. adoptive mother infamously returned her Russian son to Moscow, sending him alone on a flight with a notice that he suffered from "mental instability" and stating that she no longer wanted him. This prompted Russian officials to work to reduce international adoptions.[66] In the wake of the death of a Russian adoptee in Texas and deteriorating relations between the United States and Russia during the Sochi Olympics, Russia announced a ban on international adoptions to the United States.[67] While adoption to Canada is not banned, adoption agencies in this country have stopped accepting applications for Russian adoptions.[68]

The most recent example of an international-adoption scandal involves Haiti in the aftermath of the earthquake of January 2010. The administration of Barack Obama, moved by descriptions of abject poverty and dislocation, lifted normal visa requirements and facilitated the rapid movement of 1,150 children to the United States over a period of several months, "a babylift unlike anything since the Vietnam war." These children were released without documents illustrating that they were orphans or had been legitimately relinquished for adoption and sometimes with blatant disregard for evidence suggesting fraud. Ten Baptist missionaries from the New Life Children's Refuge, a Christian organization devoted not only to saving children from poverty but also to the notion that "heathen" children must be converted, tried to take thirty-three children to the Dominican Republic for placement in a temporary orphanage and were arrested and charged with kidnapping.[69] In Canada, 172 children were adopted from Haiti in 2010 alone,[70] but in the aftermath of international scandal New Brunswick, Nova Scotia, Prince Edward Island, and Saskatchewan have suspended all applications for adoptions from Haiti.[71]

In a context in which adoption is unlikely from the long-time leading countries with regard to relinquishment, much attention is focused on new sources of children, including sub-Saharan Africa. In these nations, an orphan crisis, caused in part by the death of parents due to AIDS, in part by sheer poverty, and in part by civil war and unrest, "has reached desperate proportions." Although historically orphans did not exist in African communities, since wider kin networks cared for children who had lost their parents, such networks are deeply strained and those who "take in orphans face worse poverty." Non-kin adoption of children within Africa is unlikely, not only because of poverty but also because it "has never been widely practiced in Africa" on account of "strong cultural barriers." Multinational organizations have played a role in educating the world about the plight of such orphans and local groups work to support families and to fund orphanages, but much of the rhetoric and imagery of such groups posits the West as saviour.[72] Nonetheless, even devout advocates of keeping African children in Africa have accepted that some international adoption may be necessary to meet the current childcare crisis. However, problems with regulation abound.[73] Canadian adoptive parents have raised concerns that children being released are not orphans. Many agencies in sub-Saharan Africa are unregulated and Dutch agencies recently suspended adoptions from Ethiopia owing to corruption.[74] In a sarcastic and angry exposé of the Ethiopian adoption racket, a child who was not an orphan, but who was nonetheless adopted to the United States, argued that the net effect of poverty and the desire of the West for babies is that Ethiopia is being pushed into a "NO CHILD policy," that the West views Ethiopians not only as poor but as inherently inferior and their children as in need of cultural rescue, and that "when [the] Ethiopian mission is complete, [Westerners] will move on to another ruined African country."[75] Despite such concerns, adoptions from sub-Saharan Africa are on the rise in Canada as well as the United States.[76]

Given the frequency of adoption from sub-Saharan Africa and Haiti in the United States, perhaps the greatest irony in Canadian international adoption is the growing proportion of U.S. children who enter Canada as adoptees. While the United States leads the world in seeking children from other nations for adoption, including interracial adoption, they also export "unwanted" children to Canada, a pattern that "exactly reverses the dominant characteristics of adoptions between the two nations through much of the twentieth century" when predominantly white children moved from Canada south.[77] Children available for adoption from the United States are overwhelmingly Black or biracial and are from southern states in which the prospects of domestic adoption for such children are dim. In 1972 the National Association of Black Social Workers decried the adoption of Black children by white families. In the 1980s sensational, racially charged reporting with "lurid images of underweight babies shaking and crying" introduced the fear of "crack babies" and a lifetime of medical needs to potential adopters of Black babies born in urban ghettos. Although doctors have argued that the "crack baby" is a media, not a medical, category, fears remain.[78] While apprehensions of Black children have increased, such children too often languish in foster care rather than finding permanent homes. Since 1994 interracial adoption has been officially encouraged in the United States under the Multiethnic Placement Act, but racial prejudice remains pervasive and babies are available for international adoption. In 2009, 52 U.S. children were adopted in Canada,[79] and by 2012 this number had grown to 152.[80]

In Ontario, to adopt a child from a foreign country, a couple (or in some cases an individual parent) must work with an accredited adoption agency. Currently there are seventeen such certified agencies in the province.[81] The agency helps the prospective adoptive parent(s) to find a child in a foreign country, to negotiate the requirements of the relinquishing country, and to prepare for the Canadian adoption process. Ontario requires that all adopting parents undergo a home assessment and parenting training. Once the couple is certified to adopt, the agency helps them to be matched with a child and to organize travel to the country for adoption. The length of stay in the relinquishing country varies dramatically, as do other conditions for adoption, and agencies provide information, support, and guidance throughout this process. Once the child has been adopted through procedures in the foreign country, Canada's Immigration Department issues the child a visa. Under the Immigration and Refugee Protection Regulations, SOR/2002–227 (the Regulations), immigration for the purpose of adoption is to be permitted when such adoption is in the best interests of the child.[82] On the arrival of the baby in Ontario, the agency continues with post-adoption supervision and the adoption is finalized in the same manner as a domestic adoption. The parents can seek citizenship or permanent residency status for the baby at the time of arrival in Canada. This process takes considerable time and money.[83] Moreover, although Ontario complies with the Hague Convention, there remains what critics have described as a "disturbing lack of oversight of adoption agencies and their policies": while we know how many children are adopted from each foreign country every year, we do not methodically collect information about the fees charged to families or the complaints and concerns of adoptive parents.[84]

Most importantly, even careful regulation of adoption proceedings in Ontario can provide little guarantee about conditions of relinquishment in home countries. International adoption is itself often contested in countries of origin and responsibility for ensuring that full and free consent is given to relinquishment belongs with countries of origin, which may, or may not, fulfil this obligation in a manner that would be acceptable in the Canadian context. In conditions of poverty, epidemic illness, dislocation, war, and/or political unrest, it can be difficult to know that children are orphans or that they have been released for adoption under conditions that meet the standards set out in the Hague Convention. Provincial courts, when faced with cases in which the conditions of surrender of children in sending countries are questionable, have few options but to formalize adoptions regardless, since the children are already landed in Canada. Perhaps not surprisingly, very few such cases have been challenged in the Ontario courts. By the time that a Canadian court deals with an international adoption, the child is already landed in Canada, bonding with the adoptive parents, and the birth parent is far away and perhaps unidentified. No mechanism exists for returning children to countries of origin and to refuse adoptions would be to render children homeless and dependent upon the Canadian state.

The first Ontario case exploring this issue was heard in Newmarket in 1982 long before the Hague Convention on Inter-Country Adoption was promulgated. Provincial Court Justice James Nevins faced a situation in which the child had been born to an unmarried mother in Bogota, Colombia. The child had been placed by the mother with the Centre for Rehabilitation and Adoption of Children, an institution similar to the Children's Aid Society. The adoptive parents travelled to Bogota to adopt the child but also wanted to confirm their status as the child's parents via an Ontario adoption. Justice Nevins found that, while the foreign adoption was valid, he did not believe that

s. 87(1) [of the *Child Welfare Act*] goes so far as to suggest that an Ontario court need not or should not inquire into the circumstances surrounding the granting of the foreign order. If I am wrong, and if s. 87 was then carried to its extreme, without any inquiry by the Ontario court into the circumstances surrounding the granting of the foreign order, then this piece of legislation would not only permit but would, I fear, encourage, 'forum shopping.' Therefore, an Applicant resident in Ontario, who for some reason could not process an adoption in Ontario, could simply temporarily move to a foreign jurisdiction which might have far less stringent pre-requisites for the granting of an adoption order, and then obtain an adoption order which, in turn, would be recognized in Ontario without question.

This case confirmed that, while courts were required to recognize foreign adoptions, an order could also be made for an adoption in Ontario to protect the child's best interests.[85] Justice Nevins's concerns about unsuitable parents avoiding Ontario screening procedures were later met through the promulgation of the Hague Convention, but neither the code, nor this decision, solved the problem of how the circumstances of relinquishment might be overseen or reviewed by the court.

In 1997 Justice Theo Wolder of the Ontario Court of Justice found that an Ontario couple who wanted to adopt an infant from Pakistan could do so despite irregularities in the relinquishment documents. The child had been born to an unwed mother and placed with an agency in Pakistan. The mother had signed a consent form for adoption but the form did not meet the requirements of Ontario legislation: the father was named on the birth record but had not consented to the adoption. The international adoption agency presented hearsay evidence that the person named as the father was not in fact the biological father and that the mother had entered her birth family's name on the birth documents in order to avoid stigma. The applicants sought an order for interim custody and eventually an order for adoption but adoption required a finding that the child did not have a male "parent." The adoptive parents had travelled to Pakistan, with the assistance of the licensed adoption agency, Adoption Agency and Counselling Service, and the child had been placed with them by the Ismailia Association for Pakistan. The adoptive parents had completed the required home study in Ontario, were duly approved for adoption, and had waited several years for a child to be available. The child had been with them continuously since placement in Pakistan and the adoption report suggested that the child was well settled and happy in the home. Justice Wolder considered that this procedure was irregular in comparison with "the usual process for adoption of foreign children ... when the child is brought back into Canada by adoptive parents, they already then have an order for adoption that is recognized in Ontario." In this case, however, the parents did not have an adoption order from Pakistan.[86] Wolder held that the hearsay evidence was adequate to dispense with the consent of the father, but expressed concern that the mother had not necessarily been "appraised of all the rights required under Ontario law." Nonetheless, he found that, under subsection 137(13) of the Child and Family Services Act, a "consent required under this section that is given outside Ontario and whose form does not comply with the requirements of subsection (12) and the regulations is not invalid for that reason alone, if its form complies with the laws of the jurisdiction where it is given."[87] Although without an order of adoption from Pakistan there was not full evidence that the birth mother's consent had complied "with the laws of the jurisdiction where it [had been] given," he found that to deny the adoption would "lead to situations of frustration, where children coming into Ontario for the purpose of adoption, where there has been no opportunity to comply with the procedural requirements of subsection 137(4), could not be adopted in Ontario."[88] There was no further discussion of the problem of ensuring that the conditions under which the child had been relinquished met the requirements of Ontario legislation.

In a 2008 case, a couple who had obtained guardianship of a three-year-old child from India had the consent of the convent caring for the child but not of the mother and father themselves (although some information about them existed in the files). Justice Wolder held that "no matter how altruistic it may appear to bring children from disadvantaged parts of the world to Ontario to be adopted by residents of Ontario ... the onus is upon the applicants ... to satisfy this court that there is sufficient evidence to allow this court to grant an adoption."[89] He noted that Ontario had recently passed a law, the Inter-Country Adoption Act of 1998, effective 2000, dealing specifically with inter-country adoptions, and that the legislation limited international adoptions to those "finalized in the child's country of origin. It therefore does not apply to children whose adoptions are not finalized in the child's country of origin, as in this case." Because India does not have statutory adoptions, compliance with this law is impossible for adopting couples. The provincial legislation may have been intended not only to bring the province into compliance with the Convention but also explicitly to prevent adoptions from countries that are not signatories to it. However, the question of how to prevent such adoptions could not be solved by the court when faced with a child already in the country. Echoing discourses of rescue, Justice Wolder asserted that international adoption "by residents of Ontario should be encouraged as a matter of public policy" and that the province should pass legislation to deal with "the various challenges that such adoption applications present under the present legislation."[90] As this case makes clear, while the Inter-Country Adoption Act ensured that adoptive parents in Ontario were screened and could not "forum shop" to evade domestic requirements for adoption, and while the court did its best to monitor standards in accordance with the Convention, neither legislation nor court oversight could solve problems with regard to standards for relinquishment in nations of origin.

The issue of conflict of law with regard to adoption was considered in a case that came before Justice Ann Nelson in the Ontario Superior Court of Justice in 2011, although this case did not involve questions of consent. The adoptive parents had made payments to the U.S. birth mother, in accordance with state law, but which under Ontario law would have made the adoption unlawful. The payments "amounted to $38,664.00" and included hospital, transportation, and housing costs. The court had to determine whether non-compliance with Ontario law prevented the adoption from being approved in this province.[91] The adoptive parents had been married for twenty years and were in their mid-forties; they had struggled for years with infertility and sought adoption through a private agency. The birth mother was a single parent with two children who had chosen the applicants and had met with them multiple times before the birth of the child and who "deposed that she was very satisfied with her choice of prospective adoptive parents for the child." The mother suffered from gestational diabetes and had lost her home in a hurricane and costs were incurred in this context. The local court had found that the expenses complied with state law. The CAS report on the adoption placement concluded that the child was thriving and that the applicants were "excellent parents and love[d] their adopted [child] unconditionally." Justice Nelson held that "there are serious deficiencies [in the Child and Family Services Act] in that it fails to address issues that arise when the rules in the child's home jurisdiction do not match Ontario's," leaving Ontario families vulnerable when they go to court in Ontario seeking an adoption order with foreign documentation that may not satisfy provincial rules. She recommended immediate amendments to the Child and Family Services Act to include such "conflict of laws" provisions and advised that future courts, when determining whether payment could preclude adoption, consider: whether the payments were fully disclosed to the ministry and the court; whether the payments induced the consent of the child's parent to the adoption; whether the expenses were reasonable; whether the consent was given freely; and the conduct of the parties, including the adoption licensee. The adoption was confirmed.[92]

Courts have expressed concern with regard to the potential exploitation of parents in other jurisdictions. Nonetheless, Ontario decisions reveal that courts are willing to facilitate adoption to meet the needs of parents in Ontario and to avoid the possibility that children already landed in Canada will be rendered homeless. Courts echo wider public assertions that "helpless and homeless children would welcome the great privilege of being taken into a Canadian family" and that such transfers are "obviously humanitarian in nature and potentially advantageous to Canada."[93] While international adoptions can be very good for individual children, such arguments elide issues of power and self-interest in the international exchange of children. It is not surprising that relinquishing nations are increasing regulation of international adoptions. It is also evident that only regulation in relinquishing countries will truly address issues of parental consent.

Conclusion

Adoption provides a model for family formation that foregrounds love, not biology or bloodlines, as the basis of the parent-child relationship; yet, simultaneously, adoption has been based upon hierarchical gender, racial, and class relations. How, historically, has the law mediated these contradictions? What does the legal history of adoption in Ontario tell us about our wider views of children, families, and ideas of belonging? Five interlinked themes emerge throughout this close study of adoption law. First, poor mothers remain stigmatized and vulnerable to coercive practices in relinquishment and to the apprehension of their children. Second, patriarchal notions of blood kinship are still powerful. Third, tensions abound between growing recognition of the importance of social parenting and that of biology. Fourth, we remain deeply wedded to the notion of the heteronormative nuclear family. And finally, race, like class, continues to be a pervasive and controversial issue in adoption. Together, these problems suggest that significant reform of adoption law is necessary but also that our commitment to children is hollow.

Historically, illegitimate and disadvantaged children were stigmatized. As children came to be viewed as innocent and malleable, however, public support for the removal of children from parents viewed as incompetent and depraved grew. In this context, unwed biological mothers were profoundly disrespected and subjected to coercion in releasing their children for adoption. While the Supreme Court recognized these problems, particularly in *Re: Mugford* in 1970, since that time protections with regard to relinquishment have been reduced, suggesting that while society has some sympathy for children, mothers, particularly sole-support mothers, continue to be subject to public and legal censure.

With fewer unmarried women relinquishing their babies after the 1960s, and in response to fears about physical child abuse, rates of apprehension of older children increased. Poor mothers, single mothers, and racialized mothers have been particularly likely to lose custody of their children. It has been, and remains, extremely difficult to challenge the powers of the state in this area. The failure of successive governments to provide economic supports, avenues for escape from abusive partners, and mental-health and addictions counselling has condemned many children to apprehension. Yet it is ironic that apprehension, while historically justified on the basis that children would have improved prospects through adoption, has too often resulted in children languishing in foster care, aging-out of the child-welfare system with limited education and few positive connections to supportive adults, rather than actually being adopted.

It is also ironic that, during the same period in which mothers' rights in revocation were restricted and rates of apprehension from sole-parent mothers skyrocketed, the rights of fathers, even unmarried fathers without social connection to their children, expanded. This reflects an ongoing, and disturbing, adherence to patriarchal notions of the importance and power of the father based on biology, not demonstrated commitment to children. Notions of kinship based primarily in blood and genetics remain rhetorically and legally powerful.

The tension between recognition of social parenting and the ongoing importance of biology to both parents and children is also illustrated in the context of debates about adoption records and open adoption. While compromise legislation has protected the privacy of those involved in adoption in an era when secrecy was assumed, the new default reality of adoption is that biological children and parents will be able to find one another once children reach adulthood; this reflects a resurgence of concern with genetic origins. Perhaps surprisingly, however, open adoption – in which children maintain contact with birth families after placement – has evolved only slowly and piecemeal and remains contested. The legislature is hesitant to endorse open adoption with regard to infants. A further contradiction is that open-adoption provisions apply only in the context of apprehension, not voluntary relinquishment. This reflects not only debates about biological versus social connection but also a hesitance to endorse non-normative family formations, particularly those involving more than two parents.

The continuing primacy of the heteronormative family is evident in debates regarding step-parent adoption and same-sex adoption. Step-parent cases raise important questions about the role of a father in contemporary society: Who is, and is not, a father and how many fathers or parents can one child have? How will rights and responsibilities be divided between multiple parents? These questions have not been resolved at law. Similarly, while lesbian couples who have conceived using anonymous sperm donation have succeeded in achieving second-parent adoption and in challenging the vital-statistics regime, such decisions conflict with the Supreme Court's affirmation of the rights of genetic fathers. Multiple-parent scenarios in queer families created through the use of a known donor or surrogacy raise issues that remain unaddressed in Ontario law.

Finally, race remains an important variable in apprehension and adoption. Indigenous children in Canada are disproportionately likely to be removed from their homes of origin but unlikely to achieve the stability of adoption in new homes (whether within or outside their communities). International adoption is based upon racial, geographic, and national hierarchies which allow white, wealthy Westerners to take the children of the poor from war-torn, impoverished, and disaster-struck nations.

While adoption in all its forms can provide tremendous opportunity and love for disadvantaged children, and while adoption is based upon the admirable notion that we can love beyond biology and genetics, ultimately adoption law has done much more to serve the needs of those seeking children than it has to meet the collective needs of children themselves. To be sure, adoption often results in very happy experiences for both individual children and their new parents, and it is a necessary option in terms of women's reproductive autonomy. However, adoption is an inadequate response to wider problems of child poverty, child neglect, and child abuse.

Notes

Introduction

1 Fiction about adoption has long been popular, with some novels achieving iconic status: Charlotte Bronte, *Jane Eyre* (London: Penguin Global 2003, original 1847); Frances Hodgson Burnett, *A Little Princess* (London: Penguin Classics 2002, original 1888); Ronald Dahl, *Matilda* (London: Jonathan Cape 1988); Charles Dickens, *Oliver Twist* (London: Penguin Classics 2003, original 1837); Charles Dickens, *Great Expectations* (Oxford: Oxford University Press 1998, original 1860); Henry Fielding, *The History of Tom Jones, a Foundling* (London: Penguin Classics 2005, original 1749); Victor Hugo, *Les Miserables* (New York: Signet Classics 1987, original 1862); John Irving, *The Cider House Rules* (Toronto: Random House 1998, original 1985); L.M. Montgomery, *Anne of Green Gables* (New York: Signet Classics 2003, original 1908); William Shakespeare, *The Winter's Tale* (Cambridge: Cambridge University Press 2007, original 1609); and Mark Twain, *The Adventures of Huckleberry Finn* (London: Penguin Classics 2002, original 1884). In most of these novels, adoption provides wealth and opportunity for a "low-born" child, reflecting the rescue theme in adoption. Beatrice Cullenton's *In Search of April Raintree* is a harrowing account of the devastation wrought by the adoption of Indigenous children (Winnipeg: Portage and Main Press 1983). Movies have tended to be more critical of adoption. Mike Leigh's *Secrets and Lies* (1996) explores the secrecy surrounding adoption; Micho Rutare's *Adopting Terror* addresses the "nightmare" of biological

parental searching; and Laurent Boileau's *Approved for Adoption* examines the complications of international adoption from a child's (and animated) perspective. These are but a few examples.
2 In his sociological study of fostering and adoption, written in 1980, H.P. Hepworth concluded that there was "extremely shaky statistical data and a dearth of good research findings" about the legalities of the transfer of children: H.P. Hepworth, *Foster Care and Adoption in Canada* (Ottawa: Canadian Council on Social Development 1980), 3.
3 Adoption Act, S.O. 1921, c.55.
4 Many cultures, including Indigenous cultures in North America or on Turtle Island, have practised what would now be referred to as open adoption, without shame or secrecy for either the birth or adoptive families. This perspective was not incorporated into adoption laws in Western law when such laws were formulated in the early twentieth century.
5 Karen Dubinsky, *Babies without Borders: Adoption and Migration across the Americas* (Toronto: University of Toronto Press 2010), 95.
6 The term Indigenous is employed throughout this book to refer to First Nations, Inuit, and Metis peoples, except when direct reference is being made to the Indian Act. Indigenous people criticize the government's use of the word "Indian" and the classification systems that have emerged from this term: Mary Ellen Turpel-Lafond, "Patriarchy and Paternalism: The Legacy of the Canadian State for First Nations Women," in Caroline Andrews and Sanda Rogers, eds., *Women and the Canadian State* (Montreal and Kingston: McGill-Queen's University Press 1997), 66.
7 Veronica Strong-Boag, *Finding Families, Finding Ourselves: English Canada Encounters Adoption from the Nineteenth Century to the 1990s* (Don Mills, ON: Oxford University Press 2006), x.
8 Dubinsky, *Babies without Borders*, 3.
9 Karen Balcom, *The Traffic in Babies: Cross-Border Adoption and Baby-Selling between the United States and Canada, 1930–1972* (Toronto: University of Toronto Press 2011), 4.
10 Strong-Boag devotes chapter 2 of *Finding Families, Finding Ourselves* to an overview of legislative developments across the country from 1873 to the 1990s.
11 Ibid., 30.
12 Criminal Law Amendment Act, S.C. 1968–9, c.38; Family Law Reform Act, R.S.O. 1980, c.152, s.1(a); and Canada Assistance Plan, 1966–7, c.45, ss. 1, 711.
13 Divorce Act, R.S.C. 1985, c.3 (2nd suppl.), s.2.2. The Ontario Family Law Act of 1986 defines a parent as "a person who has demonstrated a settled

intention to treat a child as a child of his or her family": Family Law Act, R.S.O. 1990, c. F.3, s.1.
14 Michael Wald, "Children's Rights: A Framework for Analysis," *University of California Davis Law Review* 12 (1974): 255 at 256.
15 United Nations Convention on the Rights of the Child, Art. 3, 20 November 1989, 28 I.L.M., 1448.
16 Katherine Covell and R. Brian Howe, *The Challenge of Children's Rights for Canada* (Waterloo, ON: Wilfrid Laurier University Press 2001).
17 Twila Perry, "Transracial and International Adoption: Mothers, Hierarchy, Race and Feminist Legal Theory," *Yale Journal of Law and Feminism* 10 (1998): 106.
18 Strong-Boag, *Finding Families, Finding Ourselves*, 81.
19 Karen Stote, "The Coercive Sterilization of Aboriginal Women in Canada," *American Indian Culture and Research Journal* 26 (3) (2012): 117–50.
20 An Act for the Protection of the Children of Unmarried Parents, S.O. 1921, c.54.
21 Dubinsky, *Babies without Borders*, 59.
22 Under section 15 of the Charter, "every individual is equal before and under the law and has the right to the equal protection and equal benefit of the law without discrimination and, in particular, without discrimination based on race, national or ethnic origin, colour, religion, sex, age or mental or physical disability." The application of this provision has been the subject of debate in numerous adoption cases, as will be illustrated throughout this book: Canadian Charter of Rights and Freedoms, Part 1, Constitution Act, 1982.
23 Child and Family Services Act, S.O. 1984, c.55.
24 Child and Family Services Amendment Act (Child Welfare Reform), S.O. 1999.
25 Adoption Information Disclosure Act, S.O. 2005, c.25.
26 *Cheskes v. Ontario (Attorney General)* [2007] O.J. No. 3515 (Sup. Ct.); Access to Adoption Records Act (Vital Statistics Statute Law Amendment), S.O. 2008, c.5.
27 An Act to Amend the Child and Family Services Act and Make Complementary Amendments to Other Acts, 2006, c.1, C.11, s.145.1(1); 145.1(3)(a); 145.1(3)(b); 145.1(3)(c)(i),(ii),(iii); and (iv), s.153.6(1) and 153.6(3).
28 *K (Re)* [1995] O.J. No. 1425 (Ont. Ct. J.).
29 *M.D.R. v. Ontario (Deputy Registrar General)* [2006] O.J. No. 2268 (Sup. Ct. J.).
30 *Natural Parents v. British Columbia (Superintendent of Child Welfare)* [1976] 2 S.C.R. 751.

31 An Act Respecting the Protection and Well-Being of Children and Their Families, Part VII, Adoption, S.O. 1984, 704.
32 The Hague Convention on Protection of Children and Co-Operation in Respect of Inter-Country Adoption was concluded on 29 May 1993 and entered into force on 1 May 1995.

1 The Origins of Adoption Legislation

1 Informal adoption refers to the transfer of children, often between relatives, without legal sanction. As Veronica Strong-Boag illustrates, this could occur for a multitude of reasons, including ill health, death, poverty, or simply the need for companionship in the receiving family: Strong-Boag, *Finding Families, Finding Ourselves*, chapter 1.
2 Adoption Act, c.55. Ontario was relatively early in passing such legislation in comparison to other Canadian provinces: Alberta, An Act Respecting Infants (1913), c.3, ss.1–9; British Columbia, An Act Respecting the Adoption of Children (1935), c.2, ss.1–16; Manitoba, Child Welfare Act, c.35, ss.92–9; New Brunswick, Adoption Act (1876), c.57; Newfoundland, Welfare of Children Act (1952), c.60; Northwest Territories, An Ordinance Respecting the Adoption of Children (1967), c.2, ss.1–17; Ontario, Adoption Act (1921), c.55; Prince Edward Island, Adoption Act (1950), c.2; Quebec, Loi de l'Adoption (1925), c.196, s.1.
3 Without a page-by-page review of provincial government proceedings, a project beyond the scope of this book, it is impossible to know how common adoption by private members' bills might have been.
4 Shurlee Swain and Margot Hillel, *Child, Nation, Race and Empire: Child Rescue Discourse, England, Canada and Australia, 1850–1915* (Manchester, UK: Manchester University Press 2010), 3.
5 Alan Brown, "Infant and Child Welfare Work," *Public Health Journal* 9 (April 1918): 145; editorial, "These Little Ones," *Social Welfare* 1 (1918): 53; and Helen MacMurchy, *Infant Mortality* (Toronto: Legislative Assembly, 1910).
6 An Act Respecting the Legitimation of Children by the Subsequent Intermarriage of Their Parents, S.O. 1921, c.53; An Act for the Protection of the Children of Unmarried Parents, S.O. 1921, c.54, s.10; and the Adoption Act.
7 In 1924 the Geneva Convention, promulgated by the League of Nations, for the first time affirmed the existence of rights specific to children. This convention was taken over by the United Nations in 1946 and children were included in the Universal Declaration of Human Rights, 1948. More importantly, the United Nations Declaration of the Rights of the Child,

1959, outlined the basic rights we now associate with child welfare: United Nations, Declaration of the Rights of the Child, General Assembly Resolution 1386 (XIV) (20 November 1959).
8 Max Braithwaite, "Born out of Wedlock," *Macleans* 60 (22) (1947): 64; Sidney Katz, "Why Can't You Adopt a Child?" *Chatelaine* 29 (10) (1957): 13 and 115; and Charlotte Whitton, "Child Adoption," *Chatelaine* 21 (4) (1948): 102.
9 An Act Respecting the Appointment of Guardians, 1827 U.C., 8 Geo. 4., c.6.
10 Judicature Act, 1881, S.O., 44 Vict., c.5. For further information on the fusion of common law and equity in Ontario, see Elizabeth Brown, "Equitable Jurisdiction and the Court of Chancery in Upper Canada," *Osgoode Hall Law Journal* 21 (2) (1983): 275–314.
11 Such provisions remain in Ontario law under which a parent can determine a financial guardian for a child and set out testamentary provisions for guardianship in the case of death. Today, however, guardianship after death has to be confirmed by court order within ninety days in order to protect the best interests of the child and therefore the wishes of the parent are not inviolable: Children's Law Reform Act, R.S.O. 1990, c.12, ss.47–75.
12 Russell Smandych, "Colonial Welfare Law and Practices: Coping without and English Poor Law in Upper Canada, 1792–1837," in Louis Knafla and Susan Binnie, eds., *Law, Society and the State: Essays in Modern Legal History* (Toronto: University of Toronto Press 1995), 214–46.
13 If both parents were dead or had deserted the children, they could be apprenticed by town wardens; if the father had died or abandoned the children, the mother could apprentice them. The indenture had to be signed by two justices of the peace. For further information on apprenticeship legislation, see Charlotte Neff, "Pauper Apprenticeships in Early Nineteenth-Century Ontario," *Journal of Family History* 21 (2) (1996): 144–71.
14 Xiaobei Chen, *Tending the Gardens of Citizenship: Child Saving in Toronto, 1880s–1920s* (Toronto: University of Toronto Press 2005), 3.
15 John McCullagh and Donald Bellamy, *A Legacy of Caring: A History of the Children's Aid Society of Toronto* (Hamilton, ON: Dundurn Press 2002), 29.
16 About half of the children admitted to Protestant institutions returned to parents or family, usually within a year, while many of the remainder were placed out in private homes in apprenticeships. John Bullen, "J.J. Kelso and the 'New' Child-Savers: The Genesis of the Children's Aid Society Movement in Ontario," in Russell Smandych, Gordon Dodds, and Alvin Esua, eds., *Dimensions of Childhood* (Winnipeg: Legal Research Institute 1991), 135–58.

17 *Report of the Board of Inspectors of Asylums and Prisons etc. 1861* (Quebec, 1862), http://static.torontopubliclibrary.ca/da/pdfs/37131055429989d.pdf. Under the Charity Aid Act of 1874, a funding formula for such organizations was created. In order to be eligible for funding, agencies had to accept provincial inspection: Public Aid to Charitable Institutions Act, 1874, 37 Vict., c.33.
18 Egerton Ryerson, in particular, campaigned tirelessly for a system of compulsory education for all children: Alison Prentice and Susan Houston, eds., *Family, School and Society in Nineteenth-Century Canada* (Toronto: Oxford University Press 1975).
19 An Act to Improve the Common and Grammar Schools of the Province of Ontario, S.O. 1871, ss.3, 42, and 3.
20 An Act Respecting Industrial Schools, S.O. 1883.
21 Chen, *Tending the Gardens of Citizenship*, 27 and 21.
22 The Woman's Christian Temperance Union responded directly to violence against women and posited that such violence was overwhelmingly a crime committed by working-class men under the influence of alcohol: Sharon Anne Cook, *Through Sunshine and Shadow: The Woman's Christian Temperance Union: Evangelism and Reform in Ontario, 1874–1930* (Montreal and Kingston: McGill-Queen's University Press 1995); and Ian Tyrell, *Woman's World/Woman's Empire: The Woman's Christian Temperance Union in International Perspective, 1880–1930* (Chapel Hill: University of North Carolina Press 1991).
23 Chen, *Tending the Gardens of Citizenship*, 43.
24 The legislation also created a new government position, the superintendent of neglected children, whose salary was to be paid by the provincial government: An Act for the Prevention of Cruelty to and Better Protection of Children, S.O. 1893, ss.2 and 13.
25 In Toronto, in its early years the CAS ran a shelter of its own, which, like orphanages before it, was often used by parents as a temporary source of support when they could not cope with economic or other challenges. However, the shelter was eventually closed down so that parents were forced either to reform their ways or to give up their children: Chen, *Tending the Gardens of Citizenship*, 79–101.
26 These were foster homes. They were referred to as "free" because the foster parents were not paid.
27 For an excellent review of fostering in Canada, see Veronica Strong-Boag, *Fostering Nation: Canada Confronts Its History of Childhood Disadvantage* (Waterloo, ON: Wilfrid Laurier University Press 2011).
28 Elspeth A. Latimer, "Methods of Child Care as Reflected in the Infant's

Home of Toronto, 1875–1920," MSW thesis, University of Toronto, 1953.

29 Babies who were not breastfed were vulnerable to diseases spread through tainted water and milk, such as diphtheria, and those who were housed in crowded quarters were particularly vulnerable to epidemics of communicable diseases such as measles.

30 Under this legislation, all persons running infant homes were required to keep registers and to report the deaths of infants in their care: An Act for the Protection of Infant Children, Ontario, S.O. 1887, c.36.

31 She documented that 6,932 of 52,629 infants born in 1909 had died within the first year after birth: MacMurchy, *Infant Mortality*, 30. MacMurchy served as Ontario's inspector of the "feeble-minded" (1906–18), assistant inspector of hospitals, prisons, and public charities (1913–20), investigator of infant mortality (1910–12), and inspector of auxiliary classes for the Ontario Department of Education (1915–20). In 1920 she was appointed chief of the Child Welfare Division of the federal Department of Health, a position she held until her retirement in 1934 at age seventy-two. She was also very active in the volunteer community, including the Toronto Local Council of Women, and was extremely important in promoting public-health measures for the benefit of babies. Her views were, in many ways, conservative. For example, she opposed women with children working outside the home. She also endorsed eugenic sterilization of the "unfit": Katherine Arnup, *Education for Motherhood: Advice for Mothers in Twentieth Century Canada* (Toronto: University of Toronto Press 1994); Cynthia Comacchio, *Nations Are Built of Babies: Saving Ontario's Mothers and Children, 1900–1940* (Montreal and Kingston: McGill-Queen's University Press 1993); Dianne Dodd, "Helen MacMurchy, MD: Gender and Professional Conflict in the Medical Inspection of Toronto Schools, 1910–1911," *Ontario History* 93 (2) (2001): 127–49; and Diane Dodd, "Advice to Parents: The Blue Books, Helen MacMurchy MD, and the Federal Department of Health, 1920–1934," *Canadian Bulletin of Medical History* 8 (1991): 203–30.

32 Richard Allen, *The Social Passion: Religion and Social Reform in Canada, 1914–1928* (Toronto: University of Toronto Press 1971); and Nancy Christie and Michael Gauvreau, *A Full-Orbed Christianity: The Protestant Churches and Social Welfare in Canada, 1900–1940* (Montreal and Kingston: McGill-Queen's University Press 1996).

33 Editorial, "These Little Ones," *Social Welfare* 1 (1918): 53. For detailed discussion of health and housing conditions in the early twentieth century, see Paul A. Bator, "Saving Lives on [the] Wholesale Plan: Public Health Reform in the City of Toronto, 1900–1930," PhD thesis, University of

Toronto, 1979; Paul Bator, "The Struggle to Raise the Lower Classes: Public Health Reform and the Problem of Poverty in Toronto, 1910–1921," *Journal of Canadian Studies* 14 (1) (1979): 43–9; and Terry Copp, *The Anatomy of Poverty* (Toronto: University of Toronto Press 1974). For a discussion of the public-health movement and its focus on children, see Catherine Lesley Biggs, "The Response to Maternal Mortality in Ontario, 1920–1940," MSc thesis, University of Toronto, 1983; Terry Crowley, "Madonnas before Magdalenes: Adelaide Hoodless and the Making of the Canadian Gibson Girl," *Canadian Historical Review* 67 (1986): 520–47; and Janice Dickin McGinnis, "From Health to Welfare: The Development of Federal Government Policy Regarding Standards for Public Health for Canadians, 1919–1945," PhD thesis, University of Alberta, 1980.

34 Erica Dyck, *Facing Eugenics: Reproduction, Sterilization and the Politics of Choice* (Toronto: University of Toronto Press 2013).

35 Editorial, "Infant Mortality," *Public Health Journal* 6 (1915): 510.

36 The married woman had no legal right whatsoever to her child: William Blackstone, *Commentaries on the Laws of England* (London: Kerr [1857]), 485. Under the English Poor Law Amendment Act of 1834, an illegitimate child was to be maintained solely by his or her mother. If the mother's parish became responsible for the child's support, the parish could sue the father for reimbursement. The mother's evidence as to paternity had to be corroborated by a third party: the statute provided that "no part of the monies paid by such putative father in pursuance of such order shall at any time be paid to the mother of such bastard child, nor in any way applied to the maintenance and support of such mother": Martha Bailey, "Servant Girls and Masters: The Tort of Seduction and the Support of Bastards," *Canadian Journal of Family Law* 10 (1991): 154. The Poor Laws reflected a Malthusian fear of the unruly reproductive woman as a threat to the nation: Robert Thomas Malthus, *An Essay on the Principles of Population* (1798), ed. Geoffrey Gilbert (Oxford: Oxford University Press 1993). For a detailed discussion of Malthus's arguments, see Mitchell Dean, *The Constitution of Poverty: Towards a Genealogy of Liberal Governance* (London: Routledge 1991); and Mary Jacobus, "Malthus, Matricide and the Marquis de Sade," *First Things: The Maternal Imaginary in Literature, Art and Psychoanalysis* (New York: Routledge 1995).

37 The mother had to swear an affidavit as to the child's paternity within six months of its birth: Peter Ward, "Unwed Mothers in Nineteenth-Century English Canada," Canadian Historical Association, *Historical Papers* (1981), 41.

38 The first part of the act amended the common law by making it possible

for a father to sue his daughter's employer for the daughter's seduction. Previously, only an employer had been able to sue someone in his employ who had been seduced and rendered unproductive through pregnancy. In 1877 the two parts of the original statute were severed. The civil remedy remained and a new criminal offence of seduction was created. Seduction legislation was controversial, with some commentators arguing that it provided women with unprecedented opportunity to blackmail men. This remedy was available only to a woman of previously chaste character. Ontario's Seduction Act was repealed in 1978: Bailey, "Servant Girls and Masters," 154.

39 On the social-purity movement in Canada, see John McLaren, "Chasing the Social Evil: Moral Fervour and the Evolution of Canada's Prostitution Laws, 1867–1917," *Canadian Journal of Law and Society* 1 (1986): 125–65; John McLaren, "White Slavers: The Reform of Canada's Prostitution Laws and Patterns of Enforcement, 1900–1920," *Criminal Justice History* 8 (1987), 53–119; Graham Parker, "The Legal Regulation of Sexual Activities and the Protection of Females," *Osgoode Hall Law Journal* 21 (2) (1983): 187–244; Diana Pedersen, "Keeping Our Good Girls Good: The YWCA and the Girl Problem," *Canadian Woman's Studies* 7 (4) (1986): 20–4; James Snell, "The White Life for Two: The Defence of Marriage and Sexual Morality in Canada, 1890–1914," *Histoire sociale/Social History* 16 (31) (1983): 111–28; Carolyn Strange, *Toronto's Girl Problem: The Perils and Pleasures of the City, 1880–1930* (Toronto: University of Toronto Press 1995); and Mariana Valverde, *The Age of Light, Soap and Water: Moral Reform in English Canada, 1885–1925* (Toronto: University of Toronto Press, repr. 2008).

40 U.S. Children's Bureau, *Illegitimacy as a Child Welfare Problem* (Washington, 1920), 35.

41 Wayne Carp, "Professional Social Workers, Adoption and the Problem of Illegitimacy, 1915–1945," *Journal of Policy History* 6 (3) (1994): 166.

42 Ernst Freund, "The Present Law Concerning Children Born out of Wedlock and Possible Changes in Legislation," in U.S. Children's Bureau, *Standards of Legal Protection for Children Born out of Wedlock: A Report of Regional Conferences Held under the Auspices of the U.S. Children's Bureau* (Washington, 1921), 33.

43 Balcom, *The Traffic in Babies*, 18–53.

44 Peter Bryce, "Mothers' Allowances," *Social Welfare* 8 (1925): 131.

45 During public hearings on the possible introduction of mothers' allowance legislation, conducted across the province in 1919, considerable fear was expressed that to allow support for unmarried women would provide a licence for immorality and improvident breeding. "It was in the better

interest of the (illegitimate) child," asserted one witness at the hearings, "if it were adopted into some other family": Archives of Ontario (AO), RG 7, series II–I, "Mothers' Pension Allowance: Hamilton Enquiry," 20 February 1919. To receive the mothers' allowance, a woman had to be widowed, have been deserted for seven years, or have an incapacitated husband. She had to be a British citizen and to have lived in Canada for three years, in Ontario for two. She also had to have two or more children. Birth, death, and marriage certificates were demanded as proof of eligibility, a requirement that effectively precluded First Nations mothers from collecting the allowance: Ontario Mothers' Allowance Act, S.O. 1920; Margaret Jane Hillyard Little, *No Car, No Radio, No Liquor Permit: The Moral Regulation of Single Mothers in Ontario, 1920–1997* (Toronto: Oxford University Press 1998), chapter 1.

46 J.J. Kelso, *Ontario Educational Association Yearbook* (1900), 353.

47 The rhetoric of informal adoption referred to a range of practices that were not always clearly distinguished by reformers. Informal adoption could involve the placement of a newborn child with a new family at the consent of the mother via a lawyer or physician. It could also involve commercial exchanges which were highly exploitative of birth mothers. See Balcom, *The Traffic in Babies*.

48 Charlotte Whitton, "Unmarried Parents and the Social Order," Parts I and II, *Social Welfare* (April/May 1920), 187.

49 The Stanford revision of the Binet-Simon intelligence test was particularly popular: James W. Trent, *Inventing the Feeble-Minded: A History of Mental Retardation in the United States* (Berkeley: University of California Press 1994).

50 Report by Dr Bruce Smith, 13 April 1917, AO, RG 7, "Memo on Mothers' Pensions."

51 As Strong-Boag asserts, by the 1920s "Kelso and his contemporaries across the Dominion slowly and regretfully turned to the payment of what they treated as subsidies, not salaries" to foster mothers. Such payments covered only essentials and "pecuniary advantage tainted female service." Mothers accepting money were therefore considered inferior. Children were moved from boarding homes to free homes whenever possible and institutions were still used because placements could not be found for all children who needed them: Strong-Boag, *Finding Families, Finding Ourselves*, 73–4.

52 AO, RG 4–32, 1921, 1679, Memo of the Social Service Council of Ontario to Attorney General W.E. Raney, re: Adoption bill.

53 Alberta, An Act Respecting Infants, 1913, c.13, ss.1–9; British Columbia,

An Act Respecting the Adoption of Children, 1935, c.2, ss.1–16; Manitoba, Child Welfare Act, 1924, c.35, ss.92–9; New Brunswick, Adoption Act, 1873, 36 Vict., c.30; Newfoundland, Welfare of Children Act, 1952, c.60; Northwest Territories, An Ordinance Respecting the Adoption of Children, 1967, c.2, ss.1–17; Nova Scotia, Adoption Act, 1896, 59 Vict., c.9; Prince Edward Island, Adoption Act, 1950, c.2; and Quebec, Loi de l'Adoption, 1925, c.196, s.1. While New Brunswick was the first province to enact adoption legislation, as Veronica Strong-Boag notes, "it apparently attracted little attention": Strong-Boag, *Finding Families, Finding Ourselves*, 27.

54 An Act Respecting the Legitimation of Children by the Subsequent Intermarriage of Their Parents, S.O. 1921, c.53; Children of Unmarried Parents Act; and the Adoption Act.

55 Although Drury's United Farmers of Ontario government needed the support of the Labour members of Parliament to survive – and even with such support had only a single-seat majority over the combined power of the Liberals and the Tories – the farmers could not support the central demands of Labour for an eight-hour day and a minimum wage. They were afraid that such measures would increase the flood of young farming sons to the cities and, because of the long hours required in farm work, they resented the demand for leisure time: E.C Drury, *Farmer Premier: Memoirs of the Honourable E.C. Drury* (Toronto: McClelland and Stewart 1966); Charles Johnston, *E.C. Drury: Agrarian Idealist* (Toronto: University of Toronto Press 1986).

56 Drury, *Farmer Premier*, 108.

57 In 1918 Whitton, a recent graduate of Queen's University, was handpicked as the assistant secretary of the Social Service Council of Canada. She provided the liaison between the SSCC and Toronto's welfare agencies and was assistant editor of the newly founded *Social Welfare*, one of Canada's earliest and most influential social-work journals: Balcom, *The Traffic in Babies*, chapters 1 and 3; Patricia Rooke and R.L. Schnell, *No Bleeding Heart: Charlotte Whitton: Feminist on the Right* (Vancouver: University of British Columbia Press 1988); Patricia Rooke and R.L. Schnell, "Making the Way More Comfortable: Charlotte Whitton's Child Welfare Career," *Journal of Canadian Studies* 17 (4) (1983): 33–45; and James Struthers, "A Profession in Crisis: Charlotte Whitton and Canadian Social Work in the 1930s," *Canadian Historical Review* 62 (2) (1981): 169–85.

58 Legitimation of Children Act. This lead has been followed throughout the Western world, but Ontario's statute came comparatively early. The majority of U.S. states passed such legislation only in the 1950s and 1960s:

Harry D. Krause, *Illegitimacy: Law and Social Policy* (Indianapolis, IN: Bobbs Merrill Company 1971), 14.

59 In the early decades of the twentieth century, more punitive measures had garnered considerable support. The Presbyterian Church called for adultery and lewd cohabitation to be made punishable offences under the Criminal Code. The federal Department of Justice gave some consideration to such legislation: Snell, "The White Life for Two," 111–28.

60 Blackstone, *Commentaries on the Laws of England*, 454.

61 Children of Unmarried Parents Act, ss.10, 18, 13, and 25. For an extended study of this act and its implementation, see Lori Chambers, *Misconceptions: Unmarried Motherhood and the Ontario Children of Unmarried Parents Act, 1921–1969* (Toronto: University of Toronto Press / Osgoode Society for Canadian Legal History 2007).

62 AO, box 66–3–3–14, case 89, Wentworth, 1942.

63 Children of Unmarried Parents Act, ss.18 and 11.

64 The order, when granted, imposed obligations of support on the putative father but did not give him any meaningful status with regard to his child. Neither did the child have any claim, beyond maintenance, against his or her father. In a patriarchal world in which carrying the father's name had legal, symbolic, and social importance, the Children of Unmarried Parents Act did little to reduce the stigma to which the illegitimate child was subjected: Lori Chambers, "In the Name of the Father: Children, Names, and the Law in English Canada," *University of British Columbia Law Review* 43 (1) (2010): 1–45.

65 Jamil Zainaldin, "The Emergence of Modern American Family Law: Child Custody, Adoption and the Courts, 1796–1851," *Northwestern University Law Review* 73 (6) (1979): 1042.

66 Adoption Act, s.2(a). Ultimately, the fact that the proceedings took place in lower courts faced a constitutional challenge but the legislation was upheld: "The jurisdiction exercised by these functionaries, speaking generally, touches the great mass of the people more intimately and more extensively than do the judgments of the Superior Courts; and it would be an extraordinary supposition that a great community like the province of Ontario is wanting, either in the will or in the capacity, to protect itself against misconduct by these officers whom it appoints for these duties": *Reference as to Constitutionality of the Adoption Act, The Children's Protection Act, The Deserted Wives' & Children's Maintenance Act* [1938] S.C.J. No. 21.

67 Adoption Act, s.4(1)(e). It was expressly provided, however, for the protection of the child from social censure, that the fact of illegitimacy would not be recorded on the adoption order: Adoption Act, s.4(2)(b). In 1929 this

provision was amended such that the consent of a father was required if the child resided with, and was maintained by, the father at the time of the application: Statute Law Amendment Act, S.O. 1929, c.23, s.11.
68 Adoption Act, s.5.
69 Ibid., s.10(1)(a),(b),(c); s.11(1); and 11(2). Initially, however, adoption legislation still allowed an adoptee to inherit from his or her birth parents, a seeming contradiction with closed records. While closed records precluded many children from actually claiming against the estates of birth parents, dual inheritance was explicitly eliminated by legislation in 1958: Child Welfare Amendment Act, S.O. 1958, c.11, s.3. Legislators remained hesitant to impose the adopted child on wider kin and, until 1970, with regard to wider kin, the child had no legal status.
70 Although the 1921 act was not explicit about secrecy, a revised act, passed in 1927, was: Adoption Act, S.O. 1927.
71 Katrysha Bracco, "Patriarchy and the Law of Adoption: Beneath the Best Interests of the Child," *Alberta Law Review* 35 (4) (1997): 1041.
72 Strong-Boag, *Finding Families, Finding Ourselves*, 113–17. In the early years of the century, as she illustrates, court cases involving religious placement were not unusual. Because these disputes were not about the relative merits of the parents, or their rights, but about the rights of institutions with regard to exclusive placement, they are not dealt with further in this book. Moreover, Strong-Boag provides an excellent overview of this subject.
73 Braithwaite, "Born out of Wedlock," 64.
74 Whitton, "Child Adoption," 102.
75 Child Welfare Act, R.S.O. 1954, c.8. No substantive changes were made with regard to adoption procedures: Part IV – Adoption.
76 Katz, "Why Can't You Adopt a Child?" 13 and 115.
77 Criminal Law Amendment Act, S.C. 1968–9, c.38.
78 Canada Assistance Plan, 1966–7, c.45, ss.1, 711.
79 Child and Family Services Act, Part VII, R.S.O. 1990, c.11, ss.136–77.
80 Marlene Webber, *As if Kids Mattered: What's Wrong in the World of Child Protection and Adoption* (Toronto: Key Porter Books 2002), 25.

2 Mothers and the Meaning of Consent in Adoption

1 This chapter will address the first of these questions, exploring the conditions under which birth mothers have given "consent" for the adoption of their infants. In cases involving crown wards, usually older children, the issue of consent is moot, since children are removed from their homes under child-protection legislation when they are deemed "neglected" or

"abused"; the problems inherent in apprehension will be discussed in chapter 4.
2 Strong-Boag, *Finding Families, Finding Ourselves*, 37–8.
3 For information on poor mothers, see Chambers, *Misconceptions*. For information on middle-class mothers, see Anne Petrie, *Gone to an Aunt's: Remembering Canada's Homes for Unwed Mothers* (Toronto: McClelland and Stewart 1998).
4 Strong-Boag, *Finding Families, Finding Ourselves*, 27.
5 As Strong-Boag notes, with regard to formal and informal adoption, white babies, preferably girls, have always been considered most desirable: Strong-Boag, *Finding Families, Finding Ourselves*, 8.
6 *Re: Mugford* [1970] S.C.R. 261.
7 Adoption Act, s.5.
8 Adoption Act, R.S.O. 1937, c.218, s.3(3).
9 As quoted in Andrew Jones and Leonard Rutman, *In the Children's Aid: J.J. Kelso and Child Welfare in Ontario* (Toronto: University of Toronto Press 1981), 156 and 163.
10 E. Wayne Carp, *Family Matters: Secrecy and Disclosure in the History of Adoption* (Cambridge, MA: Harvard University Press 1998), 29. See also Elaine Taylor May, *Homeward Bound: American Families in the Cold War Era* (New York: Basic Books 1988); and Elaine Taylor May, *Barren in the Promised Land: Childless Americans and the Pursuit of Happiness* (New York: Basic Books 1995).
11 John Bowlby, *Maternal Care and Mental Health*, World Health Organization Monograph Series, no. 2 (Geneva: World Health Organization 1951), 101 and 103.
12 Bette Cahill, *Butterbox Babies* (Toronto: Seal Books 1992).
13 Balcom, *The Traffic in Babies*.
14 Margaret Thornhill, "Unprotected Adoptions," *Children* 2 (5) (1955): 179.
15 This was investigated by the U.S. Congress in 1955: Kefauver's investigation uncovered the presence of a large-scale interstate commercial traffic in children that earned more than $15 million every year. The hearings also illustrated the need for legislation to protect against unethical practices by doctors, lawyers, and baby brokers. A particularly extreme example emerged in Tennessee where the Tennessee Children's Home Society in Memphis operated an adoption-for-profit scheme. Georgia Tann, the director of the society, had been a nationally respected leader in the child-welfare movement: Linda Tollett Austin, *Babies for Sale: The Tennessee Children's Home Adoption Scandal* (Westport, CT: Praeger 1993), 110.

16 AO, box 27–9–1–1, case 295, Middlesex, 1945.
17 G.F. Lemby, *Family Law* (Vancouver: International Self-Counsel Press 1974), 158.
18 L.E. Lowan, "Mail-Order Babies," *Chatelaine* 6 (4) (1932): 26.
19 In an earlier study of unwed motherhood, I explored over 4,000 case files produced under the Children of Unmarried Parents Act. For the purposes of this book, I have used evidence from 203 cases in which mothers who sought help with child support through the CAS were instead convinced to release their children for adoption: for further detail with regard to these cases, see Chambers, *Misconceptions*.
20 John L. Brown, "Rootedness," *Involvement* 6 (5) (1974): 8.
21 Child Welfare Act, S.O. 1965, c.14, s.12. See also: Hepsworth, *Foster Care and Adoption in Canada*; and N. Trocme, "Child Welfare Services," in R. Barhhorst and L. Johnson, eds., *The State of the Child in Ontario* (Toronto: Oxford University Press 1991). Only in 1998 did the provincial government assume 100 per cent of the costs involved in child welfare.
22 AO, box 24–2–3–3, case 43, Wentworth, 1944.
23 This was ironic and hypocritical since, when money was owed to mothers, the policy of the court was to allow large arrears to accrue before court action would be taken; in fact, no action would be taken until arrears reached at least $100: Chambers, *Misconceptions*.
24 N. Emily Mohr, "A Study of Illegitimacy in Ontario" (Toronto, 1921), 23. AO, RG 4–32, 1871–1947, Central Registry, no. 2023.
25 Svanhuit Josie, "The American Caricature of the Unmarried Mother," *Canadian Welfare* 29 (12) (1955): 247.
26 Strong-Boag, *Finding Families, Finding Ourselves*, 87.
27 Mary Speers, "Case Work and Adoption," *Social Worker* 16 (3) (1948): 18.
28 Editorial, "Get the Babies to Those Who Want Them," *Maclean's*, 5 February 1966, 4.
29 Josie, "The American Caricature," 249. The most prominent American critic of the adoption mandate was Clark Vincent. See Clark Vincent, "The Adoption Market and the Unwed Mother's Baby," *Marriage and Family Living* 18 (May 1956): 124–7; "Unmarried Mothers: Society's Dilemma," *Sexology* 28 (1962): 451–5; and "Illegitimacy in the Next Decade: Trends and Implications," *Child Welfare* 43 (December 1964): 513–20.
30 Josie, "The American Caricature," 248.
31 Kathleen Sutherton, "Another View," *Canadian Welfare* 31 (5) (1955).
32 Petrie, *Gone to an Aunt's*, 147.
33 AO, box 411–1–3–11, case 488, York, 1946.
34 Petrie, *Gone to an Aunt's*, 147.

35 The racial specificity of this solution was important, although non-white mothers were numerically rare in the Children of Unmarried Parents Act case files. As Karen Dubinsky illustrates so powerfully with regard to Black mothers in Montreal in this era, social workers were fearful of and hostile towards pregnant Black women (many of whom in Montreal were immigrants who had come to Canada as domestics) and considered their children undesirable for adoption, rendering the "redemption narrative ... far less available": Dubinsky, *Babies Without Borders*, 74.
36 AO, box 411–1–3–11, case 498, York, 1947.
37 AO, box 411–1–4–5, case 2316, York, 1960.
38 AO, box 411–1–2–9, case 976, York, 1959.
39 AO, box 66–3–3–14, case 111, Wentworth, 1957.
40 Leontine Young, *Out of Wedlock* (New York: McGraw-Hill, 1954), 74.
41 Petrie, *Gone to an Aunt's*.
42 *Re Fex* [1948] O.W.N. 497 at 499.
43 *Martin v. Duffell* [1950] S.C.R. 737; *Hepton v. Maat* [1957] S.C.R. 606; and *Agar v. McNeilly* [1958] S.C.R. 52.
44 *Martin v. Duffell*, 737.
45 *Hepton v. Maat*, 606 and 609.
46 *Agar v. McNeilly*, 52.
47 Svanhuit Josie, "The Unwed Mother – Her Right to her Child," *Saturday Night*, 15 August 1950, 26.
48 Adoption Amendment Act, S.O. 1951, c.2.
49 *An Act Relating to Child Welfare*, Part IV, Adoption, S.O. 1958, 47.
50 Social Planning Council of Metropolitan Toronto, *A Report on Maternity Homes in Metropolitan Toronto* (Toronto, 1960), xviii.
51 *Re: Mugford* [1970] S.C.R. 261, at paras. 6, 8, 11, and 7.
52 *Re Moores and Feldstein* (1973) 12 R.F.L. (Ont. C.A.), 273.
53 *King v. Low* [1985] 1 S.C.R. 87, at para. 16.
54 In adopting the standard of the best interests of the child, Canada was considered to be in the vanguard of child-centred legal reform. Internationally, a child-centred focus in custody decisions was endorsed in the United Nations Convention on the Rights of the Child, promulgated in 1989, which asserts that "in all actions concerning children, whether undertaken by public or private social welfare institutions, courts of law, administrative authorities or legislative bodies, the best interests of the child shall be a primary consideration": United Nations Convention on the Rights of the Child, Art. 3, 20 November 1989, 28 I.L.M., 1448.
55 For a review of these issues, see M. Woodhead, "Psychology and Social Construction of Children's Needs," in A. James and A. Prout, eds., *Con-

structing and Reconstructing Childhood: Contemporary Issues in the Sociological Study of Children (London: Falmer Press 1990, 2nd ed. 1997).
56 For the central arguments of these reformers, see Wald, "Children's Rights," 255. For a critique of the impact of gender-neutral divorce on women's access to their children, see Susan Boyd, "Demonizing Mothers: Fathers' Rights Discourses in Child Custody Law Reform Processes," *Journal of the Association of Research on Mothering* 6 (1) (2004): 52–74; Martha Fineman, "Dominant Discourse, Professional Language and Legal Change in Child Custody Decision-Making," *Harvard Law Review* 101 (4) (1988): 727–74; Noel Semple, "Whose Best Interests? Custody and Access Law and Proceedings," *Osgoode Hall Law Journal* 48 (2010): 287–336; and Barbara Bennett Wodehouse, "Child Custody in the Age of Children's Rights: The Search for a Just and Workable Standard," *Family Law Quarterly* 33 (3) (1999): 815–60. Acknowledging problems in the standard, Woodhead argues that "perfecting the best interests standard, not abandoning it for simpler alternatives that lack a child-centered justification" is the way forward: Woodhead, "Psychology and Social Construction of Children's Needs," 815.
57 *Catholic Children's Aid Society v. Pamela M.* (1983) 44 O.R. (2d) 375.
58 *Manitoba (Director of Child Welfare) v. Y* [1981] 1 S.C.R. 623; *Racine v. Woods* [1983] 2 S.C.R. 173; and *King v. Low*.
59 *Manitoba (Director of Child Welfare) v Y*, 668.
60 Child Welfare Act, 1974 (Man.), c. C80, ss.15(1)-(2), 15(4), 15(6).
61 *Manitoba (Director of Child Welfare) v. Y*, 625. Despite this ruling, in my opinion, the failure of the Children's Aid Society to respect her request for revocation was clearly unjust if not strictly unlawful.
62 Ellen Anderson, *Judging Bertha Wilson: Law as Large as Life* (Toronto: University of Toronto Press / Osgoode Society for Canadian Legal History 2001), 190.
63 *Racine v. Woods*, at 174 and 185.
64 *King v. Low*, at para. 9.

3 Putative Fathers and Newborn Adoption

1 Diana Dzwiekowski, "Casenotes: Findings of Paternity in Ontario, *Sayer v. Rollin*," *Canadian Journal of Family Law* 3 (1980): 318–26; and Family Law Act, S.O. 1978, and Family Law Reform Act, R.S.O. 1980.
2 Ontario Law Commission, *Report on Family Law, Part III – Children* (Toronto: Ministry of the Attorney General 1973).
3 A father was defined clearly under the Children's Law Reform Act, 1990, s.8(1): "Unless the contrary is proven on a balance of probabilities, there is

a presumption that a male person is, and he shall be recognized in law to be, the father of a child in any one of the following circumstances: 1. The person is married to the mother of the child at the time of the birth of the child; 2. The person was married to the mother of the child by a marriage that was terminated by death or judgment of nullity within 300 days before the birth of the child or by divorce where the decree nisi was granted within 300 days before the birth of the child; 3. The person marries the mother of the child after the birth of the child and acknowledges that he is the natural father; 4. The person was cohabiting with the mother of the child in a relationship of some permanence at the time of the birth of the child or the child was born within 300 days after they ceased to cohabit; 5. The person has certified the child's birth, as the child's father, under the *Vital Statistics Act* or a similar act in another jurisdiction in Canada; or 6. The person has been found or recognized in his lifetime by a court of competent jurisdiction in Canada to be the father of the child": Children's Law Reform Act, R.S.O. 1990, c. C.12, s.8(1). Illegitimacy had already been eliminated at law by the Family Law Reform Act, R.S.O. 1980, c.152, s.1(a). Most provincial birth registries and vital-statistics provisions still allow the mother to register an infant alone, but registration is subject to revision, even against the will of the mother. For further information on vital statistics and the registration of birth, see: Alberta, Vital Statistics Act, Alta. Reg. 322/2000, s.2.1; British Columbia, Vital Statistics Act, B.C. Reg. 69/82, s.4; Manitoba, Vital Statistics Act, C.C.S.M. c. V60, s.3, enacted as R.S.M. 1987, c. V60; New Brunswick, Vital Statistics Act, N.B. Reg. 87–30; Newfoundland and Labrador, Vital Statistics Act, S.N.L. 2009, c. V-6.01; Northwest Territories, Vital Statistics Act, R.S.N.W.T 1988, c. V-3, ss.1–11; Nova Scotia, Vital Statistics Act, R.S.N.S. 1989, c.494; Ontario, Vital Statistics Act, R.S.O. 1990, c. V.4, ss.8–17; Prince Edward Island, Vital Statistics Act, R.S.P.E.I. 1988, c. V-4.1; Saskatchewan, Vital Statistics Act, S.S. 2009, c. V-7.21; Yukon, Vital Statistics Act, R.S.Y. 2002, c.225, ss.1–15.

4 Strong-Boag, *Finding Families, Finding Ourselves,* 102. Strong-Boag devotes only five pages to the role of fathers in adoption in English Canada over the last century: 102–6. In these five pages she explores the marginality of fathers and the rise of other father's rights claims in the 1970s and 1980s. In a single paragraph she mentions briefly Charter challenges to the exclusion of fathers from decision making about adoption but does not explore the reasoning or language of these decisions, simply noting that they have been contradictory.

5 Boyd, "Demonizing Mothers," 52; Lori Chambers, "Newborn Adoption: Birth Mothers, Genetic Fathers and Reproductive Autonomy," *Canadian*

Journal of Family Law 26 (2) (2010): 339–94; Ruth Colker, "Pregnant Men Revisited or Sperms Is Cheap, Eggs Are Not," *Hastings Law Journal* 47 (1996): 1063; Karen Czapanskiy, "Volunteers and Draftees: The Struggle for Parental Equality," *University of California Los Angeles Law Review* 38 (1991): 1415; Nancy Erickson, "The Feminist Dilemma over Unwed Parents' Custody Rights," *Law and Inequality* 2 (1984): 447; Cecily Helms and Phyllis Spence, "Take Notice Unwed Fathers: An Unwed Mother's Right to Privacy in Adoption Proceedings," *Wisconsin Women's Law Journal* 20 (2005): 13; Hester Lessard, "Mothers, Fathers and Naming: Reflections on the *Law* Equality Framework and *Trociuk v. British Columbia (Attorney General),*" *Canadian Journal of Women and the Law* 16 (1) (2004): 165; and Wanda Wiegers, "Gender, Biology, and Third Party Custody Disputes," *Alberta Law Review* 47 (1) (2009), 1–37.
6 Children of Unmarried Parents Act, s.24.
7 AO, box 24–2–3–3, case 15, Wentworth, 1966.
8 AO, box 24–2–3–4, case 217, Hamilton, 1962.
9 AO, box 411–1–3–11, case 501, York, 1947.
10 AO, box 411–1–3–9, case 397, York, 1955.
11 AO, box 24–2–3–4, case 291, Wentworth, 1954.
12 AO, box 411–1–3–12, case 2050, York, 1950.
13 Statute Law Amendment Act, S.O. 1929, c.23, s.11.
14 *Children's Aid Society of Metropolitan Toronto v. Lyttle* (1973) S.C.R. 568.
15 *C.G.W. v. M.J. et al.* (1981) O.J. No. 3099 (C.A.).
16 *Re Ward* (1976) 9 O.R. (2nd) (Div. Ct.), 35.
17 They used this term as a pejorative description of men involved in one-night stands, not in the sense that we now associate with reproductive technologies.
18 *Re M.L.A. and Three Other Applicants* (1979) 25 O.R. (2d) (Prov. Ct. Fam. Div.), 779.
19 *C.E.S. v. Children's Aid Society of Metropolitan Toronto* [1988] O.J. No. 268 (Div. Ct.), at para. 4.
20 *S.(C.E.) v. Children's Aid Society of Metropolitan Toronto* [1987] O.J. No. 1251 (Prov. Ct. Fam. Div.), at paras. 2, 23, 24, and 15.
21 *Trociuk v. British Columbia (Attorney General)* [2003] S.C.J. No. 32.
22 *Trociuk v. British Columbia (Attorney General)* (2001) B.C.J. No. 1052 (C.A.), at para. 143.
23 Lessard, "Mothers, Fathers and Naming," 165; and Chambers, "In the Name of the Father."
24 *D.G.C. v. R.H.G.Y.* [2003] O.J. No. 2636 (Ct. J.), at paras. 2, 3, 4, 5, 8, 12, and 13.

25 *A.L. v. S.M.* [2009] O.J. No. 2972 (Sup. Ct. J.).
26 Ibid., at paras. 1 and 2.
27 Children's Law Reform Act, s.8(1).
28 *A.L. v. S.M.*, at paras. 21, 30, 32, 58, and 59.
29 Czapanskiy, "Volunteers and Draftees," 1427.
30 In 2006 the "Saskatchewan Dad case" "became a cause célèbre for the fathers' rights movement in Canada." The "Dad" contested adoption on the sole basis of his genetic connection to his child. At the time of the pregnancy, the mother had recently terminated a relationship with the genetic father. The relationship between the parties had ended as the result of a "violent incident." Hendricks, who initially denied the violence, later admitted to such actions but blamed his behaviour on provocation and "his problematic relationship with Rose." The mother had a history of substance abuse and limited financial resources. Justice Smith described her as "self-aware of her own failings," instead of evincing any contextualized understanding of the problems she faced as an Aboriginal woman in a society rife with colonialism. She had selected an adoptive couple to parent her son. The mother endured a complicated and life-threatening pregnancy and gave the baby to the adoptive couple directly from the hospital. After learning about the pregnancy and adoption placement, Hendricks acted immediately to assert his parental rights. Ultimately, it was determined that the best interests of the child would be met by custody remaining with the adoptive parents. This case would undoubtedly have been appealed by Hendricks had he not been killed "in a [tragic] motor vehicle accident in August 2007." Given the reasoning in *Trociuk*, the outcome of such an appeal would have been far from certain; *Hendricks* also suggests that it is inevitable that a newborn adoption case will eventually reach the Supreme Court: see Saskatoon Dad, www.saskatoondad.com; Wiegers, "Gender, Biology, and Third Party Custody Disputes," 1-37.
31 *R. v. Morgentaler* [1988] S.C.J. No. 1, at para. 243.
32 He was abusive not only of Daigle but also of other women, and has subsequently been convicted of assault: *R. v. Tremblay* [1999] A.J. No. 1486 (Q.B.); *R. v. Tremblay* [2003] A.J. No. 92 (C.A.); and *R. v. Tremblay* [2004] S.C.C.A. No. 359.
33 *Tremblay v. Daigle* [1989] S.C.J. No. 79, at para. 78.
34 Mary Shanley, *Making Babies, Making Families: What Matters Most in an Age of Reproductive Technologies, Surrogacy, Adoption and Same-Sex and Unwed Parents* (Boston: Beacon Press 2001), 47.
35 Colker, "Pregnant Men Revisited," 1071.

36 UNICEF, Statistics by Area: Maternal Mortality: http://www.childinfo
   .org/maternal_mortality_countrydata.php.
37 Colker, "Pregnant Men Revisited," 1071.
38 Chambers, "Newborn Adoption," 339–94.
39 Wiegers, "Gender, Biology, and Third Party Custody Disputes," 12.
40 *Trociuk* [2003] at para. 24.
41 Lessard, "Mothers, Fathers and Naming," 202.
42 Erickson, "The Feminist Dilemma," 460.

4 Child Apprehension

1 Both Karen Dubinsky and Karen Balcom focus almost exclusively on babies and very young children. Veronica Strong-Boag addresses the fate of older children but does not explore the legalities of apprehension in any depth in her study of adoption, although her later work on children in foster care provides unprecedented detail about this issue: Balcom, *The Traffic in Babies*; Dubinsky, *Babies Without Borders*; Strong-Boag, *Finding Families, Finding Ourselves*, and *Fostering Nation*.
2 Donald Poirier, "Social Worker Enforcement of Child Welfare Legislation: An Increasing Potential for Abuse," *Canadian Journal of Family Law* 5 (1986): 224.
3 Children also came into state care through juvenile-delinquency provisions, and in cases of institutionalization owing to severe physical and intellectual impairment, but such children were not considered adoptable.
4 Child Welfare Act, 1954, c.8.
5 *Martin v. Duffell*; *Hepton v. Maat*; *Agar v. McNeilly*.
6 Child Welfare Act, S.O. 1965, s.42. For a full review of the changes of 1965, see Freda Manson, "The Ontario Child Welfare Act of 1965," *University of Toronto Law Journal* 17 (1) (1967): 217–24.
7 Sandra Scarrth and Richard Sullivan, "Child Welfare in the 1980s: A Time of Turbulence and Change," in Leslie Foster and Brian Wharf, eds., *People, Politics and Child Welfare in British Columbia* (Vancouver: University of British Columbia Press 2007), 83–96.
8 Child and Family Services Act, S.O. 1984, c.55.
9 Report of Panel of Experts on Child Protection, *Protecting Vulnerable Children* (Ontario, March 1998), http://www.fixcas.com/social/Hatton.htm.
10 Bill 6, 1998; Child and Family Services Amendment Act (Child Welfare Reform), S.O. 1999.
11 The solutions to this problem are elusive. Social workers in child-protection services face legal consequences if they fail to intervene and a child

under their supervision is horrifically abused and/or dies. They lack adequate funds for preventive services, carry enormous caseloads, and suffer from high rates of professional burnout. As both Veronica Strong-Boag and Karen Balcom eloquently remind readers, it is important "to understand social workers' goals and objectives within their logic and their genuine concerns about how best to protect children and parents, but also to be critical of the blind spots and unchallenged assumptions shaping their world views." Balcom, *The Traffic in Babies*, 12; Strong-Boag, *Finding Families, Finding Ourselves*, xii.

12 *New Brunswick (Minister of Health and Community Services) v. G. (J.)* [1999] S.C.J. No. 47.
13 Evidence with regard to the preponderance of negligence as a reason for apprehension is extensive: http://www.cwrp.ca/provincial-studies/ontario-incidence-study.
14 Wayne Renke, "The Mandatory Reporting of Child Abuse under the Child Welfare Act," *Health Law Journal* 7 (1999): 99 at para. 40.
15 Bernd Walter, Janine Alison Isenegger, and Nicholas Bala, "Best Interests in Child Protection Proceedings: Implications and Alternatives," *Canadian Journal of Family Law* 12 (1995): 367 at para. 4.
16 For further information on apprenticeship legislation, see Neff, "Pauper Apprenticeships in Early Nineteenth-Century Ontario," 144–71.
17 Shurlee Swain, "Sweet Childhood Lost: Idealized Images of Childhood in the British Child Rescue Literature," *Journal of the History of Childhood and Youth* 2 (2) (2009): 208.
18 An Act for the Prevention of Cruelty to and Better-Protection of Children, ss.2 and 13.
19 Declaration of the Rights of the Child, United Nations General Assembly, Resolution 1386 (XIV), 1959, principle 9.
20 Mary Louise Adams, *The Trouble with Normal: Postwar Youth and the Making of Heterosexuality* (Toronto: University of Toronto Press 1997), 56 and 57.
21 *Martin v. Duffell*.
22 *Hepton v. Maat*, at 607–8.
23 *Agar v. McNeilly*, at 52.
24 C.H. Kempe et al., "The Battered Child Syndrome," *Journal of the American Medical Association* 181 (July 1962): 17. For an insightful discussion of this literature and its impact, see Sally Mennill and Veronica Strong-Boag, "Identifying Victims: Child Abuse and Death in Canadian Families," *Canadian Bulletin of Medical History* 25 (1) (2008): 316.
25 Child Welfare Act, S.O. 1965, s.42.
26 James King, Morag MacKay, Angela Sirnick, with the Canadian Shaken

Baby Study Group, "Shaken Baby Syndrome in Canada: Clinical Characteristics and Outcomes of Hospital Cases," *Canadian Medical Association Journal* 168 (2) (2003): 156. Since the 1970s, studies have illustrated that men are far more likely to shake babies to the point of damage than are women: Public Health Agency of Canada, Working Group, "Joint Statement on Shaken Baby Syndrome," http://www.phac-aspc.gc.ca/dca-dea/publications/jointstatement_web-eng.php.

27 Cyril Greenland, *Child Abuse in Ontario* (Toronto: Ministry of Community and Social Services 1973). For a discussion of this report and others, see Mennill and Strong-Boag, "Identifying Victims."

28 Mary Van Stolk, *The Battered Child in Canada* (Toronto: McClelland and Stewart 1972).

29 Ralph Garber, *The Ontario Task Force on Child Abuse* (Toronto: Ministry of Community and Social Services, Children's Services Division, 1978).

30 Benjamin Schlesinger, *Child Abuse in Canada* (Toronto: Faculty of Education, University of Toronto, 1977).

31 "Report of the Judicial Inquiry into the Care of Kim Anne Popen by the Children's Aid Society in the City of Sarnia and the County of Lambton": http://www.archive.org/details/reportofjudicial1030nta. See also Ontario Association of Children's Aid Societies, *Ontario Child Mortality Task Force – Final Report* (1997); Ontario Panel of Experts on Child Protection, *Protecting Vulnerable Children* (1998).

32 Mennill and Strong-Boag, "Identifying Victims," 324 and 326.

33 Poirier, "Social Worker Enforcement of Child Welfare Legislation," 228.

34 Factum of the Intervener, Women's Legal Education and Action Fund (LEAF), National Association of Women and the Law, and Disabled Women's Network of Canada, in *N.B. v. G. (J.)*, at para 29. LEAF is a feminist legal organization that has intervened in numerous cases involving women and children in Canada since 1985. For further information, see http://www.leaf.ca.

35 Child Welfare Act, S.O. 1978, c.85, s.28(4). This stands in stark contrast to perceptions of procedural fairness and due process, since normally you cannot be retried for the same crime.

36 The most prominent proponent of reform based on children's rights was Michael Wald. See Wald, "Children's Rights," 255.

37 For a discussion of these debates, see Scarrth and Sullivan, "Child Welfare in the 1980s," 83–96.

38 Child and Family Services Act, S.O. 1984, c.55.

39 In a unanimous all-party resolution passed on 24 November 1989, the federal Parliament committed to "achiev[ing] the goal of eliminating

poverty among Canadian children by 2000." Instead, however, federal social-policy supports were reduced and child-poverty rates increased: Colin Hughes, "Child Poverty, Campaign 2000 and Child Welfare: Working to End Child Poverty in Canada," *Child Welfare* 74 (3) (1995): 779.

40 Strong-Boag, *Fostering Nation*, 93.
41 In 1995 Premier Mike Harris reduced welfare rates for the healthy by 21.6 per cent, immediately placing many children under the low-income cutoff lines and at risk of malnutrition. Rates of child relinquishment increased immediately: Margaret Little, "A Litmus Test for Democracy: The Impact of Ontario Welfare Changes on Single Mothers," *Studies in Political Economy* 66 (autumn 2001): 9–36.
42 Jennifer Kovalsky-England was stabbed eighty-nine times by her delusional step-father, who also murdered his mother. The Clarke Institute had assessed all Jennifer's potential caregivers and had recommended that she be made a crown ward and adopted. Instead, the CAS gave custody to the step-father, whom they believed to be her biological father: Victor Malarek, "Red Tape, Bungling and Broken Bodies of Tragic Children 'Ignored to Death,'" *Globe and Mail*, 19 April 2002, http://www.theglobeandmail.com/news/national.
43 Shanay Johnson was twenty-two months old when she died in Toronto in 1993. Two other children had been removed from the mother's care in 1991, but they were all returned shortly after the birth of Shanay. Under CAS supervision, the mother nonetheless neglected Shanay by leaving her unsupervised, unfed, and unbathed in her crib for long hours. She also beat her: ibid.
44 Tiffany was four months old when she died of neglect in Trenton. Her father had been convicted of failing to provide the necessities of life, but no one informed the CAS of this fact: ibid.
45 Afua was four when she died in Toronto at the hands of her mother. Her mother had a serious psychiatric history and was delusional. A neighbour had begged the CAS to remove the child; it was this same neighbour who reported the cries that alerted the police to the child's death: ibid.
46 Margaret and Wilson, aged eight and ten, were shot to death by their father in Ottawa in 1995. The CAS had been warned that he was a ticking time bomb but had not removed the children from his care: ibid.
47 Ministry of Social Services of British Columbia, *Report of the Gove Inquiry into Child Protection in British Columbia* (1995): http://www.qp.gov.bc.ca/gove/.
48 Sara died of pneumonia but had multiple broken bones at the time of her death. In 1989 her father had been convicted of shaking her older brother

until he had brain damage but he had been released on the condition that he not have contact with his children. The conditions had been breached despite Catholic CAS supervision: Sam Pazzano, "Abusive Parents CAS Has Entrusted with Vulnerable Children," *Toronto Sun*, 21 March 2013.

49 The four children died in a house fire in Kitchener while their mother stood outside. She was a known crack addict but the CAS had determined her children to be at low risk of harm: Solicitor General and Chief Coroner, "Verdict of Coroner's Jury: Inquest into Dombroskie Deaths," 10 July 1997, http://www.fixcas.com/scholar/inquest/dombroskie.

50 Jordan died at the age of five weeks, in a homeless shelter where he was residing with his nineteen-year-old mother. She had been homeless for four years and had breastfed the child until her milk dried up; then, because of her poverty, she over-diluted the formula she fed him. She did not realize he was sick when he was tired and losing weight. Neither did the shelter workers or the CAS worker, although Jordan's mother was the one who was vilified by the press. As Krista Robson asserts, images of Renee Heikamp as a quintessential "bad mother" "deflect[ed] responsibility away from the state and social services system and, instead, heap[ed] it on an individual mother": Krista Robson, "Canada's Most Notorious 'Bad Mother': The Newspaper Coverage of the Jordan Heikamp Inquest," *Canadian Review of Sociology* 42 (2) (2005): 218. Both Heikamp and her social worker, Angela Martin, were charged in the death, but the court found no evidence of "wanton and reckless disregard" for the child's life, instead describing it as a tragedy of circumstances. The coroner's jury ruled the death a homicide but implicated the entire child-welfare system, not the mother: Chief Coroner, "Inquest Touching the Death of Jordan Desmond Heikamp," 11 April 2001.

51 Randall Dooley had recently moved from Jamaica, where he had been living with extended family, to be with his father and step-mother in Canada. A teacher and the CAS became involved when he repeatedly came to school with welts and bruises. When he died at the age of seven he had thirteen broken ribs, a developing case of pneumonia, a damaged diaphragm, fractures in his back, and torn and crushed internal organs: Christie Blatchford, "The Ruined Life of Randall, Barely 7," *National Post*, 16 November 2004 (reprint from trial, 16 January 2002). His father and step-mother were convicted of second-degree murder and appealed unsuccessfully: *R. v. Dooley* [2009] O.J. No. 5483 (C.A.).

52 Report of Panel of Experts on Child Protection, *Protecting Vulnerable Children*.

53 Cheryl Regehn et al., "Inquiries into Deaths of Children in Care: The Im-

pact on Workers and Their Organizations," *Children and Youth Services Review* 24 (11) (2002): 642 and 643. For further information, see Xenobai Chen, "Constructing Dangerous Parents through the Spectre of Child Deaths," in Deborah Brock, ed., *Making Normal: Social Regulation in Canada* (Toronto: Nelson Thompson Learning 2003), 209–33.

54 Nicholas Bala, "Reforming Child Welfare Policies: Don't Throw the Baby out with the Bathwater," *Policy Options*, 1998, 30 and 28. See also Nicholas Bala, "Reforming Ontario's *Child and Family Services Act:* Is the Pendulum Swinging Back Too Far?" *Canadian Family Law Quarterly* 12 (1999): 121–72.

55 Bala, "Reforming Child Welfare Policies," 32.

56 C.B. King et al., *Child Protection Legislation in Ontario: Past, Present and Future* (London: University of Western Ontario 2003).

57 Stephanie was thirteen, had severe autism, and was residing at Digs for Kids in Brampton. She was forced to lie face down on the floor as punishment and stopped breathing: "Inquest into 1998 Death in Brampton Group Home": http://www.ont-autism.uoguelph/jobin-inquest.html.

58 William Edgar was thirteen and had been in and out of foster care for many years. He had serious behavioural problems and was residing at Cavan Youth Services. When he refused to sit still, he was punished by being forced to lie face down with a very large man restraining him by sitting on him: Office of the Chief Coroner and Ministry of the Solicitor General, "Inquest into the Death of William Edgar, Verdict of the Jury," 6 September 2001.

59 Jeffrey Baldwin died of septic shock and pneumonia while living with his grandparents. He had been placed with them by the CAS after apprehension from his home of birth: Malarek, "Red Tape."

60 *New Brunswick (Minister of Health and Community Services) v. G. (J.).*

61 Ibid., at paras. 3 and 6.

62 Ibid., at paras. 10, 28, 38, 2, 61, and 113. This is particularly important given that women are disproportionately likely to be unrepresented under current Legal Aid guidelines which emphasize access to legal aid in the criminal law context. Rollie Thompson has argued that men are more likely to self-represent (sometimes in dangerous and vexatious ways, and often against former intimate partners), while women are likely to be unrepresented because they cannot find legal-aid support or because they eventually simply give up their claims and become invisible victims of the system: D.A. Rollie Thompson, "A Practicing Lawyer's Field Guide to the Self-Represented," *Canadian Family Law Quarterly* 19 (2002): 529.

63 Factum of the Intervener, LEAF, at paras. 18 and 51.

64 Mary Jane Mossman, "Gender Equality, Family Law and Access to Justice," *International Journal of Law and the Family* 8 (3) (1994): 366.
65 Dale Blenner-Hassett, "K.L.W. and Warrantless Child Apprehensions: Sanctioning Gross Intrusions into Private Spheres," *Saskatchewan Law Review* 67 (2004), at para. 20.
66 Anne McGillivray, "Child Physical Assault: Law, Equality and Intervention," *Manitoba Law Journal* 30 (2003–4): 148.
67 Health Canada, *Canadian Incidence Study of Reported Child Abuse and Neglect*, http://www.hc-sc.gc.ca/pphb-dgspsp/publicat/cisfr-ecirf.
68 Nico Trocmé et al., "Nature and Severity of Physical Harm Caused by Child Abuse and Neglect: Results from the Canadian Incidence Study," *Canadian Medical Association Journal* 169 (9) (2003): 911.
69 Nico Trocmé et al., *The Ontario Incidence Study of Reported Child Abuse and Neglect – 2008*, http://www.cwrp.ca/provincial-studies/ontario-incidence-study.
70 Vandna Sinha and Anne Kozlowski, "The Structure of Aboriginal Child Welfare in Canada," *International Indigenous Policy Journal* 2 (2) (2013): 3.
71 Karen Swift, *Manufacturing Bad Mothers: A Critical Perspective on Child Neglect* (Toronto: University of Toronto Press 1995), 86 and 105.
72 Kendra Nixon, "Intimate Partner Woman Abuse and Alberta's Child Protection Policy: The Impact on Abused Mothers and their Children," *Currents: Scholarship in the Human Services* 8 (1) (2001): 5.
73 Kisa Macdonald, "Returning to Find Much Wealth: Identifying the Need for a Revised Judicial Approach to Aboriginal Kinship in British Columbia," *Appeal* 15 (2010): para. 49.
74 Cheryl Farris-Manning and Marietta Zandstra, "Children in Care in Canada: A Summary of Current Issues and Trends with Recommendations for Future Research," in *The Welfare of Canadian Children* (Ottawa: Child Welfare Council of Canada 2007), 60.
75 Blenner-Hassett, "K.L.W. and Warrantless Child Apprehensions," at para. 70.
76 L. Young, "Placement from the Child's Viewpoint," *Social Casework* 31 (1950): 250.
77 For a critique of the misuse of attachment theory in apprehension, and the ways in which it obscures the difficult circumstances that mothers face, see Julia Krane et al., "The Clock Starts Now: Feminism, Mothering and Attachment Theory in Child Protection Practice," in Brid Featherstone et al., eds., *Gender and Child Welfare in Society* (New York: John Wiley and Sons 2010), 149–72.

78 On 29 May 2015, the Ontario Superior Court of Justice, Thunder Bay, denied the motion of the Province of Ontario to strike down a class-action suit by crown wards "seeking justice for the Crown's failure to protect them from the severe physical and sexual abuse they suffered as children while in the Province's care." Not surprisingly, a number of the proposed representative plaintiffs are of Indigenous descent and over five hundred class members have contacted class counsel. The government failed in its argument that they "did not owe a duty of care to the tens of thousands of children in their custody": http://www.tbnewswatch.com/News/371/720/Court_green_lights_Crown_Ward_Class_Action_against_province. This decision was confirmed by the Superior Court of Justice, on 22 January 2016: *Papassay et al. v. Ontario* 2016 ONSC 561.

79 Swift, *Manufacturing Bad Mothers*, 193.

5 Secrecy and Disclosure in Adoption

1 Strong-Boag's work explores both public demand and government investigations with regard to closed adoption. She does not, however, analyse court cases involving closed adoption in any detail, leaving significant gaps in our understanding of changes in the law. This chapter fills that gap. Strong-Boag, *Finding Families, Finding Ourselves*, 220–33.

2 United Nations Convention on the Rights of the Child, Art. 8, 20 November 1989, 28 I.L.M., 1448. This article asserts that "1. States Parties will undertake to respect the right of the child to preserve his or her identity, including nationality, name and family relations as recognized by law without unlawful interference; and 2. Where a child is illegally deprived of some or all elements of his or her identity, States Parties shall provide appropriate assistance and protection, with a view to re-establishing speedily his or her identity."

3 While curiosity about one's past may be natural, the emphasis on genetic inheritance and DNA is also a potentially troubling development with some neo-eugenic overtones. See L.B. Andres, "Past as Prologue: Sobering Thoughts on Genetic Enthusiasm," *Seton Hall Law Review* 27 (1997): 893–918.

4 Birth fathers may also participate, but far fewer of them do so. They are less likely to be named on birth certificates. They are also less likely, when named, to initiate searches.

5 Ferguson Colm O'Donnell, "The Four-Sided Triangle: A Comparative Study of the Confidentiality of Adoption Records," *University of Western Ontario Law Review* 21 (1) (1983): 135.

6 An Act to Amend the Child and Family Services Act, S.O. 1987. For further information and critique, see Shari Shneider and Michael Holosko, "Adoption Disclosure Policy: An Analysis of the Provincial Adoption Disclosure Statute Law Amendment Act," *Journal of Health and Social Policy* 3 (1) (1992): 55–76; and Marvin Bernstein and Mary Allen, "Submission to the Standing Committee on General Government Regarding Bill 77: Adoption Disclosure Amendment Act 2001," *Ontario Association of Children's Aid Societies Journal* 4 (2) (2001): 12–20.
7 Adoption Information Disclosure Act, S.O. 2005, c.25.
8 *Cheskes v. Ontario (Attorney General)* [2007] O.J. No. 3515 (Sup. Ct.).
9 Access to Adoption Records Act (Vital Statistics Statute Law Amendment) S.O. 2008, c.5.
10 Adoption Act, c.55, ss.10(1)(a),(b),(c), and 11(2).
11 Cindy Baldassi, "The Quest to Access Closed Adoption Files in Canada: Understanding Social Context and Legal Resistance to Change," *Canadian Journal of Family Law* 21 (2005), para. 1.
12 Adoption Act, s.9(3).
13 L.E. Lowman, "Mail Order Babies," *Chatelaine*, April 1932, 32.
14 *Cheskes v. Ontario*, at para. 15.
15 Adoption Act, s.9(3).
16 Jeanne House, "The Changing Face of Adoption: The Challenge of Open and Custom Adoption," *Canadian Family Law Quarterly* 1 (1996), 334.
17 Carp, *Family Matters*, 102 and 79.
18 Kate Inglis, *Living Mistakes: Mothers Who Consented to Adoption* (Toronto: Harper Collins 1985), 294.
19 AO, box 411–1–2–9, case 976, York, 1959.
20 AO, box 411–1–3–12, case 2066, York, 1952.
21 AO, box 411–1–4–1, case 455, York, 1960.
22 E. Wayne Carp, "Does Opening Adoption Records Have an Adverse Social Impact? Some Lessons from the U.S., Great Britain, and Australia, 1953–2007," *Adoption Quarterly* 10 (3/4) (2007): 31 and 32.
23 Jean Paton, *The Adopted Break Silence* (Philadelphia: Life History Study Centre 1954).
24 Strong-Boag, *Finding Families, Finding Ourselves*, 224.
25 Clare Marcus, *Adopted? A Canadian Guide for Adopted Adults in Search of Their Origins* (Vancouver: International Self-Counsel Press 1979); and Clare Marcus, *Who Is My Mother? Birth Parents, Adoptive Parents and Adoptees Talk about Living with Adoption and the Search for Lost Family* (Toronto: Macmillan 1981). The movement for open adoption records was very much a North American phenomenon, and in the 1970s, in the United States,

a new, vocal leader emerged in the adoption-rights movement, Florence Fisher, a New York City homemaker. After a traumatic but successful search for her birth parents, Fisher founded the Adoptees' Liberty Movement Association (ALMA): Carp, "Does Opening Adoption Records Have an Adverse Social Impact," 33. ALMA launched a constitutional challenge to the closed adoption-record regime: *ALMA Society Inc. v. Mellon*, 601f.2d, 1238–9 (2nd cir.) cert denied, 1101 (1986). It argued that adoptees had a fundamental right to their records, that denial of access violated the equal-protection clause of the constitution, and that such denial amounted to inhumane treatment which it likened to slavery. All of its arguments were rejected.

26 H. David Kirk, *Shared Fate: A Theory and Method of Adoptive Relationships* (Port Angeles, WA, and Brentwood Bay, BC: Ben-Simon Publications 1984, originally published 1964). For a description of his work and its importance, see Strong-Boag, *Finding Families, Finding Ourselves*, 132, 211, 218, 240, and 243.
27 June Callwood, "Adoption Not All Hearts and Flowers," *Chatelaine*, April 1976, 108.
28 Baldassi, "The Quest to Access Closed Adoption Files in Canada," para. 25.
29 Annette Baran, Rueben Pannor, and Arthur Sorosky, "Open Adoption," *Social Work* 21 (March 1976): 98.
30 Carp, *Family Matters*, 153.
31 Baldassi, "The Quest to Access Closed Adoption Files in Canada," para. 29.
32 David Kirschener, "Adoption Psychopathology and the Adopted Child Syndrome," *Directions in Child and Adolescent Therapy* 2 (6) (1995).
33 Baldassi, "The Quest to Access Closed Adoption Files in Canada," para. 29.
34 Ibid., para. 32.
35 *Cheskes v. Ontario*, at para. 65.
36 Carp, "Does Opening Adoption Records Have an Adverse Social Impact," 33.
37 United Nations Convention on the Rights of the Child, Art. 8, 20 November 1989, 28 I.L.M., 1448.
38 Carp, *Family Matters*, 159.
39 Child Welfare Act, S.O. 1978.
40 Marcus, *Adopted?* 77.
41 *Ferguson v. Director of Child Welfare et al.* (1983) 40 O.R. (2d) (Co. Ct.), 294.
42 Ibid., at 297, 295, 301, 310, 311, 315, and 317.

43 *Re Ferguson and Director of Child Welfare et al.* [1983] O.J. No. 180 (C.A.).
44 Margot Lettner, "Closing the Door on Disclosure: The Adoption Records Provisions of the Child and Family Services Act, 1984," *Reports of Family Law* (2d) 44 (1985): 28 at 30. For examples of the public outcry, see Doris Anderson, "Adoption Law Will Leave Parents, Kids in Limbo," *Toronto Star*, 13 April 1985, L1; June Callwood, "Adopted People May Never Know," *Globe and Mail*, 3 May 1985, L2; and Janice Dineen, "New Adoption Law 'Retrogressive,'" *Toronto Star*, 20 May 1985, C1.
45 *Tyler v. Ont. Dist. Ct.* [1986] O.J. No. 3074 (Co. Ct).
46 Ibid., at paras. 3, 2, and 4.
47 Ralph Garber, *Disclosure of Adoption Information* (Report of the Special Commissioner to the Honourable John Sweeney, Minister of Community and Social Services, Government of Ontario, November 1985).
48 *Ontario v. Marchand* [2006] O.J. No. 2387 (Sup. Ct.), at para. 10.
49 Baldassi, "The Quest to Access Closed Adoption Files in Canada," para. 62.
50 An Act to Amend the Child and Family Services Act, 1987.
51 Joanne Klauer, "Open Adoption Records: A Question of Empowerment," *Saskatchewan Law Review* 57 (1993): 416.
52 Nico Trocmé, "Child Welfare Services," in Richard Barnhorst and Laura C. Johnson, eds., *The State of the Child in Ontario* (Toronto: Oxford University Press 1991), 79.
53 In addition, MPPs Tony Martin, Alex Cullen, and Wayne Wettlaufer introduced bills in 1994, 1996, and 2003 respectively. See http://www.parentfindersottawa.ca/ontario-legislation/.
54 For further details regarding Marilyn Churley, see Kris Scheuer, "Churley Relives Her Son's Adoption in Tell-All Book," *My Town Crier*, 28 April 2007.
55 O'Donnell, "The Four-Sided Triangle," 135; and David Rodenhiser, "Knowing One's Origins a Right: Hamm Government Has Failed Nova Scotia's Adoptees," http://www.canada.com.
56 Strong-Boag, *Finding Families, Finding Ourselves*, 230. Further, while the popular press regularly celebrates the joys of reunion, and sociological evidence suggests that knowledge brings peace of mind, the image of "reunion" is exaggerated, since few adoptees form lasting bonds and relationships with birth parents after searching: P.S. Stevenson, "An Evaluation of Adoption Reunions in British Columbia," *Social Worker / Le Travailleur Social* 44 (1976): 9; Lou Stoneman, Jan Thompson, and Joan Webber, "Adoption Reunion: A Perspective," *Ontario Association of Children's Aid Societies Journal* 24 (December 1982): 10; Joan Webber, "Adult Adoptees Search

for Birth Parents," *Ontario Association of Children's Aid Societies Journal*, January–February 1979, 30; Jan Thompson, "Adoption Today: Viable or Vulnerable," *Ontario Association of Children's Aid Societies Journal*, January–February 1979, 7. Barbara Melosh argues that such evidence "undercuts the political agenda of adoption rights activists": Barbara Melosh, *Strangers and Kin: The American Way of Adoption* (Boston: Harvard University Press 2006), 252.

57 Adoption Information Disclosure Act, ss.48.1–48.12.
58 Anyone who violated a "no contact" notice was to be subject to criminal prosecution and fined up to $50,000. For persons who did not wish to have their identifying information disclosed, ss.48.5 and 48.7 of the Vital Statistics Act provided that birth parents and adult adoptees could apply to the Child and Family Services Review Board for a "non-disclosure order." Sections 48.5(7) and 48.7(3) of the VSA required the board to grant a non-disclosure order if it was satisfied that "because of exceptional circumstances the order is appropriate to prevent sexual harm or significant physical or emotional harm to [the adopted person or birth parent]."
59 *Hansard*, 2005, 1069–74.
60 *Ontario v. Marchand* [2006] O.J. No. 2387 (Sup. Ct.).
61 *Cheskes v. Ontario*.
62 *Ontario v. Marchand*, at paras. 1, 47, and 50.
63 Ibid., at para. 53. It is interesting to note that the applicant was difficult, at best, in her dealings with the registrar and other officials, comparing "them to Nazis and refus[ing] to speak to them because to do so would be 'like a Jew sitting down with Albert Speers'": at para. 65. Although the conduct of the registrar was not under review, the court found that "credible evidence is consistent with the employees and the Registrar having dealt with the applicant throughout in a responsive and professional manner in the face of what can be characterized as considerable abuse from the applicant": at para. 66.
64 Ibid., at paras. 40, 41, 64, and 67.
65 Ibid., at paras. 30, 70, and 74.
66 It is noteworthy that she called David Kirschner as one of her expert witnesses.
67 *Ontario v. Marchand*, at paras. 85, 96, 116, and 160.
68 *Globe and Mail*, 14 November 2007, A8.
69 *Ontario v. Marchand* [2007] O.J. No. 4440 (C.A.), at paras. 7 and 12.
70 This was further confirmed in the *Pratten* decision in British Columbia, a case involving a claim by a woman born of anonymous sperm donation that she had a right to identifying information about her donor. Pratten

Notes to pages 75–8   189

asserted that all children, except those born via sperm donation, know their genetic histories. This is erroneous and the assertion of the attorney general of British Columbia that "there is no law in B.C. guaranteeing anyone the right to know their genetic heritage and no law granting children, generally, the legal right – constitutional or otherwise – to access a parent's medical history or personal information" has significant merit. For this and other reasons, Pratten's claim was denied: *Pratten v. British Columbia (AG)* [2010] B.C.J. No. 2012 (S.C.) and *Pratten v. British Columbia (AG)* [2012] B.C.J. No. 2460 (C.A.). For further discussion of this case, see Lori Chambers and Heather Hillsburg, "Desperately Seeking Daddy: A Critique of *Pratten v. British Columbia (Attorney General)*," *Canadian Journal of Law and Society* 28 (2) (2013): 229–46.

71 Ibid., at paras. 33 and 32.
72 Ibid., at paras. 35, 33, and 34.
73 Ibid., at paras. 41 and 43.
74 Ibid., at paras. 45 and 49.
75 Ibid., at paras. 65, 82, 87, 62, 84, 107, and 138.
76 These provinces, at the time of *Cheskes*, included Quebec, Nova Scotia, New Brunswick, and Prince Edward Island. Civil Code of Quebec, S.Q. 1991, c.64, arts. 582–3; Adoption Information Act, S.N.S. 1996, c.3, s.19; Family Services Act, S.N.B. 1980, c. F-2.2, ss.91–2; Adoption Act, R.S.P.E.I. 1988, c. A-4.1, s.53.
77 Adoption Act, R.S.B.C. 1996, c.5, s.53; Child, Youth and Family Enhancement Act, R.S.A. 2000, c. C12, s.74.2(4); Adoption Act, C.C.S.M., c. A2, s.112; Adoption Act, S.N.L. 1999, c. A-2.1, s.50.
78 *Globe and Mail*, 14 November 2007, A8.
79 For more information, see http://www.ontario.ca/en/information_bundle/adoption/111872.html.

6 Open Adoption

1 Laurie Ames, "Open Adoptions: Truths and Consequences," *Law and Psychology Review* 16 (1992): 137.
2 Marianne Berry, "The Practice of Open Adoptions: Findings from a Study of 1396 Adoptive Families," *Children and Youth Services Review* 13 (1991): 379.
3 Child Welfare Act, 1978, ss.38 and 69(14).
4 In 1998 the Supreme Court of Canada confirmed that in exceptional cases access orders could survive adoption. In this case, three young girls with an absent father and a mother with limited intellectual capacity had been

placed under permanent guardianship. The court of first instance denied access; the Court of Appeal found nothing to justify such a denial; the Supreme Court overturned this decision. The Court asserted that there was no inconsistency between a permanent guardianship order and an access order, but that once a child is a crown ward access is "a right that belongs to the child and not to the parents"; the Court also noted, however, that "if adoption is more important than access for the welfare of the child and would be jeopardized if a right of access were exercised, access should not be granted": *New Brunswick (Minister of Health and Community Services) v. L.(M.)* [1998] S.C.J. No. 52, at paras. 17 and 50.

5 Bill 179, Building Families and Supporting Youth to be Successful Act, S.O. 2011, amended the Child and Family Services Act, ss.141.1.1, 145.1.1, and 145.1.2.

6 Annette Appell, "Reflections on the Movement toward a More Child-Centered Adoption," *Western New England Law Review* 32 (1) (2010): 7.

7 Carp, *Family Matters*, 202.

8 It was also recognized by the 1960s that openness in adoption has always existed to some degree, particularly in the context of private adoptions. Evidence suggests that historically often infertile couples took in unwed mothers, cared for them, and then adopted their children: "This approach expressed the principle that a mother had the right to choose the substitute parents for her child, and that their caring for her was an indication of how they would care for her child": Baran, Pannor, and Sorosky, "Open Adoption," 98.

9 Baldassi, "The Quest to Access Closed Adoption Files in Canada," para. 5.

10 Kirk, *Shared Fate*; Kirk, "Are Adopted Children Especially Vulnerable to Stress? A Critique of Some Recent Assertions," *Archives of General Psychiatry* 14 (March 1966); and H. David Kirk, *Looking Back, Looking Forward: An Adoptive Father's Sociological Testament* (Indianapolis, IN: Perspective Press 1995). For a review of his work, see Strong-Boag, *Finding Families, Finding Ourselves*, 98, 132, 211, 218, 240, and 243.

11 Baran, Pannor, and Sorosky, "Open Adoption," 98.

12 This is also evident in the United States. In 1994 the National Conference of Commissioners on Uniform State Laws promulgated the Uniform Adoption Act, but this measure generated widespread debate and was not fully adopted by states; open adoption is the subject within the Uniform Adoption Act that has caused greatest controversy; despite lobbying for full openness, the act endorses visitation and contact only in the context of step-parent adoptions: Margaret Mahoney, "Open Adoption in Context:

The Wisdom and Enforceability of Visitation Orders for Former Parents under Uniform Adoption Act #4–113," *Florida Law Review* 51 (1999): 89.
13 *Geary v. Oulton* [1995] O.J. No. 1712 (C.J.), at para. 26.
14 *C. (E.S.) v. P. (D.A.)* [1997] A.J. No. 843 (C.A.).
15 On foster care in Canada, see Strong-Boag, *Fostering Nation*.
16 Child Welfare Act, c.8.
17 Patti Phillips, "Financially Irresponsible and Obviously Neurotic Need Not Apply: Social Work, Parental Fitness and the Production of Adoptive Families in Ontario, 1940–1965," *Histoire sociale / Social History*, 2006, 354.
18 "Ontario Will Advertise Children for Adoption," *New York Times*, 14 April 1959, 3.
19 Balcom, *The Traffic in Babies*, 229. See also Strong-Boag, *Finding Families, Finding Ourselves*, 119–34.
20 Appell, "Reflections on the Movement toward a More Child-Centered Adoption," 3.
21 Deborah Silverstein and Sharon Kaplan Roszia, "Openness: A Critical Component of Special Needs Adoption," *Child Welfare* 78 (5) (1999): 639 and 640. In the United States, this recognition was formalized through the Adoption and Safe Families Act of 1997. This act asserts that it is important to work with birth families while children are in foster care, in the hope of future reconciliation of the family. Nonetheless, contingency planning should take place in case the family cannot be reunified. In many such cases, ongoing contact with members of the birth family will be necessary not only during the period of attempted reconciliation but also in the case of a formal adoption, either by the foster parents or by a third party, if reconciliation fails: Adoption and Safe Families Act, United States, 1997, Public Law 105–89, enacted 19 November 1997.
22 *C.G.W. v. M.J. et al.* (1981) 34 O.R. (2d) (C.A.), 44.
23 *Catholic Children's Aid Society of Metropolitan Toronto v. S.(T.)* [1989] O.J. No. 754 (C.A.).
24 Philip Zylberberg, "Minimal Constitutional Guarantees in Child Protection Cases," *Canadian Journal of Family Law* 10 (1992): 257–81 at para. 53.
25 Child and Family Services Act, R.S.O. 1990, c. C.11, s.58. Simultaneously the Child and Family Services Act, R.S.O. 1990, c. C.11, s.143 automatically terminated almost all previous access orders at the time of the adoption and s.160 denied the possibility of making an access order for a member of the birth family in conjunction with the adoption order.
26 *J.H. v. B.G.* [1993] O.J. No. 1497 (G.D.), at para. 37.
27 *M.A.R.P. v. A.V.* [1995] O.J. No. 421 (G.D.), at para. 24.

28 Strong-Boag, *Finding Families, Finding Ourselves*, 207. His cause was eventually taken up by the Adoption Council of Canada: http://www.adoption.ca/news/030721perez.htm.
29 *S.R. v. M.R.* [1998] O.J. No. 3385 (G.D.), at paras. 4, 5, 6, and 10.
30 An Act to Amend the Child and Family Services Act and Make Complementary Amendments to Other Acts, 2006, c.1, C.11, s.145.1(1); s.145.1(3)(a); s.145.1(3)(b); s.145.1(3)(c)(i),(ii),(iii),(iv); s.153.6(1); and s.153.6(3).
31 *S.M. (Re)* [2009] O.J. No. 2907 (Ct.J.).
32 Ibid., at paras. 2 and 7.
33 An Act to Amend the Child and Family Services Acts, s.157(2).
34 *S.M. (Re)* at para. 119. The parents suffered from HIV-related dementia as well as other ailments.
35 Ibid., at paras. 65, 106, 175, and 191. It was noted that, while attempts had been made to find African parents (but not specifically Swahili parents) for the child, none were available and the adoptive parents also did not share the boy's Islamic background.
36 Ibid., at paras. 207, 208, and 263.
37 Ontario Association of Children's Aid Societies, *Youth Leaving Care Report: An OACAS Survey of Youth and Staff* (Toronto: OACAS 2006); and Ontario Association of Children's Aid Societies, *Building Bridges to Belonging: Promising Practices for Youth Guide* (Toronto: OACAS 2009).
38 Sheilagh O'Connell, "Notable Child Protection Cases in 2012": http://www.flao.org/wp-content/uploads/2010/10/2013-01/.
39 Lisa Cowie, "Birth Parent Grief and Loss Resolution in Open Adoption," MSW thesis, University of British Columbia, 2011, 69.
40 House, "The Changing Face of Adoption," 348.
41 Cowie, "Birth Parent Grief and Loss Resolution in Open Adoption," 34 and 61.
42 Melosh, *Strangers and Kin*, 289.
43 Harriet Gross, "Open Adoption: A Research-Based Literature Review and New Data," *Child Welfare* 72 (3) (1993): 274.
44 Deborah Siegel, "Open Adoption of Infants: Adoptive Parents' Perceptions of Advantages and Disadvantages," *Social Work* 38 (1) (1993): 17 and 18.
45 Ellen Waldman, "What Do We Tell the Children?" *Capital University Law Review* 35 (2006): 526.
46 Marianne Berry, "Risks and Benefits of Open Adoption," *The Future of Children* 3 (1) (1993): 133.
47 These agencies are: Adoption Agency and Counselling Services (http://www.adoptionchoices.ca); Adoption Resource and Counselling Services (http://www.openadoption.ca); Beginnings Counselling and Adop-

tion Services in Ontario (http://www.beginnings.ca); Children's Bridge (http://www.childrensbridge.com); Children's Resource and Consultation Centre (http://www.211toronto.ca); and Jewels for Jesus (http://www.jfjhopecentre.com). This list does not include individuals who are licensed to undertake home studies and oversee adoption placements and post-adoption support services but who do not offer matching services. Nor does the list include agencies offering international adoption services, since this will be covered in a later chapter.

48 http://www.jfjhopecentre.com.
49 http://www.childrensbridge.com.
50 *New Brunswick (Minister of Health and Community Services) v. L.(M.)*, at para. 17.

7 Step-Parent Adoption

1 Adoption Act, R.S.O. 1950, c.7, s.7; Child Welfare Act, 1954, which included s.72(2), repealed the Adoption Act. The relevant section was replaced by s.64(5) of 1958, c.11, s.3. Section 64(5) is now R.S.O. 1970, c.64, s.73(5); Child Welfare Act, S.O. 1978, c.85, sub.69(15); Child Welfare Act, R.S.O. 1980, c.66, sub.69(7).
2 Alastair Bissett-Johnson, "Adoption within the Family," in Paul Sachdev, ed., *Adoption: Current Issues and Trends* (Toronto: Butterworths 1983), 217.
3 In Nova Scotia, for example, in 1977–8, half of the adoptions processed were to relatives; from 1970 to 1974 in British Columbia, 34 per cent were to step-parents (both post-divorce and unwed mothers who later married someone not named as the biological father of the child). See Wilfred Oppel, "Step-Parent Adoptions in Nova Scotia and British Columbia," *Dalhousie Law Journal* 6 (3) (1981): 633.
4 Paula Barran Weiss, "The Misuse of Adoption by the Custodial Parent and Spouse," *Canadian Journal of Family Law* 2 (1979): 156.
5 Divorce Act, R.S.C. 1985, c.3 (2nd suppl.), s.2.2. The Ontario Family Law Act of 1986 defines a parent as "a person who has demonstrated a settled intention to treat a child as a child of his or her family": Family Law Act, R.S.O. 1990, c. F.3, s.1.
6 *Chartier v. Chartier* [1998] S.C.J. No. 79.
7 Family Law Act, c.3, s.1. This section defines as a potentially legally cognizable parent anyone who "has demonstrated a settled intention to treat a child as a child of his or her family." It should be noted that Canada goes much further than other nations in recognizing social parenthood in the step-parent and other contexts, including in the context of same-sex

parentage. In particular, the various states in the United States retain a strong emphasis on the biological bases of parenthood: June Carbon, "The Legal Definition of Parenthood: The Uncertainty at the Core of Family Identity," *Louisiana State Law Review* 65 (4) (2005): 1295–344.

8 Nicholas Bala and Meaghan Thomas, "Who Is a 'Parent'? Standing in the Place of a Parent and Canada's *Child Support Guidelines s.5*," *Queen's Faculty of Law, Legal Studies Research Paper Series*, no. 07–11 (12 July 2007), http://www.ssrn.com/abstract=1023895; Brenda Cossman, "Parenting beyond the Nuclear Family: Doe v. Alberta," *Alberta Law Review* 45 (2) (2007): 501; Marie Gordon, "Third-Party Child Support: A Post-Chartier Review," *Canadian Journal of Family Law* 18 (2001): 327; Fiona Kelly, "Producing Paternity: The Role of Legal Fatherhood in Maintaining the Traditional Family," *Canadian Journal of Women and the Law* 21 (2) (2009): 328; Carol Rogerson, "The Child Support Obligation of Step-Parents," *Canadian Journal of Family Law* 18 (1) (2001): 1; Wanda Wiegers, "Fatherhood and Misattributed Genetic Paternity in Family Law," *Queen's Law Journal* 36 (2011): 623; Alison Harvison Young, "The Child Does Have 2 (or More) Fathers ... Stepparents and Support Obligations," *McGill Law Journal* 45 (1) (2000): 107.

9 For example, in her excellent social history of adoption in English Canada, Veronica Strong-Boag, while acknowledging the importance of step-parent adoption, devotes a scant two paragraphs to its history: Strong-Boag, *Finding Families, Finding Ourselves*, 44.

10 *Re L. et al. and C.* [1972] O.J. No. 1760 (C.A.).

11 *W.A. et al. v. W.B.* (1982) 4 O.R. (2d) (Prov. Ct.), 716.

12 *Re Kennette and Munro* [1973] 3 O.R. (Co. Ct.), 156 at 161, 163, and 166.

13 *P.C.S. v. D.B.H.* [1974] O.J. No. 1291 (Co. Ct.); confirmed on appeal: [1975] O.J. No. 305 (C.A.).

14 *Re McWhannel et al. and Kerr* [1974] B.C.J. No. 190 (S.C.), at para. 11.

15 *North v. North* [1978] B.C.J. No. 50 (S.C.), at para. 12.

16 *J.H.S. v. G.R.S.* [1979] M.J. No. 395 (Co. Ct.), at para. 17.

17 *A.E.C. (Re)* [1975] N.S.J. No. 23 (Co. Ct.), at para. 7.

18 Catherine Williams, "Step-Parent Adoptions and the Best Interests of the Child in Ontario," *University of Toronto Law Journal* 32 (2) (1982): 226.

19 S.M. 1979, c.22, s.70, assented to on 15 June 1979. The new section 100(6), (7), and (8) read as follows: "Where the marriage entered into by 2 persons is dissolved by a decree absolute granted by a court of competent jurisdiction in Canada and the court grants custody of their children to the wife who remarries, if the wife and her husband apply for and obtain an order of adoption of those children, the former husband may apply to a judge of

the County Court for an order granting him the right to visit those children."
20 S.N.B. 1980, c. C-2.1, s.8(2), which reads as follows: "Except where a person adopts a child of his spouse, an adoption order, from the date it is made, (a) severs the tie the child had with his natural parent or guardian or any other person in whose custody the child has been, by divesting the parent, guardian or other person of all parental rights in respect of the child, including any right of access that is not preserved by the court, and freeing that person from all parental responsibilities for the support of the child; (b) frees the child from all obligations, including support, with respect to his natural parent or any other person in whose custody he has been; and (c) unless specifically preserved by the order in accordance with the express wishes of the natural parent, severs the right of the child to inherit from his natural parent or kindred."
21 B. (Re) [1981] O.J. No. 1989 (Prov. Ct. Fam. Div.), at para. 7.
22 M.W. v. T.C. [1981] O.J. No. 1057 (Prov. Ct. Fam. Div.), at paras. 30 and 33.
23 W. et al. v. C. (1982) 35 O.R. (2d) (Prov. Ct. Fam. Div.), 730.
24 W.A. et al. v. W.B. (1982) 34 O.R. (2d) (Prov. Ct. Fam. Div.), 716.
25 H.R.E.R. v. M.A.P. [1983] O.J. No. 776 (Prov. Ct. Fam. Div.), at paras. 12, 24, and 25.
26 C.S.B. v. G.R.B. [1980] O.J. No. 1798 (Prov. Ct. Fam. Div.), at para 10.
27 M. v. B. [1984] O.J. No. 899 (Co. Ct.), at paras. 15 and 18.
28 Re L. and L. (1985) 51 O.R. (2d) (U.F.C.), 345 at 359.
29 P. (R.C.) v. M. (S.A.) [1986] O.J. No. 1730 (Prov. Ct. Fam. Div.).
30 Lawrence Ganong et al., "Issues Considered in Contemplating Stepchild Adoption," *Family Relations* 47 (1998): 64, 66, and 69.
31 Rogerson, "The Child Support Obligation of Step-Parents," para. 29.
32 The Divorce Act, 1985, for example, defines as a child of the marriage "a) any child for whom two spouses or former spouses both stand in the place of a parent; and b) any child of whom one is the parent and for whom the other stands in the place of a parent": Divorce Act, R.S.C. 1985, c.3 (2nd suppl.), s.2.2. The Ontario Family Law Act of 1986 defines a parent as "a person who has demonstrated a settled intention to treat a child as a child of his or her family": Family Law Act, R.S.O. 1990, c. F.3, s.1. It should be noted that British Columbia has been more explicit in defining who is, and is not, considered to be *in loco parentis*. Any person who has contributed to the support of a child for a year, or who has been in a marital or quasi-marital relationship with the parent of the child for two years (same-sex or opposite sex), will be considered to be a parent liable for child support: Family Relations Act, R.S.B.C. 1996, c.128, s.1(1) and 1(2); this means that

the threshold is significantly lower in British Columbia since, in cases with fact situations covered under the statute, no threshold inquiry is necessary.
33 Federal Child Support Guidelines, 1997 SOR/97–175.
34 Rogerson, "The Child Support Obligations of Step-Parents," para. 29.
35 *Carignan v. Carignan* [1989] M.J. No. 557 (C.A.), 557.
36 It should be noted that, despite the fact that this case was heard after the promulgation of the Federal Child Support Guidelines, it did not depend upon them since it originated before their passage.
37 *Chartier v. Chartier*, at paras. 2 and 3.
38 Bala and Thomas, "Who Is a 'Parent?'" 26.
39 *Chartier*, at paras. 4, 5, 11, and 17. The court cited, in particular, *Theriault v. Theriault* [1994] A.J. No. 187 (C.A.), in which it was found that once a step-parent "has made at least a permanent or indefinite unconditional commitment to stand in the place of a parent, the jurisdiction of the courts to award support under the *Divorce Act* is triggered and that jurisdiction is not lost by a subsequent disavowal of the child by the parent": at para. 213.
40 *Chartier*, at para. 37.
41 Young, "The Child Does Have 2 (or More) Fathers," 127 and 121.
42 Rogerson, "The Child Support Obligations of Step-Parents," paras. 87–8. Similarly, she notes that a poor relationship between the step-parent and child, the fact that a child is older, the presence of an involved biological parent, and/or the fact that the step-parent is female can make the finding that a person stands *in loco parentis* less likely: ibid., para. 90. This list was officially endorsed by the Ontario Superior Court of Justice in 2009: *Proulx v. Proulx* [2009] O.J. No. 1680 (Sup. Ct. J.), at para. 27.
43 Bala and Thomas, "Who Is a 'Parent?'" 61.
44 Gordon, "Third-Party Child Support," paras. 94 and 92.
45 Rogerson, "The Child Support Obligation of Step-Parents," para. 59.
46 It should also be noted that calculating the threshold for recognition of the *in loco parentis* status of a step-parent is only the first part of the determination of child support. Once a person has been determined to be *in loco parentis*, the decision with regard to quantum must be made and the Guidelines do not apply. This has led to decisions that are "extremely unpredictable": Brian Burke and Stephanie Chipeur, "The More the Merrier? Multiple Parents and Child Support," *Canadian Family Law Quarterly* 29 (2) (2010): 185 at 193.
47 Wiegers, "Fatherhood and Misattributed Genetic Paternity in Family Law," para. 28.
48 Bala and Thomas, "Who Is a 'Parent'"? 49.

8 Same-Sex Parents, Assisted Reproduction, and Adoption

1 While Karen Dubinsky makes brief reference to the propensity of lesbian families to seek children internationally, she does not deal with domestic same-sex adoption (reasonably so, given the subject of her work). Strong-Boag's failure to engage with this subject is more surprising given her wider arguments about the changing face of adoption. She discusses only the increasing ability of same-sex parents to adopt from the CAS: Dubinsky, *Babies without Borders*; Strong-Boag, *Finding Families, Finding Ourselves*, 67 and 96. For discussion of assisted reproductive technologies and their impact on legal parenthood, see Susan Boyd, "Gendering Legal Parenthood: Bio-Genetic Ties, Intentionality and Responsibility," *Windsor Yearbook of Access to Justice* 25 (2007): 63; Angela Cameron, "Regulating the Queer Family: *The Assisted Human Reproduction Act*," *Canadian Journal of Family Law* 24 (2008): 10; Fiona Kelly, "(Re)forming Parenthood: The Assignment of Legal Parentage within Planned Lesbian Families," *Ottawa Law Review* 40 (2008–9): 185; Fiona Kelly, "Equal Parents, Equal Children," *University of New Brunswick Law Journal* 64 (2013): 253; Kelly, "Producing Paternity," 320; and Fiona Kelly, *Transforming Law's Family: The Legal Recognition of Planned Lesbian Motherhood* (Vancouver: University of British Columbia Press 2011).
2 Civil Marriage Act, S.C. 2005, c.33.
3 It should be noted that the litigation with regard to second-parent adoption and the rights of same-sex parents overwhelmingly involves lesbian families. "The prominence of lesbian couples – and the corresponding under-representation of gay male couples – in the case law on same-sex adoption are partially rooted in human biology and biotechnology": Malcolm Dort, "Unheard Voices: Adoption Narratives of Same-Sex Male Couples," *Canadian Journal of Family Law* 26 (2010): 289 at para. 11.
4 *K (Re)* [1995] O.J. No. 1425 (Prov. Ct.).
5 *M.D.R. v. Ontario (Deputy Registrar General)* [2006] O.J. No. 2268 (Sup. Ct. J.).
6 Boyd, "Gendering Legal Parenthood," 63.
7 Kelly, "(Re)forming Parenthood," 185 at para. 11.
8 Family Law Act, S.B.C. 2011, c.25, Part III, in force 18 March 2013. This act was based upon a new uniform parentage act developed by the Uniform Law Conference of Canada (ULCC): http://www.ulcc.ca/en/2009-ottawa-on/192-civil-section-documents/396-assisted-human-reproduction-working-group-report-2009?start=12 and http://www.ulcc.ca/images/stories/2010_pdf?en/2010ulcc0021.pdf. The Law Commission

of Manitoba has also recently completed a report on this issue: http://www.digitalcollection.gov.mb.ca/pdfopener?smd=1&did=23464&md=1. See in particular the arguments of Kelly in "(Re)forming Parenthood," "Equal Parents, Equal Children," "Producing Paternity," 320, and *Transforming Law's Family*.

9 *K (Re)*, 679.
10 Here he was referring to Parts III and VII of the Child and Family Services Act and the Family Law Act, R.S.O. 1990, c. F.3, s.1(1).
11 *K (Re)*, 679.
12 Ibid., at 688, 703, 701, 710, 707, 708, and 718.
13 *Re S.C.M.* [2001] N.S.J. No. 261 (S.C. Fam. Div.); Adoption Act, S.M. 1997, c.47, C.C.S.M. c. A2, s.10 (Manitoba); Adoption Act, S.N.L. 1999, c. A-2.1, s.20 (Newfoundland and Labrador); Adoption Act, S.S. 1998, c. A-5.2, s.23 (Saskatchewan); Adoption Act, R.S.B.C. 1996, c.5, ss.5, 29 (British Columbia); Adoption Act, S.N.W.T. 1998, c.9, s.5 (Northwest Territories); and art. 555 C.C.Q. (Quebec).
14 Kelly, "(Re)forming Parenthood," 185 at para. 6.
15 Charles Neville, "Is It Adultery?" *Maclean's* 62 (4) (1949): 9, 43, and 44.
16 Legal parentage is not required to reflect biology. Effectively, if the mother is not married to a third party, any man she chooses can sign a statement of live birth and therefore become the presumptive parent of a child by recognizing paternity. Fathers are further protected, even when mothers wish to exclude them from the lives of children, by presumptions of paternity that apply to all men in extended relationships with birth mothers. In Ontario a father is clearly defined under the Children's Law Reform Act, s.8(1). See chapter on fathers.
17 In so doing, they based much of their argument upon the proceedings in *Gill and Murray*, a British Columbia human-rights complaint filed by two lesbian couples after the Vital Statistics Department in that province refused to register the co-mothers as parents. Testimony revealed that only same-sex couples were questioned about their biological connection to children, despite the known use of sperm donation in heterosexual relationships. The government's claim that the intent of the registration system was to record biological or genetic facts was thus effectively challenged. The Human Rights Tribunal found that the purpose of registration was "to ensure that live births are recorded accurately and promptly" and the province was required to amend its vital-statistics legislation: *Gill and Murray* [2001] British Columbia Human Rights Tribunal 34.
18 *M.D.R. v. Ontario (Deputy Registrar General)*, at paras. 9, 14, 38, and 85. It is ironic that, in making the argument that they were discriminated against,

they depended heavily upon the Supreme Court of Canada's decision in *Trociuk* in which the right of an uninvolved biological father to register his children was upheld. This decision, discussed in chapter 3, has been widely criticized as inimical to women's autonomy rights: Chambers, "In the Name of the Father"; and Lessard, "Mothers, Fathers and Naming."

19 *M.D.R. v. Ontario (Deputy Registrar General)*, at paras. 104, 51, 52, 143, 106, 272, 261, and 267. He did not, however, rule with regard to the claim that their s.7 rights had been violated, asserting that there was potential for such an argument but that the applicants had "not adequately pleaded" for him to make a determination.

20 Ontario Regulation 401/06, ss.1, 2, 3 of Reg. 109, Vital Statistics Act, amending Reg. 1094 of R.R.O., 1990, *Ontario Gazette*, 9 September 2006.

21 Kelly, "(Re)forming Parenthood," 185 at para. 10.

22 Not surprisingly, this period of legal limbo also creates potential problems for the social mother, who can be excluded by the birth mother if she changes her own mind about adoption during this period, whatever relationship is developing between the child and the social parent. For an example of a case in which such concerns arose, see *K.G.T. v. P.D.* [2005] B.C.J. No. 2935 (S.C.). "The case raises the broad question of what is a parent and who should be entitled to parental rights, and the nature of those rights. In particular, it raises the issue if those rights include a right to become an adoptive parent of a child against the wishes of the birth parent with whom the child primarily resides." The court found that it "is fundamental to the scheme that the birth parent either consents to the adoption or the court dispenses with that consent" (69). Nonetheless, the court affirmed the social mother's right to ongoing access.

23 Kelly, *Transforming Law's Family*, 36.

24 For further information, see Family Law Act, S.A. 2003, c. F-4.5, s.51(1)(a); Family Law Act, S.B.C. 2011, c.25, s.30; Vital Statistics Act, C.C.S.M. v.60, s.3(6); Civil Code of Quebec, S.Q. 1992, c.64, arts. 538–42; and Child Status Act, R.S.P.E.I. c. C-6, ss.9(5) and 9(6).

25 It should be noted that British Columbia provides for the possibility that a child may have more than two parents: Family Law Act, S.B.C. 2011, c.25, s.30. In order to avoid the possibility that this will invite interference in the families of lesbian couples, parties who wish to have a third parent recognized must enter into a written agreement to that effect before the birth of the child.

26 *M.A.C. et al. v. M.K.* (2009) 94 O.R. (3d) (Ct. J.), 756 at paras. 1, 2, 4, 6, and 16.

27 Ibid., at paras. 25, 29, 33, 35, 64, 73, 74, 45, and 69.

28 *Ss.M. (Re)* [2007] O.J. No. 4290 (Ct.J.), at paras. 4, 9, 42, and 41.
29 *A.A. v. B.B.* [2003] O.J. No. 1215 (Sup. Ct. J. Fam. Div.), at paras. 1, 8, 13, 14, and 41.
30 *A.A. v. B.B. et al.*, 83 O.R. (3d) (C.A.), 561 at paras. 1, 21, 27, 34, and 38.
31 Donna Bouchard, "The Three-Parent Decision: A Case Commentary on A.A. v. B.B.," *Saskatchewan Law Review* 70 (2007): 459–78 at para. 21.
32 Cameron, "Regulating the Queer Family," para. 29.
33 Assisted Human Reproduction Act, S.C. 2004, c.2. While other aspects of the legislation were deemed to be ultra vires under a challenge from Quebec, regulation of payment was considered to be legitimately within the criminal law: Assisted Human Reproduction Act [2010] 3 S.C.R. 457.
34 *Rypkema v. British Columbia* [2003] B.C.J. No. 2721 (S.C.), at para. 31.
35 *K.G.D. v. C.A.P.* [2004] O.J. No. 3508 (Sup. Ct. J.), at para. 16.
36 *J.R. v. L.H.* [2002] O.J. No. 3998 (Sup. Ct. J.), at para. 29.
37 Family Law Act, c.25, s.30.

9 Indigenous Children and Adoption

1 Hadley Friedland, "Tragic Choices and the Division of Sorrow: Speaking about Race, Culture and Community Traumatization in the Lives of Children," *Canadian Journal of Family Law* 25 (2009): 223 at para. 1.
2 Customary (or custom) adoption, however, was common in many Indigenous, particularly Inuit, communities. This was a variable practice by which children were transferred from birth parents to the care and custody of other adults for a variety of reasons, but in which the children were always aware of their adopted status and often knew their birth relatives: Cindy Baldassi, "The Legal Status of Aboriginal Customary Adoption across Canada: Comparisons, Contrasts, and Convergences," *University of British Columbia Law Review* 39 (2006): 63–100 at para. 13. By the 1960s, legal decisions in some jurisdictions recognized customary adoptions; for the first such case, see *Re Adoption of Katie 7–1807* [1961] N.W.T.J. No. 2. In the Northwest Territories and Nunavit, Aboriginal customary adoption has been given statutory recognition: Aboriginal Custom Adoption Recognition Act, S.N.W.T. 1994, c.26, as duplicated for Nunavut by s.29 of the Nunavut Act, S.C. 1993, c.28. In British Columbia, the Adoption Act 1996, c.5, s.46(1) allows judges the discretion to recognize customary adoptions. A decision of the British Columbia Court of Appeal suggests that customary adoption may be an Aboriginal right protected under s.35, and the same result could prevail in Ontario in the case of a legal challenge: see *Casimel v. Insurance Corp. of British Columbia* [1994] B.C.C.A. It

is interesting to note that "Nunavut, the Canadian jurisdiction with the highest incidence of customary adoption, engineered public consultations on possible increased regulation of the extremely common practice." Baldassi, "The Legal Status of Aboriginal Customary Adoption," 64. See also Denise Rideout, "Commission Considers Rules for Custom Adoptions: Nunavummiut Seek Balance between Legal Regulations and Longstanding Tradition," *Nunatsiaq News*, 8 December 2000, http://www.nunatsiaq.com/archives/nunavut001231/nvt21208_11.html.

3 Marlee Kline, "Child Welfare Law: Best Interests of the Child Ideology and First Nations," *Osgoode Hall Law Journal* 30 (2) (1992): 381 and 387.
4 Saskatchewan, Department of Welfare, Child Welfare Branch, *Annual Report* (1964–5), 17.
5 Raven Sinclair, "Identity Lost and Found," *First Peoples Child and Family Review* 3 (1) (2007): 66.
6 I use the term "settler law" since this legal system has been imposed on First Nations, Inuit, and Metis communities without their consent.
7 An Act respecting the Protection and Well-Being of Children and Their Families, Part VII, Adoption, S.O. 1984, 704.
8 Assembly of First Nations, *Kiskisik Awasisak: Remember the Children*, http://www.cwrp.ca/, x.
9 Friedland, "Tragic Choices and the Division of Sorrow," para. 19.
10 And status itself is a fraught and contested issue. Under the Indian Act, women who married out, and their children, lost status. Even recent reforms only delay such results for a further generation. For a trenchant critique of the Indian Act and revisions to it, see Martin Cannon, "Race Matters: Sexism, Indigenous Sovereignty and *McIvor*," *Canadian Journal of Women and the Law* 26 (1) (2014): 23–50.
11 Sinclair, "Identity Lost and Found," 68.
12 *Brown v. Attorney General (Canada)* [2010] (S.C.) 102 O.R. (3rd) 493.
13 Constitution Act, 1867 (UK), 30 and 31 Vict., c.3, reprinted in R.S.C. 1985, app. II, no. 5.
14 Underlying the "Indian Problem," as described by MP Duncan Campbell Scott, was the idea that "our object is to continue until there is not a single Indian in Canada that has not been absorbed into the body politic and there is no Indian question, and no Indian Department, that is the whole object of this Bill": as quoted in John Leslie and Ron Maguire, *The Historical Development of the Indian Act* (Ottawa: Department of Indian Affairs and Northern Development, Treaties and Historical Research Centre, 1978), 114. A primary purpose of the Indian Act was not only to identify who was and who was not "Indian" but also to promote enfranchisement, de-

fined as absorption into the "normative" body politic; the colonial agenda "purported to force an Aboriginal person to exit the legal classification of an 'Indian' and become a full citizen of Canada. Legislation in the area of enfranchisement came in 1857, under the *Gradual Civilization Act* ... Under s.3 of the Act, enfranchisement could occur if the 'Indian' was twenty-one years of age, could speak, read and write English or French, a person of 'good moral character,' and had no debts": Brian Pfefferle, "The Indefensibility of Post-Colonial Aboriginal Rights," *Saskatchewan Law Review* 70 (2007): 393 at para. 14. See also An Act to Encourage the Gradual Civilization of the Indian Tribes in This Province, and to Amend the Laws respecting Indians, S. Prov. C. 1857, 20 Vict., c.26. This act was consolidated into the 1876 Indian Act.
15 An Act to Amend the Indian Act, 1920, A10.
16 *Hansard*, no. 110 (11 June 2008), 1519 (Peter Milliken).
17 John MacDonald, "The Spallumcheen Indian Band By-Law and Its Potential Impact on Native Indian Child Welfare Policy in British Columbia," *Canadian Journal of Family Law* 4 (1983): 77.
18 Universal Declaration of Human Rights, United Nations General Assembly, Res. 217 A (III), 10 December 1948. It should be noted that, during this period, the government of Canada refused to sign the Convention on the Prevention and Punishment of Genocide precisely because it condemned residential schools as a form of genocide. Art. 2(e) forbids "forcibly transferring the children of the group to another group": Convention on the Prevention and Punishment of Genocide, United Nations General Assembly, Res. 26A (III), Art. 2(e), 9 December 1948, entered into force 12 January 1951. Canada signed a revised version which excluded this clause in 1952.
19 Strong-Boag, *Finding Families, Finding Ourselves*, 143.
20 While this move symbolically located First Nations, Inuit, and Metis as people rather than as resources to be exploited, it nonetheless considered such people as immigrants rather than as original inhabitants.
21 Indian Act, 1952, s.88.
22 Jessa Chupick-Hall, "Good Families Do Not Just Happen: Indigenous People and Child Welfare Services in Canada, 1950–1965," MA thesis, Trent University, 2001, 38.
23 H.P. Hepworth, "Trends in Provincial Social Service Expenditures, 1963–1982," in J.S. Ismael, ed., *Canadian Social Welfare Policy: Federal and Provincial Dimensions* (Montreal and Kingston: McGill-Queen's University Press 1985), 140–1. It should be noted that Indigenous people "consistently rejected the federal position that provinces had responsibility to provide child welfare services, using as evidence their treaty relationship" with

the crown as well as the latter's constitutional responsibility for "Indians and lands reserved for Indians": Allyson Stevenson, "Vibrations across a Continent: The 1978 Indian Child Welfare Act and the Politicization of First Nations Leaders in Saskatchewan," *American Indian Quarterly* 37 (1/2) (2013): 226. The Canada Assistance Plan was debated throughout 1965, became law on 15 July 1966, and was in operation for the 1967–8 fiscal year: Canada Assistance Plan, 1966–7, c.45, s.1.

24 Sinclair, "Identity Lost and Found," 67.
25 Philip Zylerberg, "Who Should Make Child Protection Decisions for the Native Community?" *Windsor Yearbook of Access to Justice* 11 (1991): 77.
26 Kline, "Child Welfare Law," 387.
27 Saskatchewan, Department of Welfare, Child Welfare Branch, *Annual Report* (1964–5), 17.
28 Hepworth, *Foster Care and Adoption*, 120.
29 Richard Lee, "The Transracial Adoption Paradox: History, Research and Counseling Implications of Cultural Socialization," *Counseling Psychologist* 31 (6) (2003): 712–13.
30 Saskatchewan, Department of Welfare, Child Welfare Branch, *Annual Report* (1964–5), 17.
31 As others have argued, "accusations of genocide and racism have come to rest on the shoulders of adoptive parents and have filled them with feelings of guilt and isolation." For those who began the process with naive, but honest, good faith, this has been extremely painful: McGillivray, "Transnational Adoption and the Status Indian Child," *Canadian Journal of Family Law* 4 (1985): 466. Some accounts of the experiences of adoptive parents have started to emerge, particularly in the Australian context. Damien Riggs is critical of such works, not for speaking to the experiences of white adoptive parents who were devastated when adoptions did not work, but for "analogizing their experiences to those of Indigenous mothers." The pain of adoption was not a shared pain and the emphasis on the experiences of white mothers erases the violence perpetuated against Indigenous mothers whose children were stolen. These voices have not been given much credence in historical or sociological discourse, or even in the rhetoric of Indigenous rights groups who have focused instead on cultural loss for children themselves and damage to communities, paying little attention to the pain experienced by individual women who lost their children. This is in sharp contrast to work on relinquishing mothers in white, middle-class communities: Damien Riggs, "White Mothers, Indigenous Families and the Politics of Voice," *Critical Race and Whiteness Studies* 4 (1) (2008).

32 Sinclair, "Identity Lost and Found," 78.
33 Emily Carasco, "Canadian Child Welfare Laws: Have Canadian Child Welfare Laws Broken the Circle?" *Canadian Journal of Family Law* 5 (1986): 4.
34 Suzanne Fournier and Ernie Crey, *Stolen from our Embrace: The Abduction of First Nations Children and the Restoration of Aboriginal Communities* (Vancouver: Douglas and McIntyre 1997), 81.
35 Ibid., 64.
36 This paragraph summarizes the provisions of the Adoption Act, c.55, ss.10(1)(a),(b),(c), and 11(2).
37 Indian Act, 1952, s.87.
38 *Natural Parents v. British Columbia (Superintendent of Child Welfare)* [1976] 2 S.C.R. 751.
39 Ibid., at 755, 756, 766, and 768. Philip Girard has argued that "in other decisions dealing with the rights of native peoples, Laskin displayed either a neutral or an overtly hostile approach to the whole system of Indian status created by the *Indian Act*": Philip Girard, *Bora Laskin: Bringing Law to Life* (Toronto: University of Toronto Press / Osgoode Society for Canadian Legal History 2005), 396.
40 Bracco, "Patriarchy and the Law of Adoption," 1041.
41 Indian and Northern Affairs Canada, *Adoption and the Indian Child* (Ottawa: Minister of Indian Affairs and Northern Development 1981).
42 McGillivray, "Transracial Adoption and the Status Indian Child," 445 and 447.
43 Ovide Mercredi is Cree and has been the chief of the Assembly of First Nations of Canada. Clem Chartier has served as president of the Metis National Council and the International Council of Indigenous Peoples.
44 Ovide Mercredi and Clem Chartier, "The Status of Child Welfare Services for the Indigenous Peoples of Canada: The Problem, the Law and the Solution," presented at the National Workshop on Indian Child Welfare Rights, March 1981, 45.
45 Patrick Johnston, *Native Children and the Child Welfare System* (Ottawa: Canadian Council on Social Development 1983), 23.
46 Sinclair, "Identity Lost and Found," 66.
47 Kathryn Irvine, "Supporting Aboriginal Parents: Teachings for the Future" (National Collaborating Centre for Aboriginal Health 2009), 25. When the experiences of adoptive parents are discussed in the Canadian media, the failure of adoptions is too often blamed on Indigenous mothers and their supposed addiction problems. For example, "Virtually every native child adopted over the past 20 years has some degree of alcohol damage. It is

that, and not the pain of alienation from white society, that accounts for their frequent estrangement from their adoptive families and their terrible problems in life": Margaret Wente, "Our Poor Ruined Babies: The Hidden Epidemic," *Globe and Mail*, 7 October 2000.
48 Patricia Monture, "A Vicious Circle: Child Welfare and First Nations," *Canadian Journal of Women and the Law* 3 (1989), 3.
49 Joan H. Hollinger, "Beyond the Best Interest of the Tribe," *University of Detroit Law Review* 60 (1988): 451 at 454. Under the act, tribal courts have control over child placement in cases of involuntary surrender and adoption by non-Indigenous people is allowed only as a last resort. It should be noted, however, that the Indian Child Welfare Act has been implemented very unevenly owing to the weakness of tribal governments (and their complete non-existence in some cases), the failure of state governments to have much sympathy with tribal governments and/or priorities, and the lack of funds to address underlying problems in communities (ibid., 472).
50 Stevenson, "Vibrations across a Continent," 219 and 222.
51 Carasco, "Canadian Native Children: Have Canadian Child Welfare Laws Broken the Circle?" 112.
52 Strong-Boag, *Finding Families, Finding Ourselves*, 164. See also Technical Assistance and Planning Associates, "*Starving Man Doesn't Argue,*" Report Prepared for Policy, Research and Evaluation Division, Department of Indian Affairs and Northern Development (1979).
53 Editorial, "Social Work on Reserve," *Ontario Association of Children's Aid Societies* 22 (February 1979): n.p.
54 Janet Budgell, *Research Project: Repatriation of Aboriginal Families – Models and a Workplan. Final Report* (Toronto: Native Child and Family Services of Toronto, March 1999), n.p. Tom's commitment to the cause led to his reputation as the "father of repatriation." He was, it should be noted, grieving his own losses, since four of his children had been apprehended by the very Children's Aid Society for which he ultimately came to work.
55 *Woods v. Racine and Racine* [1983] 2 C.N.L.R. (Man. C.A.), 157 at 187.
56 Kline, "Child Welfare Law," 402.
57 For a discussion of the homogenized Indian in law, see Marlee Kline, "The Colour of Law: Ideological Representations of First Nations in Legal Discourse," *Social and Legal Studies* 3 (1994): 451–76.
58 *Racine v. Woods* [1983] 2 S.C.R. 173 at 185. While the concerns about respect for Aboriginality might have greater weight given statutory reform since 1983, *Racine v. Woods* has yet to be overturned by the Supreme Court. See Tae Mee Park, "In the Best Interests of the Aboriginal Child," *Windsor Review of Legal and Social Issues* 16 (2003): 43.

59 *Racine v. Woods*, 189 and 190. At the trial of first instance, not only was the ability of the birth mother to maintain her sobriety questioned, but also she was accused of "using the adoption battle as a political issue." Marlee Kline asserted that this case reveals a fear of a successful, activist First Nations woman "who acknowledged, confronted and attempted to resist what she perceived as harsh treatment of herself and her people by the child welfare system": Kline, "Child Welfare Law," 409.
60 *Racine v. Woods*, 191 and 190.
61 *L.M.C. v. Catholic Children's Aid Society of Metropolitan Toronto* [1984] O.J. No. 2503 (Prov. Ct. Fam. Div.), at paras. 4, 7, 8, 10, 12, 16, 17, 23, 26, and 35.
62 These concerns helped to prompt the investigation of adoption-disclosure laws undertaken by Ralph Garber for the Ontario government: Ralph Garber, *Disclosure of Adoption Information* (Report of the Special Commissioner to the Honourable John Sweeney, Minister of Community and Social Services, Government of Ontario, November 1985). For a discussion of these hearings with regard to non-Indigenous adoption and disclosure, see the previous chapter on secrecy. These events are also described by Strong-Boag in *Finding Families, Finding Ourselves*, 164.
63 An Act respecting the Protection and Well-Being of Children and Their Families, Part VII, Adoption, S.O. 1984, 704.
64 Ashley Smith, "Aboriginal Adoptions in Saskatchewan and British Columbia," *Canadian Journal of Family Law* 25 (2009): para. 23.
65 Jocelyn Downie, "A Choice for K'aila: Child Protection and First Nations Children," *Health Law Journal* 2 (1994): 99–120 at para. 40.
66 *Children's Aid Society of Owen Sound and County of Grey v. M.B.* [1985] O.J. No. 737 (Prov. Ct. Fam. Div.), at paras. 9, 12, 20, 21, and 22.
67 *C.J.K. v. Children's Aid Society of Metropolitan Toronto* [1989] 4 C.N.L.R. (Ont. Prov. Ct. Fam. Div.), 75 at 82.
68 For information on the challenges faced by urban First Nations people, see Bonita Lawrence, *"Real" Indians and Others: Mixed-Blood Urban Native Peoples and Indigenous Nationhood* (Lincoln: University of Nebraska Press 2004).
69 *C.J.K. v. Children's Aid Society of Metropolitan Toronto*, 81.
70 *Aboriginal Child and Family Services v. E.G.D* [2004] 1 C.N.L.R. 1 (Ont. Ct. J.), at paras. 16, 23, 25, and 18.
71 *Algonquins of Pikwakanagan First Nation v. Children's Aid Society of Toronto* [2004] 3 C.N.L.R. 1 (Ont. Sup. Ct. J.), at para. 1. It should be noted that a Saskatchewan court had recently considered a similar claim and rejected a band's refusal to authorize adoptions by non-First Nations foster parents. At the heart of the Saskatchewan case were five First Nations siblings

who were in protective care and were going to continue without permanent homes. Although the court acknowledged that "the policy reflected a desire to keep First Nations children in their communities in response to historical injustices suffered by Aboriginal people at the hands of the child welfare system," it was nevertheless critical of the policy's practical effect, asserting that the band policy was unconstitutional: "There was no evidence that the policy itself was an 'aboriginal right' and it was found to be in breach of the children's equality rights under section 15(1) of the *Charter*, and not prescribed by law within the meaning of section 1. A violation of the children's section 7 rights to security of the person was also found since the children were kept in continued foster care without a permanent home, due to the policy": *R.T. (Re)* as quoted in Smith, "Aboriginal Adoptions in Saskatchewan and British Columbia," paras. 35 and 36. Further, the question of what constitutes an "aboriginal right" worthy of constitutional protection has been the subject of extensive litigation and jurisprudence: Russel Lawrence Barsh and James Youngblood Henderson, "The Supreme Court's Van der Peet Trilogy: Naïve Imperialism and Ropes of Sand," *McGill Law Journal* 42 (1997): 993; Gordon Christie, "Aboriginal Rights, Aboriginal Culture and Protection," *Osgoode Hall Law Journal* 36 (1998): 447–84; Robert Groves and Bradford Morse, "Constituting Aboriginal Collectivities: Avoiding New Peoples 'In Between,'" *Saskatchewan Law Review* 67 (2004): 257–99; Constance MacIntosh, "From Judging Culture to Taxing 'Indians': Tracing the Legal Discourse of the 'Indian Mode of Life,'" *Osgoode Hall Law Journal* 47 (3) (2009): 401; Ronald Niezen, "Culture and the Judiciary: The Meaning of the Culture Concept as a Source of Aboriginal Rights in Canada," *Canadian Journal of Law and Society* 18 (2) (2003): 1; and D'Arcy Vermette, "Colonialism and the Process of Defining Aboriginal People," *Dalhousie Law Journal* 31 (spring 2008): 211.
72 *Algonquins of Pikwakanagan First Nation*, at paras. 40, 1, 4–6, 15, 42, 44, and 57.
73 Emily Grier, "Aboriginal Children in Limbo," *Saskatchewan Law Review* 68 (2005): 435 at para. 34.
74 Garber, *Disclosure of Adoption Information*, 59.
75 Dubinsky, *Babies without Borders*, 87; Strong-Boag, *Finding Families, Finding Ourselves*, 236.
76 A tragic case from Manitoba illustrates why such compromises remain necessary. In this case, a child, born in 1972, was placed in foster care initially because she required medical care that was not available on her reserve. She lived with the family for thirteen years, but was then removed from her home, against her will, by Awasis, a First Nations child-welfare

agency, and returned to her home reserve. She did not speak the local Dene language and her parents did not speak English. She was treated as an outcast in the community. She was sexually assaulted by a number of the male residents of the reserve and contracted venereal disease. Her foster parents attempted to remove her from the community but were prevented from doing so by the band. She was eventually removed by a doctor, and the foster parents sought, and obtained, a court order that she not be returned. However, she was seriously depressed, resulting in hospitalization: *Doe v. The Awasis Agency of Northern Manitoba* [1990] 4 C.N.L.R. (Man. Q.B.), 10. Her foster parents sought an order that the records of the case be closed, but this was denied: "Anything that the courts can do to protect her from further humiliation should be done in her interest. I would not want, in any way, to see her publicly identified through these proceedings. That can be accomplished by referring to her as Jane Doe, and by removing from the pocket and sealing or expunging only those documents or portions of documents which might tend to identify her": *Doe v. The Awasis Agency of Northern Manitoba*. To avoid the requirement that Jane Doe continue to relive her assaults during litigation, the foster parents settled with the government for $75,000 to assist with counselling costs rather than pursuing civil action. For an extended discussion of this case, see Christine Davies, "Native Children and the Child Welfare System in Canada," *Alberta Law Review* 30 (1992): 120.

77 Vic Satzewich and Terry Witherspoon, *First Nation: Race, Class and Gender Relations* (Saskatoon: Canadian Plains Research Center 2000), 93.

78 Val Napoleon, "Aboriginal Feminism in a Wider Frame," *Canadian Dimension* 41 (3) (2007): 44. In her recent and extended critique of self-determination arguments in the Aboriginal community, Brenda Gunn asserts that women's interests have too often been ignored by male leaders and that "incorporating Indigenous women's issues into self-determination requires addressing violence against women, women's educational attainment, and access to economic and employment opportunities": Brenda Gunn, "Self-Determination and Indigenous Women: Increasing Legitimacy through Inclusion," *Canadian Journal of Women and the Law* 26 (2) (2014): 271.

79 Hollinger, "Beyond the Best Interest of the Tribe," 501.

80 For a particularly disturbing example of the vulnerability of an Indigenous mother who was threatened not only with the apprehension of her child but also with involuntary drug treatment in order to protect her child, see *Winnipeg Child and Family Services v. D.F.G.* [1996] M.J. No. 398. For an analysis of the problems in this decision, including blatant racism, see

Vera J. Roy, "The Erasure of Ms. G," *Canadian Journal of Law and Society* 20 (1) (2005): 107–38.
81 Sinha and Kozlowski, "The Structure of Aboriginal Child Welfare in Canada," 2.
82 Irvine, "Supporting Aboriginal Parents," 12.
83 Assembly of First Nations, *Kiskisik Awasisak*, 5.
84 The federal government has spent millions of dollars trying to avoid this hearing since proceedings were launched in 2007. Nonetheless, the Human Rights Commission began hearing evidence on 25 February 2013. See First Nations Caring Society, http://www.fncaringsociety.ca/I-am-witness. Initially the case was dismissed by the Human Rights Tribunal on the grounds that there was no comparator group "as the government of Canada does not provide welfare funding for any other children." The Federal Court set aside this decision as "substantively unreasonable." The federal government again attempted to halt proceedings through an appearance at the Federal Court of Appeal on 6 March 2013, but the right of the appellants to proceed was confirmed. The decision dismissing the appeal was released on 11 March 2013: http://www.fncaringsociety.com/sites/default/files/Federal%20Court%20of%20Appeal/. According to the *Globe and Mail*, as of 1 October 2012, the federal government had spent more than $3 million in its "unsuccessful attempts to keep a high-stakes battle over first nations child welfare out of the courts": Heather Scoffield, "Ottawa Spends $3 Million to Battle First Nations Child Welfare Case," *Globe and Mail*, 1 October 2012, http://www.theglobeandmail.com/news/national/ottawa-spends-3-million-to-battle-first-nations-child-welfare-case/. The evidence amassed by the litigants includes reports from the auditor general in 2008 and 2011, from the Standing Committee on Public Accounts in 2009 and 2012, and from the United Nations Committee on the Rights of the Child. The litigants sought equitable funding for child welfare and a trust fund of $112 million to assist the children and families who have already been harmed by government negligence: Andy Cosby, "Human Rights Tribunal Hears Indigenous Child Welfare Case to the Ire of Harper Government," *The Leveller*, 12 March 2013, http://www.leveller.ca/2013/03/human-rights-tribunal-hears-child-welfare-case-to-the-ire-of-Harper-government/. On 26 January 2016 the Canadian Human Rights Tribunal handed down a landmark decision accepting the arguments of the FNCFCS and acknowledging that funding for Indigenous children on reserve has been inadequate for decades and must immediately be increased to that which other children in Canada take for granted: *First Nations Child and Family Caring Society of Canada et al. v. Attorney General of*

Canada (for the Minister of Indian and Northern Affairs Canada), 2016, CHRT 2, T1340/7008.
85 *Brown v. Attorney General (Canada)*, at paras. 2, 3, and 48; *First Nations Child and Family Caring Society of Canada v. Attorney General of Canada (for the Minister of Indian and Northern Affairs Canada)*, 26 January 2016, CHRT 2, T1340/7008.
86 Ibid., at paras. 49–51.
87 Strong-Boag, *Finding Families, Finding Ourselves*, 237. See also Aboriginal Healing and Wellness Strategy Research Project, "Repatriation of Aboriginal Families – Issues, Models and a Workplan," *Final Report*, prepared by Native Child and Family Services of Toronto, Stevenato and Associates, Janet Budgell (n.p., March 1999), 76.
88 *Brown v. Attorney General (Canada)*, at paras. 82 and 155–67.
89 The practical effect of making the case a test case, instead of a class-action suit, would be to limit its impact and to require all other potential litigants to sue independently. With a class-action suit, hearings are much shorter and individual evidence is taken in a context in which, if the class action has been successful, the merits of the wider issue do not have to be reproven in each case by individual litigants, who instead only have to prove that they are members of the affected class.
90 *Brown v. Attorney General (Canada)*, at paras. 184 and 9. Under this act, the court shall certify a class-action suit only if: "(a) the pleadings disclose a cause of action; (b) there is an identifiable class; (c) the claims of the class members raise common issues of fact or law; (d) a class proceeding would be the preferable procedure; and (e) there is a representative plaintiff who would adequately represent the interests of the class without conflict of interest and who has produced a workable litigation plan": at para. 71.
91 Ibid., at paras. 120–49 and 150–4. It is noteworthy that, in reframing the pleadings, Justice Perell rejected as uncertifiable the claim that the crown had breached its honour (paras. 84–7); the claim that the federal government had endorsed cultural genocide (paras. 88–107); the claim that the crown had violated the Aboriginal rights of the complainants (paras. 108–19); and the claim that the government had failed in its fiduciary duty with regard to spending power. He found nonetheless that a failure of protection might be actionable (paras. 120–49); similarly, the claim that the federal government was negligent was not rejected but was deemed to be inadequately evidenced and pleaded (paras. 150–4).
92 http://www.kleinlyons.com/class/aboriginal-sixties-scoop/; http://www.ammsa.com/publications/saskatchewan-sage/class-action-lawsuit/; Linda Diebel, "Legal Setback for Ontario Aboriginals Taken

from Their Families during the 'Sixties Scoop,'" *Toronto Star*, 25 January 2012, http://www.thestar.com/news/canada/2012/01/25/legal_setback_for_ontario_aboriginals/.

93 http://www.thestar.com/news/canada/2012/01/25/legal_setback_for_ontario_aboriginals/.
94 http://www.sixtiesscoopclaim.com/2013/02/07/update-on-the-decision-from-the-court-of-appeal/.
95 *Brown v. Canada (Attorney General)* [2013] O.J. No. 4381 (Sup. Ct. J.).
96 *Brown v. Canada (Attorney General)* [2014] O.J. No. 1128 (Sup. Ct. J.).
97 *Brown v. Canada (Attorney General)* [2014] O.J. No. 6967 (Sup. Ct. J.).

10 International Adoption

1 There is a long history of cross-border adoption, much of it illegal, between Canada and the United States, but such adoptions were rarely cross-racial: Karen Balcom, "Constructing Families, Creating Mothers: Gender, Family, State and Nation in the History of Child Adoption," *Journal of Women's History* 18 (1) (2006): 219–32. See also Elizabeth Bartholet, "International Adoption: Propriety, Prospects and Pragmatics," *Journal of the American Academy of Matrimonial Lawyers* 13 (winter 1996): 181; Herman, *Kinship by Design*, 217; John Caldwell, *Children of Calamity* (New York: John Day 1957); Tobias Hubinette, *Comforting an Orphaned Nation: Representations of International Adoption and Adopted Koreans in Korean Popular Culture* (Seoul: Jimoondang 2006); Christina Klein, *Cold War Orientalism: Asia in the Middlebrow Imagination* (Berkeley and Los Angeles: University of California Press 2003); and Arissa Oh, "A New Kind of Missionary Work: Christians, Christian Americanists, and the Adoption of Korean GI Babies," *Women's Studies Quarterly* 33 (fall/winter 2005): 161–88. A foundational text with regard to the analysis of empire and intimate relations remains Ann Laura Stoler, *Carnal Knowledge and Imperial Power: Race and the Intimate in Colonial Rule* (Berkeley and Los Angeles: University of California Press 2002).
2 Bartholet, "International Adoption," 182 and 165.
3 Dubinsky, *Babies without Borders*, 99.
4 In the United States, increasingly, international adoption is also about Christian evangelism, with far-right political movements asserting that adoption is salvation. For an exposé of both the extreme rhetoric of this movement and its political power, see Katherine Joyce, *The Child Catchers: Rescue, Trafficking and the New Gospel of Adoption* (New York: Public Affairs 2013).

5 Canada was an early signatory. The Hague Convention on Protection of Children and Co-operation in Respect of Inter-Country Adoption was concluded on 29 May 1993 and entered into force on 1 May 1995: United Nations Convention on the Rights of the Child, United Nations General Assembly, Session 44, Res. 25, 20 November 1989.
6 Rita Simon and Howard Alstein, "Intercountry Adoption: A Multinational Perspective 1," in Euthymia Hibbs, ed., *Adoption: International Perspectives* (New York: International Universities Press, 1991), 93.
7 Mark Eade, "Inter-Country Adoption: International, National and Cultural Concerns," *Journal of the American Academy of Matrimonial Lawyers* 13 (winter 1996): 381.
8 Citizenship and Immigration Canada, "International Adoptions," *Monitor* (fall 2003), http://www.cic.gc.ca/english/monitor/issue03/06-feature.html.
9 Canada 2012, C-14, Citizenship Adoption and Permanent Residence, as reported to the Hague: http://www.hcch.net/index.en/php?act=publications. It is also perhaps not surprising that international adoption has received more than its proportional share of attention from historians of adoption. Karen Balcom's exploration of trans-border adoptions between Canada and the United States, Veronica Strong-Boag's long chapter on "Foreign Affairs," and Karen Dubinsky's *Babies without Borders* all highlight the heightened moral dilemmas implicit in international adoption.
10 Joy Parr, *Labouring Children: British Immigrant Apprentices to Canada, 1869–1924* (Montreal and Kingston: McGill-Queen's University Press 1980). Veronica Strong-Boag asserts that 76,416 children were sponsored for emigration to Canada between 1868 and 1922, by eleven major agencies, including Barnardo with 25,456 children, as well as a number of unnamed minor agencies: Strong-Boag, *Finding Families, Finding Ourselves*, 182. In the early 1920s, however, such programs came under criticism both in Canada and in Britain and in 1925 Britain forbade the emigration of unaccompanied minors under the age of fourteen: Patrick Dunae, "Waifs: The Fairbridge Society in British Columbia, 1931–1951," *Histoire sociale / Social History* 21 (42) (1988): 224–50.
11 Geoffrey Bilson, *The Guest Children: The Story of British Child Evacuees Sent to Canada during World War II* (Saskatoon: Fifth House 1988).
12 Fraidie Martz, *Open Your Hearts: The Story of Jewish War Children in Canada* (Montreal: Véhicule 1996). They were also often adolescent males, the children most likely to have survived the death camps but the least desirable from the perspective of potential adoptive families. See also Irving

Abella and Harold Troper, *None Is Too Many: Canada and the Jews of Europe* (Toronto: Key Porter 2002; originally published 1983); and Ben W. Lappin, *The Redeemed Child: The Story of the Rescue of War Orphans by the Jewish Community of Canada* (Toronto: University of Toronto Press 1963).

13 Tara Brookfield, *Cold War Comforts: Canadian Women, Child Safety and Global Insecurity* (Waterloo, ON: Wilfrid Laurier University Press 2012), 193. Strong-Boag also provides an overview of these developments in *Finding Families, Finding Ourselves*, 176–9.

14 Richard Carlson, "Transnational Adoption of Children," *Tulsa Law Review* 23 (3) (1988): 325 and 327. Strong-Boag also discusses these developments in *Finding Families, Finding Ourselves*, 179–97.

15 Refugee Relief Act of 1953, Public Law no. 203, 67 Stat. 400 (1953). See also Kirsten Lovelock, "Intercountry Adoption as a Migratory Practice: A Comparative Analysis of Intercountry Adoption and Immigration Policy and Practice in the United States, Canada and New Zealand in the Post-WWII Period," *International Migration Review* 34 (3) (2000): 912. The origins of international adoption are in the evangelical right. The early Save the Children program, intended to promote foster parenting at a distance through the provision of funds to poor families, inspired those who wished to take support a step further and remove children from impoverished families and countries and to absorb them into Christianity. The Reverend Billy Graham first popularized such sentiments. The movement for adoption from Korea was spearheaded by the Holts, an evangelical Christian couple inspired by Graham who viewed their work as a mission. They managed to adopt eight children themselves and then, from humble beginnings, developed what is now the world's longest-running (and perhaps largest) international adoption agency: Laura Briggs and Dianna Marre, *International Adoption: Global Inequalities and the Circulation of Children* (New York: New York University Press 2009), 7.

16 Carlson, "Transnational Adoption of Children," 328.

17 Act of 26 September 1961, Public Law no. 87–301, ss.1–4, 75 Stat. 650, 650–1 (1961).

18 Dubinsky, *Babies without Borders*, 95.

19 *Hansard*, 26 May 1954, 6796–7.

20 Sidney Katz, "Why Can't You Adopt a Child?" *Chatelaine* 29 (10) (1957): 119.

21 Lovelock, "Intercountry Adoption as a Migratory Practice," 920.

22 In the United States "the consensus against transracial adoption was so complete before the 1960s that only two states – Texas and Louisiana – bothered to pass statutes explicitly prohibiting them, a stark contrast to

anti-miscegenation laws, which aggressively policed the color line in marriage": Herman, *Kinship by Design*, 238. Texas stated that "no white child can be adopted by a negro person nor can a negro child be adopted by a white person." This law was declared unconstitutional in 1967 in the case *In re Gomez*, 4244 SW 2d 656 (Tex. Cir. Ct. App. 1967). Louisiana's law was struck down in 1972: *Compos v. McKeithen*, 341 F.Suppl. 264 (E.D. La. 1972). See also "Federal Court Voids a Law Prohibiting Biracial Adoptions," *New York Times*, 25 March 1972.
23 Social Planning Council of Metropolitan Toronto, "The Adoption of Negro Children: A Community Wide Approach" (mimeo, July 1966), 3, Dalhousie Library: Dalhousie University.
24 "Project on Adoption of Negro Children," *Canadian Welfare* 38 (15 July 1962): 187.
25 Elizabeth Bartholet, "Where Do Black Children Belong? The Politics of Race Matching in Adoption," *University of Pennsylvania Law Review* 139 (5) (1991): 1180. So far scholars have unearthed few cases of non-whites adopting white children. Disturbingly, "although Black women have functionally served as the mothers of white children, the idea of a Black woman raising a white child in an adoptive home as an adoptive mother is one that is seldom explored in the literature on transracial adoption, even for the limited purpose of exploring perceptions about race and parenthood. The contemplation of such a scenario seems to exceed our cultural imagination": Perry, "Transracial and International Adoption," 125. Limitations on the adoption of Black children by white families have been rescinded because so many children of colour were languishing in foster care: Multiethnic Placement Act (MEPA), 1994, Public Law no. 104–88 and 551–5, 108 Stat. 3518, 4056–8 (20 October 1994).
26 Veronica Strong-Boag, "Today's Child: Preparing for the 'Just Society' One Family at a Time," *Canadian Historical Review* 86 (4) (2005): 698.
27 For information on immigration reform, see Vic Satzwich, ed., *Racism and Social Inequality in Canada: Concepts, Controversies and Strategies for Change* (Toronto: Thompson Educational Publications 1998); and Ninette Kelley and Michael Trebilcock, *Making the Mosaic: A History of Canadian Immigration Policy* (Toronto: University of Toronto Press 2010). While these reforms ostensibly created a racially neutral immigration system based on points, the point system itself favours particular ethnic groups, those with English-language skills who are well educated, and men: Naomi Alboim, *Adjusting the Balance: Fixing Canada's Economic Immigration Policies* (Toronto: Maytree Foundation 2009).
28 Women could also come as primary immigrants and bring dependent

husbands and children, but, owing to disparities in educational opportunities, language acquisition, and marketable job skills, this was much less common.

29 Dubinsky, *Babies without Borders*, 94.
30 Brookfield, *Cold War Comforts*, 204. See also Helke Ferrie, "Crusader for the World's Children," *Chatelaine*, October 1978, 33. Ferrie ultimately went on to establish her own private adoption agency, the Kuan Yin Foundation, although she eventually moved her organization to the United States: Tarah Brookfield, "Maverick Mothers and Mercy Flights: Canada's Controversial Introduction to International Adoption," *Journal of the Canadian Historical Association* 19 (1) (2008), at para. 24. See also Strong-Boag, *Finding Families, Finding Ourselves*, 204.
31 Brookfield, *Cold War Comforts*, 190 and 210.
32 Legal actions by birth mothers of Vietnamese Babylift children adopted in the United States resulted in the return of twenty such children to Vietnam: M. Brown, "Operation Babylift and the Exigencies of War: Who Should Have Custody of Orphans?" *Northern Kentucky Law Review* 7 (1980): 81–91.
33 Brookfield, "Maverick Mothers," 210.
34 For example, in Ontario, the Adoption Agency and Counselling Services, an agency undertaking both domestic and international adoptions was established in 1982: http://www.adoptionchoices.ca.
35 Katherine McDade, "International Adoption in Canada: Public Policy Issues," discussion paper 91.B.1, *Studies in Social Policy* (Ottawa, April 1991), 25, Table 3.
36 The women involved, silenced for many years, have started to tell their stories of coercion and manipulation in such homes. These stories are disturbing to adopted children and adoptive parents and there is a growing movement of Korean adoptees back to Korea, where some have become involved in efforts to provide more choice and financial support for unwed mothers: Joyce, *The Child Catchers*, 267–90. Recent works stress cultural dislocation that echoes the experience of Indigenous children in out-of-community adoptions: Eleana Kim, *Adopted Territory: Transnational Adoption and the Politics of Belonging* (Durham, NC: Duke University Press 2010).
37 U.S. Bureau of the Census, *Statistical Abstract of the United States: 1992* (112th ed.) (Washington, D.C., 1992).
38 R. Pastor, "The Honduran Baby Market," *Sojourner: The Women's Forum*, May 1989, 19.
39 Jorge Carro, "Regulation of Intercountry Adoption: Can the Abuses Come

to an End?" *Hastings International and Comparative Law Review* 18 (1994): 126–7. In particular, an article in the *New York Times*, "Babies for Export," 21 April 1988, was infamous.
40 Dubinsky, *Babies without Borders*, 97. See also Strong-Boag, *Finding Families, Finding Ourselves*, 195.
41 Human Rights Watch, *Romania's Orphans: A Legacy of Oppression* (New York: Human Rights Watch 1990).
42 Eade, "Inter-Country Adoption," 381.
43 Lovelock, "Intercountry Adoption as a Migratory Practice," 932.
44 Citizenship and Immigration Canada, "International Adoptions."
45 Sharon Marcovitch and Laura Cesaroni, "Romanian Adoption: Parents' Dreams, Nightmares and Realities," *Child Welfare* 74 (5) (1995): 993–8; and Jeffrey Haugaard, Julie Wojslawowicz, and Megan Palmer, "International Adoption: Children from Romania," *Adoption Quarterly* 3 (3) (2000): 73–84.
46 United Nations Convention on the Rights of the Child, United Nations General Assembly, Session 44, Res. 25, 20 November 1989.
47 Lovelock, "Intercountry Adoption as a Migratory Practice," 940–42.
48 Balcom, *The Traffic in Babies*, 238.
49 On 1 April 2000 the Intercountry Adoption Act, 1998, S.O. 1998, c.29, as amended by s.25 of S.O. 1999, c.12, Sched. G, was proclaimed in force.
50 Intercountry Adoption Act, S.O. 1998, c.29.
51 Richard Carlson, "The Emerging Law of Intercountry Adoptions," *Tulsa Law Journal* 30 (2) (1994): 252 and 253.
52 For example, "if same-sex couples wish to adopt internationally, they must give the foreign adoption agency through which they apply the appearance that they are not gay. In order to create this appearance, applicants must live separately from each other during the adoption process, and they must designate one partner to adopt the child as a single parent. Married gay couples, however, cannot misrepresent their public conjugal status; their public status effectively bars them from applying to adopt internationally": Dort, "Unheard Voices," para. 35.
53 Adoption in Guatemala, explored in detail by Karen Dubinsky in *Babies without Borders*, expanded exponentially as a result of civil war and poverty. Adoptions were completely private and unregulated and tactics used to obtain children were often unethical, even violent, creating what Dubinsky describes as a "culture of 'missingness.'" The removal of children created a violent backlash against foreigners who were suspected of taking children: Dubinsky, *Babies without Borders*, 108.
54 Brazil's children were rendered "adoptable" by "conditions of sheer poverty" and civil unrest, but it was not an improvement in the economy, or

international regulation, that prompted the drop in international adoption. In 1998 a scandal revealed that a judge had undertaken summary hearings, declared children abandoned, and released them for international adoption: Claudia Fonseca, "An Unexpected Reversal: Charting the Course of International Adoption in Brazil," *Adoption and Fostering* 26 (3) (2002): 29.
55 Citizenship and Immigration Canada, "International Adoptions."
56 Anita Andrew, "China's Abandoned Children and Transnational Adoption: Issues and Problems for U.S.-China Relations, Adoption Agencies and Adoptive Parents," *Journal of Women's History* 19 (1) (2007): 127.
57 Sara Wallace, "International Adoption: The Most Logical Solution to the Disparity between the Numbers of Orphaned and Abandoned Children in Some Countries and Families and Individuals Wishing to Adopt in Others," *Arizona Journal of International and Comparative Law* 20 (3) (2003): 714. While outsiders have assumed that domestic adoption of abandoned Chinese girl babies is unlikely, some researchers contest this belief, tracing a long history of informal adoption of unrelated baby girls despite official policy sanctioning only adoption of blood-related boys for the purpose of inheritance: Kay Johnson, "Politics of International and Domestic Adoption in China," *Law and Society Review* 36 (2) (2002): 379–96. Also, not only did China promote a one-child policy, but also the domestic adoption of foundlings was limited to those over thirty-five, a weapon meant to "shore up the one-child policy by eliminating adoption as a potential loophole for those who sought to hide the birth of a child": ibid., 389. The age for adoption was reduced to thirty in 1999, at which time families with children were also allowed to adopt foundlings: ibid., 390. Because all adopters must pay fees to the orphanage, however, domestic adoption remains too expensive for many Chinese families.
58 Wallace, "International Adoption," 715.
59 Andrew, "China's Abandoned Children and Transnational Adoption," 123, 125, and 126. Funds obtained from adoptions are substantial, not in terms of total revenue in China but as a percentage of that available for domestic child-welfare programs: "Orphanage donations have been significant from the perspective of the welfare institutions that reap the lion's share of these funds for funding improvements and daily operations": Johnson, "Politics of International and Domestic Adoption in China," 388.
60 Wallace, "International Adoption," 722.
61 Citizenship and Immigration Canada, "International Adoptions."
62 Kevin Voigt and Sophie Brown, "International Adoptions in Decline as Number of Orphans Grows," CNN, 17 September 2013, http://www

.edition.cnn.com/2013/09-16/world/international-adoption-main-story-decline/.
63 Hansa Apparao, "International Adoption of Children: The Indian Scene," *International Journal of Behavioral Development* 20 (1) (1997): 3 and 4.
64 http://www.cornerstoneadoption.ca.
65 Human Rights Watch, *Abandoned to the State: Cruelty and Neglect in Russian Orphanages* (New York: Human Rights Watch December 1998).
66 This scandal led to a temporary suspension of adoptions from Russia to the United States. The offending mother was ordered to pay child support by a Tennessee court, since the child is a U.S. citizen, and the woman remains his legal mother, despite his return to Russia, where he is institutionalized: http://www.forbes.com/sites/dianeclehane/2012/u-s-mother-who-returned-her-adopted-son-to-russia/.
67 The coroner determined the death to be accidental, and the parents reported a history of self-harming actions by the boy: Greg Botelho, "Texas Investigator Found 30+ Bruises, Cuts on Dead Boy Adopted from Russia," CNN, 29 March 2013, http://www.cnn.com/2013/03/29/texas-investigator-found-30+-bruises-cuts-on-dead-boy-adopted-from-russia/.
68 Voigt and Brown, "International Adoptions in Decline."
69 Ginger Thompson, "After Haiti Quake, the Chaos of U.S. Adoptions," *New York Times*, 3 August 2010, http://www.nytimes.com/2010/08/04/world/americas/04adoption.html. For a detailed critique of the role of the religious right in international adoption, in particular in Haiti, see Joyce, *The Child Catchers*, 1–38.
70 http://www.adoption.ca/adoption-news?news_id=56.
71 http://www.cic.gc.ca/english/immigration/adoption/index.asp.
72 Jini L. Roby and Stacey A. Shaw, "The African Orphan Crisis and International Adoption," *Social Work* 51 (3) (2006): 199, 200, 202, and 203.
73 Joyce, *The Child Catchers*, 129–75.
74 "Canadian Parents Raise Concerns," CBC News, 19 March 2009.
75 The Grio, "Stop 'Rescuing' African Children through Corrupt Adoptions," *The Clutch*, 6 May 2013, http://www.clutchmagonline.com/2013/05/stop-rescuing-african-children-through-corrupt-adoptions/.
76 In Canada 93 children were adopted from Ethiopia in 2012 and 183 children from greater sub-Saharan Africa. In 2002, 102 children were adopted to the United States from Ethiopia; 441 in 2005. Four U.S. agencies currently operate in Ethiopia to facilitate adoptions. South Africa, Kenya, and Liberia also allow foreign adoptions: U.S. Department of State, "Immigrant Visas Issued to Orphans Coming to the U.S." (2006), http://www.travel.state.gov/family/adoption_resources_02.html.

77 Balcom, *The Traffic in Babies*.
78 Anne Collinson, "The Littlest Immigrants: Cross-Border Adoption in the Americas, Policy and Women's History," *Journal of Women's History* 19 (1) (2007): 132. The parallels with constructions of First Nations mothers as producers of children plagued by Fetal Alcohol Syndrome are profound. For further information on the "crack baby" construct, see Enid Logan, "The Wrong Race, Committing Crime, Doing Drugs, and Maladjusted for Motherhood: The Nation's Fury over 'Crack Babies,'" *Social Justice* 26 (1) (1999): 115–30.
79 http://www.hcch.net/upload/wop/adop2010pdf.
80 Canada 2012, C-14, Citizenship Adoption and Permanent Residency. A 2013 exposé of adoption in the United States found that 315 U.S. children were sent abroad for adoption in 2009, three times the number in 2004: Voigt and Brown, "International Adoptions in Decline."
81 These agencies are: 1. Adoption Agency and Counselling Services, specializing in adoptions from Peru and Columbia. This agency was established in 1982 and also undertakes domestic adoptions. The agency has currently suspended acceptance of new clients because of a decline in the availability of children in Peru and Columbia: http://www.adoptionchoices.ca; 2. Adoption Horizons Inc., specializing in adoptions from Kazakhstan and Russia. This agency was established in 1995 by parents who had undertaken international adoption. They have averaged twenty-five to thirty adoptions per year since that time but have currently suspended acceptance of new applications owing to tightened regulations in Russia with regard to international adoption: http://www.adoptionhorizons.com; 3. Adoptionworx Inc., specializing in adoptions from Albania. This agency was established in 1999 by the parents of the first Albanian child adopted in Canada. They have an exclusive agreement with the Albanian government. The Albanian government will consider only married, opposite-sex couples as adoptive parents, who must also be between the ages of twenty-five and fifty. Parents must spend several months in Albania to complete the adoption process: http://www.adoptionworx.com; 4. CARC-International Adoption, specializing in adoptions from Bulgaria, Kazakhstan, Romania, and Ukraine. Children placed by this agency are exclusively from orphanages and are usually three years of age or older (with special-needs children sometimes being placed at a younger age). The website asserts that waiting periods of twelve to sixteen months for Bulgaria, seven to nine months for Kazakhstan, and eight to twelve months for Ukraine can be expected. Only parents of Romanian descent are eligible for adoption of Romanian children. In all countries, prospec-

tive adoptive parents must spend several weeks in the country to finalize the relinquishment and home-country adoption: http://www.carc-ia.com; 5. Cheryl Appell, specializing in adoptions from the United States. Cheryl Appell is a lawyer who has worked in private-adoption placement since 1979. She also completes domestic adoptions: http://www.dicksonlawyers.com/profiles/cappell.shtml; 6. Children's Resource and Consultation Center of Ontario, specializing in adoptions from the United States but also completing adoptions from Bangladesh, Iran, Lebanon, and Pakistan on a case-by-case basis. This agency was founded in 1980 and deals also with domestic adoptions. It is not accepting any new applications for adoptions from Pakistan: http://www.ontarioadoptions.com; 7. Cornerstone Adoption Agency, specializing in adoptions from Barbados, Guyana, India, Jamaica, the Philippines, Sri Lanka, and St Vincent and the Grenadines. Adoptions from India have been suspended by CARA as of 1 December 2012 and only special-needs children are available for international placement; Barbados is not currently accepting new applications for international adoption; Guyana accepts opposite-sex married and single female applicants, and children are two years of age and older; St Vincent and the Grenadines accept opposite-sex married and single female applicants, but the waiting period for placement is a minimum of two years; the Philippines lifted a moratorium on the international adoption of children aged under two in September 2012, but quotas are low and waits are long: http://www.cornerstoneadoption.ca; 8. Family Outreach International, specializing in adoptions from China, with applications currently suspended. The agency is currently processing applications dating from 2006 in which parents still await infants for adoption: http://familyoutreach.com; 9. From the Heart Adoption Agency, specializing in adoptions from Ukraine: http://fromtheheartadoption.com; 10. Loving Heart International Adoption Agency, specializing in adoptions from Bulgaria, Lithuania, Poland, and Serbia: http://lovingheartadoption.com; 11. Mission of Tears, specializing in adoptions from Ghana, Haiti, Kenya, Nigeria, South Africa, and Ukraine. This agency is run as a non-profit, charitable organization which describes its work as a "humanitarian aid program." It has been in operation since 1993 and runs orphanages and other services in a number of the countries in which it operates. The organization estimates the cost of international adoption at between $28,000 and $36,000 per child, depending upon the country from which a child is adopted: http://www.missionoftears.ca; 12. Open Arms to International Adoption, specializing in adoptions from China, with applications currently suspended: http://www.open-arms.com; 13. Paul Conlin, specializing in adoptions from Algeria, India, Lebanon, the Philippines, Portugal, South Korea, and the United States. He also facilitates domestic adoptions: http://www.pconlin.conlinlaw.ca; 14. Terres des Hommes, specializing in adoptions from Haiti, Honduras, New York, Russia, Ukraine, and Vietnam. Children from Haiti are between six and twelve months of age and often have special needs; only married, opposite-sex couples are eligible for adoption; wait times average seven to eighteen months. Children from Honduras are five years of age or older; only married, opposite-sex couples may apply; and wait times are one to three years. Children from Russia are fourteen months or older; only married, opposite-sex couples may apply; and wait times average one year. Children from Ukraine are five years of age or older or have special needs; only married, opposite-sex couples may apply; and wait times average one year. Children from the United States are exclusively black and biracial infants; all individuals and couples are eligible to apply for adoption; and wait times range from six to twenty-four months. Children from Vietnam have special needs, increasingly HIV; only married opposite-sex couples may apply; and wait times average one year: http://www.tdhontario.tdh.ca; 15. The Children's Bridge, specializing in adoptions from China, India, Jamaica, South Korea, Thailand, Vietnam, Florida, and Zambia. The program for U.S. children is currently full and not accepting applicants. Children from Ethiopia are aged a few months to ten years; single female applicants are accepted; and a two-year wait can be expected. The South Korean program is also full. When operational, children from South Korea are between eighteen and twenty-four months of age; only married, opposite-sex applications are accepted; and wait times average two to three years. Children from Thailand are of varied ages; only opposite-sex married couples can apply; the wait averages three to four years; and the cost is advertised as $12,000 to $14,000. Adoptions from India have been suspended owing to changes in CARA. The Children's Bridge is not currently accepting applications for adoption from Vietnam. Children from Jamaica are generally males over the age of four; married couples and single women may apply; waits are unpredictable; and costs are between $9,000 and $11,000. The program with China is not accepting new applications because of long wait times. Children from Zambia are eight months of age or older; parents must stay in Zambia for six months to finalize the adoption; opposite-sex married couples and single women may apply; the wait is six to twelve months; costs are not estimated since they vary dramatically on account of the long required stay in the country: http://www.childrensbridge.com; 16. Tzivos Hashem, specializing in adoptions from Russia, applications currently suspended. This organization focuses on finding Jewish children for Jewish parents: http://www.tzivoshashem.com; and 17. Worldview Adoptions, which operates on a case-by-case basis, often facilitating relative adoptions or adoptions by families who originate in the relinquishing country: http://www.worldviewadoptions.com.

82 Immigration and Refugee Protection Regulations, SOR/2002–227 (the Regulations): The adoption of the child is considered to be in the child's best interests when:
   (a) a competent authority has conducted or approved a home study of the adoptive parents;
   (b) before the adoption, the child's parents gave their free and informed consent to the child's adoption;
   (c) the adoption created a genuine parent-child relationship;
   (d) the adoption was in accordance with the laws of the place where the adoption took place;
   (e) the adoption was in accordance with the laws of the sponsor's place of residence and, if the sponsor resided in Canada at the time the adoption took place, the competent authority of the child's province of intended destination has stated in writing that it does not object to the adoption;
   (f) if the adoption is an international adoption and the country in which the adoption took place and the child's province of intended destination are parties to the Hague Convention on Adoption, the competent authority of the country and of the province have stated in writing that they approve the adoption as conforming to that Convention; and
   (g) if the adoption is an international adoption and either the country in which the adoption took place or the child's province of intended destination is not a party to the Hague Convention on Adoption, there is no evidence that the adoption is for the purpose of child trafficking or undue gain within the meaning of that Convention.

83 The cost of adopting internationally varies significantly but in the United States the National Adoption Information Clearinghouse lists a range of $7,000 to $30,000 for international adoption: Johnson, "International Adoption," 1230. International adoption agencies advertise their children. As Lisa Cartwright notes, photographs and brochures for international adoption agencies function as "lures, drawing prospective clients into the adoption market … [and] children of poor countries become commodities": Lisa Cartwright, "Photographs of 'Waiting Children,'" *Social Text* 21 (1) (2003): 83.

84 Andrew, "China's Abandoned Children," 128.
85 *A.R. (Re)* [1982] O.J. No. 766 (Prov. Ct. Fam. Div.), at paras. 3, 4, 5, 22, and 25.
86 *A.S. (Re)* [1997] O.J. No. 2793 (Ct. J.), at paras. 1, 2, 3, 12, and 38.
87 Under the Child and Family Services Act, subsection 137(4), where a child is being placed for adoption by a society or licensee, a consent under clause (2)(a) shall not be given until the society or licensee has advised the parent of his or her right,
   (1) to withdraw the consent under subsection (8),
   (2) to be informed, on his or her request, whether an adoption order has been made in respect of the child, and to obtain non-identifying information under section 166 and to participate in the adoption disclosure register maintained under clause 163(2)(a); and the society or licensee has given the parent an opportunity to seek counseling and independent legal advice with respect to the consent.
88 *A.S. (Re)*, at paras. 46 and 50.
89 *G. (Re)* [2008] O.J. No. 1906 (Ct. J.), at para. 9.
90 Ibid., at paras. 10 and 11.
91 *A.C. (Re)* [2011] O.J. No. 727 (Sup. Ct. J.), at para. 1. Payment to birth mothers is prohibited under s.175 of the Child and Family Services Act:
   175. No person, whether before or after a child's birth, shall give, receive or agree to give or receive a payment or reward of any kind in connection with,
      (a) the child's adoption or placement for adoption;
      (b) a consent under section 137 to the child's adoption; or
      (c) negotiations or arrangements with a view to the child's adoption, except for,
      (d) the prescribed expenses of a licensee, or such greater expenses as are approved by a Director;
      (e) proper legal fees and disbursements.
92 *A.C. (Re)*, at paras. 2, 7, 8, 13, 17, 30, 40, and 44.
93 Reginald Stackhouse, Conservative MP from Ontario, future chair of the House of Commons Standing Committee on Human Rights, delegate to the UN, and member of the Ontario Human Rights Commission Canada, *Hansard*, 18 March 1988, 1390.

Index

Aboriginal. *See* First Nations; Indigenous children; Indigenous communities; Indigenous mothers
Aboriginal Affairs and Northern Development Canada, 118
abortion, 6, 24, 49–51, 140–1
abuse, 73, 131. *See also* child abuse
access orders, 78, 80, 82–5, 87, 91, 95–7, 103, 189–90n4, 191n25
Act for the Prevention of Cruelty to and Better Protection of Children [1893], 17, 54, 162n24
Act for the Protection of Children of Unmarried Parents. *See* Children of Unmarried Parents Act [1921]
Act for the Protection of Infant Children [1887], 18, 163n30
Act Respecting Industrial Schools [1883], 16
Act to Amend the Child and Family Services Act [2006], 85
Act to Improve the Common and Grammar Schools of Ontario [1871], 16
Adams, Mary Louise, 54
Adopt Indian Metis (AIM), 116, 119–20, 131
Adopted Break Silence, The (Paton), 66
adopted child syndrome, 67
Adopted? A Canadian Guide (Marcus), 67
adoptees, 80; adult, 10, 64, 68, 70–2, 74, 79, 188n58; inheritance, 169n9; non-searching, 76
Adoptees' Liberty Movement Association (ALMA), 186n25
adoption: "black market," 28; domestic, 9, 12, 26–7, 89, 136, 141–2, 144, 147, 150, 197n1, 215n34; domestic, China, 217n57; domestic, Peru and Columbia, 219n81; domestic, U.S., 220n81; free, full consent and validity in foreign, Canada, 147–50; Indigenous, 4, 11–12, 24, 39, 116–34, 140, 215n36; informal,

13, 15, 33, 160n1, 166n47, 170n5, 217n57; international, 4, 12, 24, 114, 135–52, 155, 211n4, 212n9, 213n15, 216n52, 217–18n54, 219–22nn81–3; interracial, 4, 138, 146–7; open, 4, 8, 10–11, 71, 74, 76–90, 92, 95, 105, 112–13, 115, 127–8, 130, 158n4, 190n8, 190–1n12; same-sex, 155, 197n1, 197n3; same-sex parents, and assisted reproduction, 104–15; same-sex, second-parent, 11, 107; secrecy and disclosure in, 63–77; step-parent, 11, 79–80, 91–107, 155, 190n12, 193n3, 194n9; third-party, 9; three-parent, 112–13, 114
Adoption Act: repealed, 54
Adoption Act [1921], 3, 6–7, 11, 13–14, 21–2, 24, 27, 42–3, 54, 64, 121, 168n66, 168–9n67, 169n69, 169n70
Adoption Act [1927], 64–5, 169n70
Adoption Act [1937], 27
Adoption Disclosure Registry, 68, 70–3
Adoption Disclosure Statute Law Amendment Act [1987], 71
Adoption Information Disclosure Act [2005], 10, 64, 72, 74, 76–7
adoption-rights movement, 4, 10, 63, 66, 68, 70, 80, 185–6n25. *See also* open-records movement; search movement
Africa, 218n76, 220n81; orphan crisis, 145–6; orphanages, 146. *See also* sub-Saharan Africa
Ahenakew, Dave, 125
AIDS, 145. *See also* HIV
Alberta, 80, 110, 133; baby-selling to U.S., 28
Algonquins of Pikwakanagan First Nation, 128

apprehension, 4, 10, 52–62, 81, 153–5; Black and mixed-raced children, Canada and U.S., 138, 147; critiques of, and government response, 57–60; critiques, and use of attachment theory, 183n77; Indigenous children, 116, 118–23, 125, 131–3, 208–9n80; and social worker responsibilities, 177–8n11; and voluntary surrender, 56–7. *See also* Children's Aid Society; neglect; social workers
Assembly of First Nations (AFN), 125, 131, 204n43
Assisted Human Reproduction Act [2004], 115, 200n33
assisted reproduction: and same-sex parents, and adoption, 104–15. *See also* surrogacy
Australia, 13, 65, 203n31

babies, 5, 7, 17–18, 31, 52, 94, 142; adoption, 12, 24, 27–9, 89; biracial, 140; Chinese, 144, 217n57; "crack," 146–7, 219n78; domestic, 6, 135; foreign, 135, 143; illegitimate, 20; relinquishment, 9, 34, 154; shaken, 178–9n26; vulnerable to disease, 163n29; white, 170n5. *See also* baby-selling; black market in babies; infants
Babies without Borders (Dubinski), 4–5, 172n35, 177n1, 197n1, 212n9, 216n53
baby-selling, 28, 170n15. *See also* black market in babies
Backhouse, Nancy (Justice; Canada), 108
Bala, Nicholas, 58–9, 101
Balcom, Karen, 19, 138, 177–8n11,

177n1, 211n1, 212n9; *Traffic in Babies*, 5, 166n47
Baldassi, Cindy, 79, 200n2
Baldwin, Jeffrey: death, septic shock and pneumonia (Toronto, 2002), 59, 182n59
Bangladesh, 139, 220n81
Baran, Reuben, 67, 80
Bartholet, Elizabeth, 135
Bastarache, Michel (Justice; Canada), 59–60, 102
bastard, 18, 164n36
Battered Child in Canada, The (Van Stolk), 56
battered child syndrome, 56
Belobaba, Edward (Justice; Canada), 133
best interests of the child, 7–8, 30, 32, 36–8, 40, 50, 60, 69–70, 79–87, 91–4, 96–9, 103–4, 106, 111–12, 114, 172n54, 173n56, 176n30; and guardianship after death, 161n11; Indigenous, 12, 117, 121, 123–4, 126; in international adoption, 147, 149, 222n82
Big Grassy First Nation, 123
birth certificates, 48, 65, 101, 108, 166n45, 184n4; gender-neutral, 109
birth control, 6, 24, 139
birth mothers: and consent in adoption, 26–41
black market in babies, 20, 28–9, 141
Blackstone, William, 18
Blenner-Hassett, Dale, 60
Boateng, Afua: death (Toronto, 1995), 58, 180n45
Bogota, Colombia: Centre for Rehabilitation and Adoption of Children, 148

Bowlby, John, 28, 38–9
Bracco, Katrysha, 23
Brazil, 142, 216–17n54
Britain, 136, 212n10
British Columbia, 58, 61, 95, 121–2, 133, 188–9n70, 193n3, 198n17; Adoption Act [1996], 200n2; customary adoption recognition, 200–1n2; liability for child support, 195–6n32; Parent Finders, 67; parentage legislation, 11, 105, 110, 112, 114–15; recognition of multi-parent families, 199n25; step-parent adoption (stats), 193n3. *See also* cases, discussed
British North America Act [1867], 117–18
Brown, Marcia, 131–3
Bryce, Peter, 19
Burns, Devin: death, in house fire (Kitchener, 1996), 58, 181n49

Canada: adoption from Ethiopia, sub-Saharan Africa, 218n76; British children, 136–7; child-rescue discourse, 13; Child, Family and Community Division, Human Resources Development, 142; cross-border adoption, with U.S., 5, 146–7, 211n1; Federal Child Support Guidelines, 100; Gradual Civilization Act [1857], 201–2n14; interracial adoption, 138, 146–7; Jewish children, 136–7, 212–13n12, 221–2n81; maternal mortality, 50–1; recognition of social parenthood, 193–4n7; refusal to sign UN Convention on Genocide [1948], 202n18; sixties scoop, 10–12, 116–17, 122–3, 131–2, 138; sponsorship of emigrating children, 212n10. *See also* cases, discussed; Supreme Court of Canada (SCC); Upper Canada

Canada Assistance Plan, 118, 203n23; expansion of welfare benefits (1966), 24

Canadian Human Rights Tribunal: 2016 ruling, Indigenous child welfare case, 131, 209n84

Canadian Public Health Journal, 18

Canadian Welfare Council, 31–2

Carp, Wayne, 28, 65, 67

cases, discussed: *A.A. v. B.B.* [2003], 105, 113–14; *A.L. v. S.M.* [2009], 48–50; *Agar v. McNeilly* [1958], 35–6, 55; *Algonquins of Pikwakanagan First Nation v. Children's Aid Society of Toronto* [2004], 128–30, 206–7n71; *Brown v. Attorney General (Canada)* [2010], 117, 131–3, 210nn89–91; *C.J.K. v. Children's Aid Society of Toronto* [1989], 127; *Carignan v. Carignan* [1989], 101; *Chartier v. Chartier* [1998], 92–3; *Chartier v. Chartier* [1999], 101–2; *Cheskes v. Ontario* [2007], 64, 68, 72, 74–7; *Children's Aid Society of Metropolitan Toronto v. Lyttle* [1973], 45–6; *Doe v. The Awasis Agency of Northern Manitoba* [1990], 207–8n76; *Ferguson v. Director of Child Welfare et al.* [1983], 68–70; *FNCFCS et al. v. Attorney General of Canada* [2016], 131, 209–10n84; *Hepton v. Maat* [1957], 35–6, 55; *K (Re)* [1995], 104–6; *Kerr v. McWhannel* [1974], 95; *King v. Low* [1985], 40; *L.M.C. v. Catholic Children's Aid Society of Toronto* [1984], 124–5; *M.A.C. et al. v. M.K.* [2009], 111–12; *M.D.R. v. Ontario* [2006], 104, 107–9, 198–9nn18–19; *Manitoba (Director of Child Welfare) v. Y* [1981], 39; *Martin v. Duffell* [1950], 35–6, 55; *Natural Parents v. British Columbia (Superintendent of Child Welfare)* [1976], 121–3, 128–9; *New Brunswick (Minister of Health and Community Services) v. G. (J.)* [1999], 59–60; *North v. North* [1978], 95; *Ontario v. Marchand* [2006], 72–4, 188n63; *P.C.S. v. D.B.H.* [1974], 95; *R. v. Tremblay* [1999; 2003; 2004], 50, 176n32; *Racine v. Woods* [1983], 39, 124, 205n58, 206n59; *Re L. et al. and C.* [1972], 93; *Re: Mugford* [1970], 37, 40–1, 154; "Saskatchewan Dad case," 176n30; *S.M. (Re)* [2009], 86–7; *Ss.M (Re)* [2007], 112–13; *Tremblay v. Daigle* [1989], 51; *Trociuk v. British Columbia (Attorney General)* [2003], 47–50, 105, 109–10, 176n30, 199n18

Catholic Children's Aid Society, 24, 84, 125, 181n48

Cavoukian, Ann, 72

Charter rights, 8, 43, 48–50, 53, 60, 73–6, 83, 85, 99, 106–7, 109, 125, 128–30, 159n22, 174n4, 207n71

Chartier, Clem, 122, 204n43

Chatelaine, 24, 29, 64, 161n8, 171n18, 185n13, 186n27, 213n20, 215n30

Chen, Xiaobei, 15

child abuse, 10, 16–17, 23, 52–6, 59, 61–2, 82, 106, 121, 125, 154–5, 177–8n11; as public health issue, 61; sexual, 62, 73, 118, 131, 184n78. *See also* neglect

Child Abuse in Canada (Schlesinger), 56

Index   229

child deaths, 10, 53, 58–9, 144–5, 163n30. *See also* infant mortality; *individual cases*; *individual victims*

child mortality. *See* child deaths; infant mortality

child saving, 3, 6, 15–21, 18, 23, 27, 54; and Christianity, 213n15; and international adoption, 141, 145–6. *See also* Operation Babylift; rescue narrative

child welfare, 5–6, 9–10, 13, 25, 28–9, 42, 52–62, 160–1n7, 189–90n4; government involvement in, 15–23, 81; and Indigenous children, 116–17, 120, 123, 126, 130–1, 206–7n71, 209n84. *See also* Children's Aid Society; children's rights; social workers

child welfare movement, 170n15

child-rescue discourse, 13, 150. *See also* child saving; rescue narrative

children: Black, 138, 146–7, 221n81; boarding homes, 166n51; disabled, 6; institutionalized, 14–15, 17–18, 20, 30, 81–2, 117, 141, 145, 166n51, 177n3, 218n66; mixed-race, 6, 137–8; older, 4, 6, 9–10, 14–15, 17, 24, 30, 38, 42, 52, 54, 57, 79, 81–2, 84, 87, 89, 90, 154, 169–70n1, 177n1, 196n42; as property, 38, 40, 88; as property of legal father, 13, 53; special-needs, 10, 24, 79, 82, 89, 144, 220–1n81

Children of Unmarried Parents Act [1921], 7, 9, 21–3, 29, 32, 43, 45–6, 65, 168n64, 171n19, 172n35

Children's Aid Society, 7, 16, 22, 56, 76, 81–2, 84, 89, 91, 94, 140; and baby-selling to U.S., 28; closed adoption files, 65–6, 69–70, 72; established [1892], 17, 54; Fort Frances, 123; and Indigenous children, 118, 123, 127, 129, 131; investigations into, 58–9; Kenora District, 123; Ohsweken, 123; openness orders, 85–7; power of, 60; removal privileges (1893), 20; Supreme Court censuring of, 27, 37; Toronto, 24, 31–4, 138; treatment of fathers, 43–7; young unwed mothers pressured by, 27–34, 37. *See also* coercion; social workers

Children's Bridge, 89, 221n81

Children's Law Reform Act [1990], 48–9, 108, 113, 161n11; definition of a father, 173–4n3, 198n16

children's rights, 6–8, 14, 19, 38–9, 41, 54, 68, 108, 122, 129, 160–1n7, 184n2, 206–7n71. *See also* adoption-rights movement

China, 220–1n81; informal adoption of girls, 217n57; orphanages, 143–4, 217n57, 217n59; signatory to Hague Convention on Inter-Country Adoption, 143

Christian organizations: New Life Children's Refuge, 145; Save the Children program, 213n15

Christian-based reform movements, 18, 211n4

Christianity: and international adoption, 211n4, 213n15. *See also* Christian organizations

Churley, Marilyn, 71

Citzenship and Immigration Canada: Immigration and Refugee Protection Regulations, 147, 222n82

class, 3, 5, 7, 12, 14, 17–18, 26, 34, 53–4, 60, 118, 153, 162n22, 203n31

Co-operative Commonwealth Federation (CCF), 137
coercion, 7, 9, 26–7, 38, 41, 44, 57, 153, 215n36
cohabitation, 21, 42, 100–1, 168n59; step-parents, 102–3
Cohen, Marion (Justice; Canada), 111–12
Cold War, 12, 28, 54, 135
Coldwell, Major, 137
Commanda, Robert, 131–3
conflict of law: and adoption, 51, 110, 144, 151
conjugal relationship, 106
consent: and birth mothers, in adoption, 26–41
Coville, Tiffany: death, neglect (Trenton, 1993), 58, 180n44
"crack baby" construct, 146–7, 219n78
Cree, 125, 204n43
Crey, Ernie, 120
cross-racial adoption, 7, 138–9, 211n1
crown ward, 9–10, 17, 22, 27, 29, 62, 78–9, 82–7, 89–90, 169–70n1, 180n42, 184n78, 190n4; Indigenous children, 129
custody, 6, 17, 23, 28, 45–9, 50, 64, 86, 91–4, 104, 111, 113, 115, 120, 172n54, 176n30, 180n42, 194–5nn19–20; biological parents' right to, 55; denial of, 127–8; fathers', 42; interim, 40, 124, 149; joint, 100, 105; maternal, 11, 33–9; mothers' loss of, 22, 59, 61, 154; protective, 83; removal from parental, 54, 121; voluntary, agreement, 56. *See also* divorce
Czapanskiy, Karen, 50

Diefenbaker, John, 138
disclosure vetos, 64, 71, 74–5, 77
divorce, 6, 11, 39, 79, 92–5, 100–1, 112, 173n56, 174n4, 193n3, 195n32, 196n39. *See also* custody
DNA, 51, 109, 184; evidence, use of, 105
Dombroskie, Angela: death, in house fire (Kitchener, 1996), 58, 181n49
Dombroskie, David: death, in house fire (Kitchener, 1996), 58, 181n49
domestic violence, 61. *See also* abuse
Dominican Republic, 145
Dooley, Randall: death, abuse (Scarborough, 1998), 58, 181n51
Drea, Frank, 70
Drury, E.C., 21, 167n55
Dubinsky, Karen, 3–5, 8, 130, 135, 138–9, 141, 172n35, 177n1, 197n1, 216n53; *Babies without Borders*, 4–5, 172n35, 177n1, 197n1, 212n9, 216n53

Edgar, William: death, by restraint (Peterborough, 1999), 59, 182n58
England: guardianship provisions, 14; Poor Law Amendment Act [1834], 164n36; Poor Laws, 15, 18, 53
Erickson, Nancy, 51
Ethiopia, 146, 218n76, 221n81
eugenics, 20, 163n31, 184n3

families: alternative, 104; birth, 4, 79, 80, 149, 154; cohabiting, 45; gay men, 114–15; multiple parent, 11, 115, 155; natural, 99; queer, 90, 105, 110, 114–15, 155; same-sex, 106, 140; single-parent, 140. *See also* gay

men; lesbian; lesbian couples; stepparent
father: defined, 173–4n3
fathers, 23, 114, 129, 150, 169n67; adoptive, 124; biological, 46–8, 96, 98, 111–12, 139, 149, 180n42, 199n18; birth, 6, 8, 11, 51, 73, 87, 109, 142, 174n4, 184n4; cohabiting, 42, 45, 51, 174n3; foster, 124; gay, 110, 111, 115; genetic, 7, 9, 42–3, 46, 51, 105, 155, 176; marital, 93–4; married, 18, 42, 46, 91, 173–4n3; natural, 79, 95–8, 98, 101, 174n3; and parentage, 198n16; putative, 21–2, 30, 32–3, 41, 64, 72–6, 164n36, 168n64; putative, and newborn adoption, 42–62; rights, 154; social, 9, 42, 47, 51, 103; sperm donor/biological, 11, 110; unmarried, 9, 42, 45–6, 65, 154; unwed, 6, 42–3, 45, 47, 105
fathers' rights movement, 176n30
feminism, 7, 8, 47, 49–51, 88, 179n34. *See also* formal equality; Women's Legal Education and Action Fund (LEAF)
Ferrie, Helke, 139, 215n30
Fetal Alcohol Syndrome (FAS): and First Nations mothers, 219n78
Finding Families, Finding Ourselves (Strong-Boag), 4, 169n72
First Nations, 122, 158n6, 201n6; child welfare, 209n84; children, 116–20, 123–7, 129, 131–2, 138, 206–7n71; communities, and repatriation, 132; families, 128, 130–2; identity, 133; mothers, 166n45, 219n78. *See also* Indigenous children; Indigenous communities; Indigenous mothers
First Nations Child and Family Caring Society of Canada (FNCFCS), 131, 209n84
Fish, Morris (Justice; Canada), 74
formal equality, 6, 47, 51
foster care, 8, 10, 15, 17, 20, 25, 54, 82–3, 158n2, 182n58, 191n21; Black children, 147, 214n25; Indigenous children, 12, 117, 119–20, 128, 130–4; outcomes, 14, 52–3, 57, 62, 81, 87, 154
foster father, 124
foster mother, 121, 124, 166n51
foster parents, 35, 38, 40, 62, 78, 80, 84, 86, 162n26, 213n15; and First Nations children, 206–7n71, 207–8n76; and Indigenous children, 126, 128–9, 133
Fournier, Suzanne, 120
Freund, Ernst, 19

Gammell, John (Justice; Canada), 126–7
Garber, Ralph, 56, 70, 206n62; report on adoption disclosure, 130
gay men: adoption, international, 216n52; couples, 197n3; family creation, 114–15; married, 216n52; surrogacy, 104, 110–11, 115. *See also* families; fathers; same-sex
gender, 3
gender-neutral laws, 6, 8, 51, 92, 114
genetics, 9, 42, 51, 80, 109, 114–15, 154–5, 184n3, 188–9n70, 198n17. *See also* fathers; mothers
genocide: cultural, Indigenous, 122–3, 210n91; identity, Indigenous, 132; Indigenous peoples, 203n31; residential schools as form of, 202n18
gestation, 39, 51, 88

gestational mother, 114–15, 151
Gillese, Eileen (Justice; Canada), 133
Gonthier, Charles (Justice; Canada), 60
Good Women of China – Hidden Voices, The, 143
Gordon, Marie, 102–3
Great War, The (1914–1918), 5, 14, 18–19, 21
guardianship, 14, 17–18, 96, 112, 137, 144, 150, 161n11, 189–90n4
Guatemala, 142–3, 216n53

Hague, The: Convention on Protection of Children and Cooperation in Respect of Inter-Country Adoptions [1993], 12, 136, 141–4, 147–9, 160n32, 212n5, 222n82
Haiti, 143, 146, 220–1n81; international adoption scandal, 145
Health Canada: *Canadian Incidence Study of Reported Child Abuse and Neglect*, 61
Heikamp, Jordan: death, homocide (Toronto, 1997), 58, 181n50
Hillel, Margot, 13
HIV, 192n34, 221n81
Huband, Charles (Justice; Canada), 101
Human Rights Watch, 141, 145

illegitimacy, 6, 9, 13–14, 18–23, 27, 30, 42, 65, 174n3
illegitimate: child, 19, 20–1, 35, 55, 107, 164n36, 165–6n45, 168n64; children, 13, 17–21, 23, 28, 46, 109, 137, 153. *See also* adoption
immigrant mothers, 18, 44, 56
immigrant status, 61

immigrants, 35, 172n35; women, 214–15n28
immigration, 4–5, 13; of adopted children, 138–40, 147, 222n82; evacuee and refugee children, to Canada, 136–7; reforms, 214n27; United States, 137
impoverished, 3, 13, 18, 28, 61, 125, 127, 136, 141, 155, 213n15
India, 143, 150, 220–1n81; Central Adoption Resource Agency (CARA), 144, 220–1n81; orphanages, 144
Indian Act [1876], 117, 132, 158n6, 201n10, 201–2n14, 204n39
Indian Act [1952], 118, 120–1
Indian Affairs and Northern Development (Canada), 123
Indian status, 12, 117, 120–2, 124–6, 131–2, 201n10, 204n39
Indigenous children: adoption of, 4, 11–12, 24, 39, 116–34, 140, 215n36; apprehension of, 62, 116, 118–23, 131–3, 155, 208–9n80; best interests of, 12; crown wards, 129; foster care, 12, 62; funding for, 209n84; racialization of, 10; repatriation, 132; sixties scoop, 10–12, 116–17, 122–3, 131–2, 138
Indigenous communities: poverty, 116–17, 119, 131; and social workers, 118–19, 125
Indigenous mothers, 3, 203n31, 204–5n47, 208n80
Indo-Pakistani War, 139
industrial schools, 16
industrialization, 5, 13
infant mortality, 18, 163n30; early 1900s, 163n31
infants, 25, 30–1, 34–6, 121; adoption,

28, 46, 54, 78–9, 88, 90, 136, 140, 143–4, 149, 154, 169n1, 220–1n81; domestic, 140; healthy, 6; illegitimate, 9, 17–19, 22; institutionalized, 145; private placement of, 23; relinquished, 84; screening, for adoption, 20
infertility, 4, 6, 25, 27, 54, 107, 135, 140, 151, 190n8
inheritance, 217n57
inheritance rights, 19, 21, 169n69
Inuit, 12, 118–20, 122–4, 138, 158n6, 200n2, 201n6, 202n20

Jamaica, 56, 143, 181n51, 220–1n81
Jewels for Jesus, 89
Jewish children, 136–7, 212–13n12, 221–2n81
Jewish children's aid agencies, 24
Jobin, Stephanie: death, by restraint (Brampton, 1998), 59, 182n57
Johnson, Shanay: death, neglect (Toronto, 1993), 58, 180n43
Johnston, Patrick, 122–3
Josie, Svanhuit, 31, 36
juvenile delinquency, 16–17, 54, 177n3

Kasonde, Margaret: death, by shooting (Ottawa, 1995), 58, 180n46
Kasonde, Wilson: death, by shooting (Ottawa, 1995), 58, 180n46
Katz, Sidney, 138
Kelly, Fiona, 107, 110, 112, 198n8
Kelso, J.J., 16–17, 19–20, 27
Kempe, C.H., 55
Kirk, David, 67, 80
Kirschner, David, 67, 188n66
Korea, 142–3. *See also* South Korea

Korean children: adoption of, 137, 140–1, 213n15, 215n36, 221n81
Korean War, 137
Kovalsky-England, Jennifer: death, stabbing (Toronto, 1990), 58, 180n42

L'Heureux-Dube, Claire (Justice; Canada), 60
Laskin, Bora (Justice; Canada), 121, 204n39
Lee, Jamie: death, in house fire (Kitchener, 1996), 58, 181n49
Legal Aid, 182n62
Legal Education and Action Fund (LEAF), 60, 179n34
legislation: parentage, 11, 42, 105, 110–15. *See also* Canada; Ontario; United States
Legitimation of Children Act [1921], 21, 167n58
lesbian: co-mothers, 108–9, 198n17; co-parents, 107, 111; families, 107n3, 197n1, 199n25; family creation, 114–15; mothers, 112; mothers, non-biological, 107
lesbian couples, 11, 106, 197n3, 198n17; anonymous sperm donation, 11, 104, 106, 155; artificial insemination, 8; known donor cases, 110, 112; parental rights, 104–5; second-parent adoption, 104, 155; third parent recognition, 199n25
Lessard, Hester, 47
Lewis, Stephen, 139

Macdonald, John Kidson, 16–17
Maclean's, 31, 107, 161n8, 171n28, 198n15
MacMurchy, Helen, 18, 163n31

Manitoba, 39, 95–6, 101, 110, 207–8n76
Marcus, Clare, 66–7; *Adopted? A Canadian Guide*, 67; *Who Is My Mother?*, 67
Matas, Roy Joseph (Justice; Canada), 124
maternal mortality: Canada, 50–1
Matheson, Wendy (Justice; Canada), 133
McLachlin, Beverley (Justice; Canada), 60, 74
Meilleur, Madeleine, 77
Mendes de Costas, Virginia (Justice; Canada), 98–9
Mennill, Sally: on Kim Anne Popen case, 56
Mercredi, Ovide, 122, 204n43
Mesbur, Ruth (Justice; Canada), 128–9
Metis, 118–20, 122–4, 138, 158n6, 201n6, 202n20
Monnin, Alfred (Justice; Canada), 39
Montreal: black market in babies, 28; Black mothers, 172n35; interracial adoption, 138; Open Door Society, 138; social workers, 172n35
Mossman, Mary Jane, 60
mothers, 150; bad, 56, 181n50; biological, 47; birth, 8, 41, 51, 65, 65–6, 72–3, 75, 80–1, 87, 106, 108–11, 111, 114–15, 124, 142, 150, 199n22; Black, 172n35; constructed as delinquent and unstable, 30–1; genetic, 114–15; immigrant, 18; married, 11, 65, 91, 107, 164n36, 174n3; natural, 36, 40, 70, 95–7, 126–7; neglectful, 21; poor, 154; racialized, 154; single, 29, 154; social, 199n22; social, lesbian, 107–8, 110–12; unmarried, 11, 18–41, 91, 148, 154, 165–6n45; unwed, 3, 6, 9, 18–41, 44, 47, 55, 66, 125, 131, 140–1, 149, 153, 164n37, 171n19, 190n8, 193n3; unwed, constructed as sick, 30–1; unwed, Korea, 215n36
Mothers' Allowance Act [1920], 19, 165–6n45

Napoleon, Val, 130
Nasmith, A.P. (Justice; Canada), 125
neglect, 9–10, 13, 16–17, 21–3, 27, 52–4, 58–9, 61–2, 82, 106, 125, 155, 169–70n1, 180nn43–4
Nelson, Ann (Justice; Canada), 151
Nevins, James (Justice; Canada), 105–6, 148–9
New Brunswick, 96, 133, 145, 167n53
New Democractic Party (NDP), 137, 139
New Zealand, 65
newborns, 17–18, 45, 88; and consent, 26; and putative fathers, adoption, 9, 42–62. *See also* consent
Newfoundland, 61
Nordheimer, Ian (Justice; Canada), 133
Nova Scotia, 71, 95, 145; baby-selling to U.S., 28; step-parent adoption (stats), 193n3

Obama, Barack, 145
Ojibwa, 124, 131
Ontario: 1998 Panel of Experts' Report on Child Protection, 58; lack of oversight, adoption agencies, 147; Mike Harris's Common Sense Revolution, 58; origins of adoption legislation, 13–25; over-

apprehension in, 53; private adoption agencies, 89–90, 192–3n47; ratification of Hague Convention on Inter-Country Adoption, 142, 144; reporting of child abuse mandatory in, 55; York County, Family Court, 46, 124–5
Ontario Child and Family Services Act [1984], 53, 57
Ontario Child and Family Services Act [1985], 126–7
Ontario Child and Family Services Act [1990], 25, 78, 84; treatment of access orders, 191n25
Ontario Child and Family Services Act [2011], 78, 87–8
Ontario Child and Family Services Amendment Act [1999], 59
Ontario Child and Family Services Amendment Act [2006], 78, 87–8, 112
Ontario Child Mortality Task Force, 58
Ontario Child Welfare Act [1954], 24, 52, 54, 126
Ontario Child Welfare Act [1978], 68, 78, 83
Ontario Child Welfare Act [1987], 71
Ontario Child Welfare Amendment Act [1958], 169n69
Ontario Divorce Act [1968], 92, 100
Ontario Divorce Act [1985], 92, 100, 195n32
Ontario Family Law Act [1986], 92, 195n32; definition of a parent, 158–9n13, 193n5, 193–4n7
Ontario Family Law Reform Act [1978], 42, 83, 92, 100
Ontario Family Law Reform Act [1980], 174n3

Ontario Inter-Country Adoption Act [1998], 150
Ontario Task Force on Child Abuse, 56
open adoption, 78–90
Open Door Society (Montreal), 138
open-records movement, 79, 185–6n25. *See also* adoption-rights movement; children's rights; search movement
openness agreements, 78–9, 86, 88–90, 112
openness orders, 79, 85–7
Operation Babylift, 139, 215n32
orphanages, 85, 135, 162n25; Africa, 146; China, 143–4, 217n57, 217n59; India, 144; Romania, 141, 219–20n81; Russia, 145; Vietnam, 139
orphans, 15, 137–9, 145–6, 148

Pakistan, 139, 149–50, 220n81
Pannor, Arthur, 67, 80
Parent Finders, 67
parentage, 43, 108–9; legal, 110, 198n16; legislation, 11, 42, 105, 111–15; same-sex, 193–4n7
parents: adoptive, 4–6, 8, 11, 20, 23, 39, 41, 62–3, 65–7, 79–80, 84–90, 95, 119–22, 126–7, 133, 141–51, 176n30, 199n22, 203n31, 222n82; birth, 4, 8, 56, 64, 72–6, 79, 86–7, 169n69, 199n22; foster, 191n21; gay, 106; genetic, 115; heterosexual, 108; indigent, 59; lesbian, 8, 11, 104–5, 106; lesbian, third parent recognition, 199n25; natural, 23, 35, 64, 80, 82–3, 88, 94–9, 102, 120–1, 129, 195n20; same-sex, 104–15, 193–4n7, 198n17; social, 115, 199n22. *See also* fathers; mothers; step-parent

paternity, 9, 19, 21, 33, 42–6, 48–50, 65, 72, 76, 96, 105, 164, 198n16
Paton, Jean M.: *Adopted Break Silence, The*, 66
Perell, Paul (Justice; Canada), 132–3, 210n91
Perry, Twila, 7, 214n25
Philippines, 143, 220–1n81
placement, 15, 24, 52, 54, 62; adoption, 8, 10, 20, 29, 49, 223n91; adoption, informal, 166n47; Asian children, Canada, Vietnam War, 139; Black children, Canada, 138; British children, Second World War, 136–7; foster, 81; Indigenous children, 11–12, 116–17, 122, 124–30, 205n49; institutional, 53; and international adoption, 140, 144–5; Jewish children, post-Second World War, 136–7; private, 23; religious, 169n72. *See also* Catholic Children's Aid Society; Children's Aid Society
Podniewicz, Sara: death, pneumonia and abuse (Toronto, 1996), 58, 180–1n48
poor, 10; children, 13–15; countries, 142, 146; families, 17–18, 53, 213n15; and marginalized communities, 60–1; mothers, 8, 16, 20, 53, 58–9, 153–4; nations, 4, 155; pregnant, unmarried women, 26; white women, 7
Popen, Kim Anne: death, multiple contusions and abrasions (Ontario, 1976), 56
poverty, 15, 20, 22, 31–3, 41–2, 57, 61, 87, 125, 160n1, 181n50; child, 9, 13, 18, 53, 58, 155, 179–80n39; Indigenous communities, 116–17, 119, 131; international, 142, 144–6, 148
pregnancy, 46–50, 70, 88, 96, 112, 165n38, 176n30
Prince Edward Island, 110, 145
privacy rights, 10, 63–4, 71–7, 154
Pupatello, Sandra, 72

Quebec, 61, 110. *See also* Montreal

race, 3, 5, 61, 119–21, 135, 138–9, 153, 155, 214n25
racialization: birth mothers, 8; Indigenous children, 10; minority women, 7; mothers, 154
racism, 119–20, 124–5, 127, 130, 203n31, 208n80; structural, 12
Rand, Ivan (Justice; Canada), 35, 55
Raney, W.E., 20
religion, 18; and adoption, 139, 144–5; Protestant institutions, 15, 24, 161n16
religious institutions, 15, 17, 24, 118
relinquishment, 4, 9–10, 22, 24, 26–7, 34–5, 38, 66–7, 153, 154; and fathers, 42–4; impact of welfare cuts on, Ontario, 180n41; in international adoption, 136, 141, 143, 145–9, 220n81; voluntary, 29, 58, 78, 88, 90, 115, 130, 154–5. *See also* consent
repatriation: of Indigenous people, 132
reproductive autonomy, 7–8, 43, 49–51, 155
reproductive technologies, 108, 113–14; artificial insemination, 8, 107; new, 4, 110. *See also* assisted reproduction; same-sex; surrogacy
rescue narrative: and adoption, 3–4,

13, 118, 135, 150, 157n1; and international adoption, 145–6. *See also* child saving; orphanages; orphans
residential schools, 116, 118, 120, 123, 130, 132; as genocide, 202n18
reunion, 4, 63, 67–8, 70, 74, 139, 187–8n56
revocation: of relinquishment, 36–7, 39, 41, 55, 115, 154, 173n61
Rivard, Paul (Justice; Canada), 108–9
Rogerson, Carol, 102, 196n42
Romania, 142–3; orphanages, 141, 219–20n81
Rosenberg, Marc (Justice; Canada), 113–14, 133
Rothstein, Marshall (Justice; Canada), 74
Russia, 143, 218nn66–7, 219n81, 221n81; orphanages, 145

same-sex: adoption, 155, 197n1, 197n3, 216n52; couples, 115, 135, 198n17; families, 106, 140; parentage, 193–4n7; parents, 197n1, 197n3, 198n17; parents, assisted reproduction and adoption, 104–15; relationships, 4; second-parent adoption, 11, 107; social mothers, 107–8, 110–12. *See also* gay men; lesbian; lesbian couples
Saskatchewan, 83, 133, 145; "Saskatchewan Dad case" [2006], 176n30; Adopt Indian Metis (AIM), 116, 119–20, 131
Save the Children, 213n15
Schlesinger, Benjamin: *Child Abuse in Canada*, 56
Scott, Duncan Campbell: on "the Indian problem," 201–2n14

search movement, 66–8, 80. *See also* adoption-rights movement
Second World War (1939–1945), 28, 52, 58, 116, 118, 135–7
secrecy, 4, 6, 8, 10, 23, 26, 34, 79–80, 84, 107, 154, 158n4, 169n70; and disclosure, adoption, 63–77
settler law, 12, 116, 201n6
shaken baby syndrome, 55, 178–9n26
shame, 4, 6, 10, 21, 23, 26, 158n4
Six Nations of the Grand River, 123
sixties scoop, 10–12, 116–17, 122–3, 131–2, 138. *See also* Indigenous children
social parenthood, 92, 193–4n7
social parenting, 39, 41, 103, 153–4
Social Service Council of Ontario, 20
social workers, 8, 177–8n11; British Columbia, 75–6; Canadian, 19, 20, 31–2, 36, 53, 57–8; construction of unwed mothers as sick, 30–1; and Indigenous communities, 118–19, 125; Montreal, 172n35; Ontario, 14, 17, 22, 24, 28–34, 37, 41, 43–5, 56, 58, 62, 66, 68, 71, 181n50; United States, 31, 65, 138, 146. *See also* Catholic Children's Aid Society; Children's Aid Society
social-purity movement (Canada), 165n39
Sorosky, Annette, 67, 80
South Korea, 140–1, 143, 221n81
Spence, Robert (Justice; Canada), 112
spouse, 93, 102, 105–6, 110, 114–15, 195n20, 195–6n32; defined, 106
step-children, 98, 99–100
step-daughter, 101
step-father, 79, 92, 93, 97, 98, 101–2
step-parent, 4, 8, 111, 113, 193n3, 193n7, 196n39, 196n42

step-parent adoption, 11, 79–80, 91–107, 155, 190n12; British Columbia, 193n3; Nova Scotia, 193n3
sterilization, 7, 163n31
stigma, 60, 149; birth mothers, 41; illegitimacy, 13, 19, 21, 65, 168n64; infertility, 6; poor mothers, 153; unwed mothers, 24, 26, 28, 30, 32, 34, 141. *See also* Children's Aid Society; coercion; social workers
Strong-Boag, Veronica, 5, 26, 58, 79–80, 167n53, 177n1, 184n1, 194n9, 197n1; Aboriginal history and adoption, 118, 123, 130, 132; adoption-rights movement, 63, 66–7; control of women's reproduction, 7; fathers and adoption, 43, 174n4; *Finding Families, Finding Ourselves*, 4, 169n72; history of fostering, 166n51; informal adoption, 160n1; international adoption, 212n10; interracial adoption, Montreal, 138; Kim Anne Popen case, 56; mothers and consent, 30–1; preferences for white babies, 170n5; social workers, 178n11
sub-Saharan Africa, 145–6, 218n76
Supreme Court of Canada (SCC), 9, 12, 27, 35–41, 45, 47, 50–2, 55, 59–60, 74, 95, 101, 105, 110, 117, 121–4, 144, 153, 155, 189–90n4, 199n18. *See also* cases, discussed; *individual justices*
surrogacy, 11, 104–5, 110, 114–15, 155
Swain, Shurlee, 13
Sweeney, John, 70–1

Thailand, 143, 221n81
Thomas, Meaghan, 101

Tom, Moses, 123; "father of repatriation," 205n54
Toronto, 125, 163n31, 167n57, 180n43, 180n45; Children's Aid Society, 24, 31–4; homes for children (1851–1859), 15; interracial adoption, 138; Social Planning Council of Metropolitan Toronto, 36; Toronto Humane Society (1887), 16–17; Toronto Infants' Home (1875), 17–18
Toronto Star, 187n44, 210–11n92
Toronto Telegram, 81
Traffic in Babies (Balcom), 5, 166n47
Tulloch, Michael (Justice; Canada), 133

U.S. Children's Bureau: *Illegitimacy as a Social Welfare Problem* (1920), 19
United Kingdom, 13, 65
United Nations (UN): Convention on the Prevention and Punishment of Genocide [1948], 202n18; Convention on the Rights of the Child [1989], 6–7, 63, 68, 141, 172n54, 184n2, 212n5; Declaration of the Rights of the Child [1959], 54, 160–1n7; Universal Declaration of Human Rights [1948], 118, 160n7, 202n18
United States, 19, 49, 65–6, 66, 130, 136, 139; adopting out of children, 219n80; Adoption and Safe Families Act [1997], 191n21; Adoption Assistance and Child Welfare Act [1980], 81–2; babies sold to, from Canada, 28; Children's Code of Minnesota, 22; cross-border adoption, with Canada, 211n1; cross-racial adoption, 7; Displaced

Persons Act [1948], 137; emphasis on biological basis of parenthood, 194n7; exchange of children with Canada, 5; feminist scholars, 49–50; immigration, 137; Immigration and Nationality Act [1961], 137; Indian Adoption Project, 119; Indian Child Welfare Act [1978], 123, 205n49; international adoption, 140, 143, 145–6, 215n32, 218n66, 222n83; interracial adoption, 146–7; interstate trafficking of children, 170n15; Massachusetts, formalizing of adoptions in, 22; Multiethnic Placement Act, 147; National Association of Black Social Workers, 138, 146; secrecy provisions, adoption law, 65; social workers, 31, 65; trans-border adoption, with Canada, 212n9; transracial adoption, prohibition of, 213–14n22; Uniform Adoption Act [1994], 190n12. *See also* social workers

Upper Canada: apprenticeship legislation (1851), 15; child indentureship, 15, 53; creation of Children's Aid Society (1892), 17; guardianship legislation [1827], 14; mandatory education, 16; Seduction Act legislation [1837], 18–19, 164–5n38

Van Stolk, Mary: *The Battered Child in Canada*, 56

Vaudreuil, Matthew John: death, abuse and torture (Vancouver, 1992), 58
Vietnam, 143; children, 221n81; Operation Babylift children, 139, 215n32
Vietnam War, 139, 145
visitation orders, 95–6. *See also* access orders
Vital Statistics, 11, 49, 69, 104, 108–9, 155, 174n3, 198n17
voluntary relinquishment. *See* relinquishment

Wald, Michael, 6, 57, 173n56, 179n36
Weigers, Wanda, 103
Whitton, Charlotte, 20–1, 24, 167n57
Who Is My Mother? (Marcus), 67
Wilson, Bertha (Justice; Canada), 40, 124
Wolder, Theo (Justice; Canada), 149–50
Woman's Christian Temperance Union, 162n22
women: access to legal aid, 182n62; Black, 214n25. *See also* Indigenous mothers; lesbian; lesbian couples; mothers
Women's Legal Education and Action Fund (LEAF), 60, 179n34
women's liberation movement, 6

PUBLICATIONS OF THE OSGOODE SOCIETY FOR CANADIAN LEGAL HISTORY

2016   Lori Chambers, *A Legal History of Adoption in Ontario, 1921–2015*
       Bradley Miller, *Borderline Crime: Fugitive Criminals and the Challenge of the Border, 1819–1914*
       James Muir, *Law, Debt, and Merchant Power: The Civil Courts of Eighteenth-Century Halifax*
2015   Barry Wright, Eric Tucker, and Susan Binnie, eds., *Canadian State Trials, Volume IV: Security, Dissent, and the Limits of Toleration in War and Peace, 1914–1939*
       David Fraser, *"Honorary Protestants": The Jewish School Question in Montreal, 1867–1997*
       C. Ian Kyer, *A Thirty Years War: The Failed Public/Private Partnership that Spurred the Creation of the Toronto Transit Commission, 1891–1921*
       Dale Gibson, *Law, Life, and Government at Red River: Settlement and Governance, 1812–1872*
2014   Christopher Moore, *The Court of Appeal for Ontario: Defining the Right of Appeal, 1792–2013*
       Paul Craven, *Petty Justice: Low Law and the Sessions System in Charlotte County, New Brunswick, 1785–1867*
       Thomas GW Telfer, *Ruin and Redemption: The Struggle for a Canadian Bankruptcy Law, 1867–1919*
       Dominique Clément, *Equality Deferred: Sex Discrimination and British Columbia's Human Rights State, 1953–1984*
2013   Roy McMurtry, *Memoirs and Reflections*
       Charlotte Gray, *The Massey Murder: A Maid, Her Master, and the Trial that Shocked a Nation*
       C. Ian Kyer, *Lawyers, Families, and Businesses: The Shaping of a Bay Street Law Firm, Faskens 1863–1963*
       G. Blaine Baker and Donald Fyson, eds., *Essays in the History of Canadian Law, Volume XI: Quebec and the Canadas*
2012   R. Blake Brown, *Arming and Disarming: A History of Gun Control in Canada*
       Eric Tucker, James Muir, and Bruce Ziff, eds., *Property on Trial: Canadian Cases in Context*
       Shelley Gavigan, *Hunger, Horses, and Government Men: Criminal Law on the Aboriginal Plains, 1870–1905*
       Barrington Walker, ed., *The African Canadian Legal Odyssey: Historical Essays*
2011   Robert J. Sharpe, *The Lazier Murder: Prince Edward County, 1884*

Philip Girard, *Lawyers and Legal Culture in British North America: Beamish Murdoch of Halifax*

John McLaren, *Dewigged, Bothered, and Bewildered: British Colonial Judges on Trial, 1800–1900*

Lesley Erickson, *Westward Bound: Sex, Violence, the Law, and the Making of a Settler Society*

2010 Judy Fudge and Eric Tucker, eds., *Work on Trial: Canadian Labour Law Struggles*

Christopher Moore, *The British Columbia Court of Appeal: The First Hundred Years*

Frederick Vaughan, *Viscount Haldane: 'The Wicked Step-father of the Canadian Constitution'*

Barrington Walker, *Race on Trial: Black Defendants in Ontario's Criminal Courts, 1858–1958*

2009 William Kaplan, *Canadian Maverick: The Life and Times of Ivan C. Rand*

R. Blake Brown, *A Trying Question: The Jury in Nineteenth-Century Canada*

Barry Wright and Susan Binnie, eds., *Canadian State Trials, Volume III: Political Trials and Security Measures, 1840–1914*

Robert J. Sharpe, *The Last Day, the Last Hour: The Currie Libel Trial* (paperback edition with a new preface)

2008 Constance Backhouse, *Carnal Crimes: Sexual Assault Law in Canada, 1900–1975*

Jim Phillips, R. Roy McMurtry, and John T. Saywell, eds., *Essays in the History of Canadian Law, Volume X: A Tribute to Peter N. Oliver*

Greg Taylor, *The Law of the Land: The Advent of the Torrens System in Canada*

Hamar Foster, Benjamin Berger, and A.R. Buck, eds., *The Grand Experiment: Law and Legal Culture in British Settler Societies*

2007 Robert Sharpe and Patricia McMahon, *The Persons Case: The Origins and Legacy of the Fight for Legal Personhood*

Lori Chambers, *Misconceptions: Unmarried Motherhood and the Ontario Children of Unmarried Parents Act, 1921–1969*

Jonathan Swainger, ed., *A History of the Supreme Court of Alberta*

Martin Friedland, *My Life in Crime and Other Academic Adventures*

2006 Donald Fyson, *Magistrates, Police, and People: Everyday Criminal Justice in Quebec and Lower Canada, 1764–1837*

Dale Brawn, *The Court of Queen's Bench of Manitoba, 1870–1950: A Biographical History*

R.C.B. Risk, *A History of Canadian Legal Thought: Collected Essays*, edited and introduced by G. Blaine Baker and Jim Phillips

2005 Philip Girard, *Bora Laskin: Bringing Law to Life*
      Christopher English, ed., *Essays in the History of Canadian Law: Volume IX – Two Islands: Newfoundland and Prince Edward Island*
      Fred Kaufman, *Searching for Justice: An Autobiography*
2004 Philip Girard, Jim Phillips, and Barry Cahill, eds., *The Supreme Court of Nova Scotia, 1754–2004: From Imperial Bastion to Provincial Oracle*
      Frederick Vaughan, *Aggressive in Pursuit: The Life of Justice Emmett Hall*
      John D. Honsberger, *Osgoode Hall: An Illustrated History*
      Constance Backhouse and Nancy Backhouse, *The Heiress versus the Establishment: Mrs Campbell's Campaign for Legal Justice*
2003 Robert Sharpe and Kent Roach, *Brian Dickson: A Judge's Journey*
      Jerry Bannister, *The Rule of the Admirals: Law, Custom, and Naval Government in Newfoundland, 1699–1832*
      George Finlayson, *John J. Robinette, Peerless Mentor: An Appreciation*
      Peter Oliver, *The Conventional Man: The Diaries of Ontario Chief Justice Robert A. Harrison, 1856–1878*
2002 John T. Saywell, *The Lawmakers: Judicial Power and the Shaping of Canadian Federalism*
      Patrick Brode, *Courted and Abandoned: Seduction in Canadian Law*
      David Murray, *Colonial Justice: Justice, Morality, and Crime in the Niagara District, 1791–1849*
      F. Murray Greenwood and Barry Wright, eds., *Canadian State Trials, Volume II: Rebellion and Invasion in the Canadas, 1837–1839*
2001 Ellen Anderson, *Judging Bertha Wilson: Law as Large as Life*
      Judy Fudge and Eric Tucker, *Labour before the Law: The Regulation of Workers' Collective Action in Canada, 1900–1948*
      Laurel Sefton MacDowell, *Renegade Lawyer: The Life of J.L. Cohen*
2000 Barry Cahill, *'The Thousandth Man': A Biography of James McGregor Stewart*
      A.B. McKillop, *The Spinster and the Prophet: Florence Deeks, H.G. Wells, and the Mystery of the Purloined Past*
      Beverley Boissery and F. Murray Greenwood, *Uncertain Justice: Canadian Women and Capital Punishment*
      Bruce Ziff, *Unforeseen Legacies: Reuben Wells Leonard and the Leonard Foundation Trust*
1999 Constance Backhouse, *Colour-Coded: A Legal History of Racism in Canada, 1900–1950*
      G. Blaine Baker and Jim Phillips, eds., *Essays in the History of Canadian Law: Volume VIII – In Honour of R.C.B. Risk*
      Richard W. Pound, *Chief Justice W.R. Jackett: By the Law of the Land*
      David Vanek, *Fulfilment: Memoirs of a Criminal Court Judge*

1998 Sidney Harring, *White Man's Law: Native People in Nineteenth-Century Canadian Jurisprudence*
Peter Oliver, *'Terror to Evil-Doers': Prisons and Punishments in Nineteenth-Century Ontario*
1997 James W.St.G. Walker, *'Race,' Rights and the Law in the Supreme Court of Canada: Historical Case Studies*
Lori Chambers, *Married Women and Property Law in Victorian Ontario*
Patrick Brode, *Casual Slaughters and Accidental Judgments: Canadian War Crimes and Prosecutions, 1944–1948*
Ian Bushnell, *The Federal Court of Canada: A History, 1875–1992*
1996 Carol Wilton, ed., *Essays in the History of Canadian Law: Volume VII – Inside the Law: Canadian Law Firms in Historical Perspective*
William Kaplan, *Bad Judgment: The Case of Mr Justice Leo A. Landreville*
Murray Greenwood and Barry Wright, eds., *Canadian State Trials: Volume I – Law, Politics, and Security Measures, 1608–1837*
1995 David Williams, *Just Lawyers: Seven Portraits*
Hamar Foster and John McLaren, eds., *Essays in the History of Canadian Law: Volume VI – British Columbia and the Yukon*
W.H. Morrow, ed., *Northern Justice: The Memoirs of Mr Justice William G. Morrow*
Beverley Boissery, *A Deep Sense of Wrong: The Treason, Trials, and Transportation to New South Wales of Lower Canadian Rebels after the 1838 Rebellion*
1994 Patrick Boyer, *A Passion for Justice: The Legacy of James Chalmers McRuer*
Charles Pullen, *The Life and Times of Arthur Maloney: The Last of the Tribunes*
Jim Phillips, Tina Loo, and Susan Lewthwaite, eds., *Essays in the History of Canadian Law: Volume V – Crime and Criminal Justice*
Brian Young, *The Politics of Codification: The Lower Canadian Civil Code of 1866*
1993 Greg Marquis, *Policing Canada's Century: A History of the Canadian Association of Chiefs of Police*
Murray Greenwood, *Legacies of Fear: Law and Politics in Quebec in the Era of the French Revolution*
1992 Brendan O'Brien, *Speedy Justice: The Tragic Last Voyage of His Majesty's Vessel Speedy*
Robert Fraser, ed., *Provincial Justice: Upper Canadian Legal Portraits from the Dictionary of Canadian Biography*
1991 Constance Backhouse, *Petticoats and Prejudice: Women and Law in Nineteenth-Century Canada*

1990   Philip Girard and Jim Phillips, eds., *Essays in the History of Canadian Law: Volume III – Nova Scotia*
       Carol Wilton, ed., *Essays in the History of Canadian Law: Volume IV – Beyond the Law: Lawyers and Business in Canada, 1830–1930*
1989   Desmond Brown, *The Genesis of the Canadian Criminal Code of 1892*
       Patrick Brode, *The Odyssey of John Anderson*
1988   Robert Sharpe, *The Last Day, the Last Hour: The Currie Libel Trial*
       John D. Arnup, *Middleton: The Beloved Judge*
1987   C. Ian Kyer and Jerome Bickenbach, *The Fiercest Debate: Cecil A. Wright, the Benchers, and Legal Education in Ontario, 1923–1957*
1986   Paul Romney, *Mr Attorney: The Attorney General for Ontario in Court, Cabinet, and Legislature, 1791–1899*
       Martin Friedland, *The Case of Valentine Shortis: A True Story of Crime and Politics in Canada*
1985   James Snell and Frederick Vaughan, *The Supreme Court of Canada: History of the Institution*
1984   Patrick Brode, *Sir John Beverley Robinson: Bone and Sinew of the Compact*
       David Williams, *Duff: A Life in the Law*
1983   David H. Flaherty, ed., *Essays in the History of Canadian Law: Volume II*
1982   Marion MacRae and Anthony Adamson, *Cornerstones of Order: Courthouses and Town Halls of Ontario, 1784–1914*
1981   David H. Flaherty, ed., *Essays in the History of Canadian Law: Volume I*